A LIFE OF PHILIP K. DICK
THE MAN WHO REMEMBERED THE FUTURE

ANTHONY PEAKE

ARCTURUS

I would like to thank Anne Dick, Ray Nelson, Tim Powers, Claudia Krenz-Bush and Brad Steiger for their kindness in responding to my various questions regarding their experiences with Phil. I would also like to thank writer Jamelle Morgan and film-maker John Alan Simon for their assistance. However, my special thanks go to PKD scholar Nick Buchanan and Phil's last wife, Tessa B. Dick, for their amazing support throughout this project. Nick kindly give me access to his huge collection of PKD material; Tessa was always available on points of clarification and to give me fascinating personal insights into her life with Phil.

For those interested in an ongoing analysis of the life and work of Philip K. Dick, a wonderful source of information is the fanzine *PKD Otaku*, past copies of which can be downloaded for free from the Philip K. Dick fansite: http://www.philipkdickfans.com/resources/journals/pkd-otaku/.

ARCTURUS
This edition published in 2013 by Arcturus Publishing Limited
26/27 Bickels Yard, 151–153 Bermondsey Street,
London SE1 3HA

ISBN: 978-1-78212-242-5
AD002653EN

Printed in China

CONTENTS

Foreword

'My major preoccupation is the question, what is reality?'

Philip K. Dick

On 21 February 2008 the fourth episode of Season 4 of the hugely popular TV series *Lost* was broadcast for the first time in the USA. A character, John Locke, wakes up in the barracks and, after making breakfast, chooses a novel from the bookshelf. He carries the book down to the basement and gives it to another character, Ben, telling him he ought to read it. Ben replies that he's already done so, at which Locke suggests reading it again. 'You might catch something you missed, second time round.' Clearly Ben takes this advice to heart because in a later episode ('The Other Woman') we see him immersed in the pages of the book.

The novel in question was *VALIS* by Philip K. Dick. Fittingly for a man who was always ahead of his time, it was written in the late-1970s but first published in 1981. Its appearance in *Lost* is a subtle but significant nod to the debt the series owed to the author as well as yet another acknowledgement of the immense contribution PKD has made to popular culture in the 21st century.

In the age of 24-hour news coverage where weird events are transmitted live to a worldwide internet audience, corporations and governments have the technology to know far too much about all of us, ordinary people 'wear' advanced technology in the shape of Google Glass and adverts that follow you around actually exist, PKD's time has well and truly arrived.

As Paul Verhoeven, director of the first *Total Recall* film, put it, '[we live in a time when] people can't put their finger on what is real and what is not real.' That was exactly how PKD felt, and now millions have come to the same conclusion.

On 5 July 2007 I was invited to give a talk in the North of England on my first book, *Is There Life After Death?: The Extraordinary Science of What Happens When We Die*. This book explored the idea that all human beings have two centres of consciousness: the 'Eidolon', the everyday part that lives time in a linear fashion and knows nothing other than the sum total of its experiences, and the Daemon, the part that exists within a timeless location somewhere in the borderlands between life and death. The Daemon knows about the life-route of its Eidolon in the way that a first-person computer game player knows the previous lives of his or her on-screen 'avatar'. In this way the Daemon can assist the Eidolon in negotiating the game we call 'life'.

The last chapter of the book touches upon the life and experiences of

Philip K. Dick. In the various biographies that had been written about this enigmatic cult writer I had found amazing parallels regarding my Daemon-Eidolon model. Not only that, but his books *VALIS* and *UBIK* also contained fictionalized accounts of the overall hypothesis proposed in my book.

It was as if in some bizarre way Philip K. Dick was aware of my books and had used them to frame his plots. But I knew this to be impossible. PKD had died in March 1982 and my first book was published in September 2006.

That particular summer's evening, I had been talking for about an hour when I flashed my second-to-last slide up on to the screen. This showed Philip K. Dick flanked on either side by the covers of the books *UBIK* and *VALIS*. As the slide appeared there was an audible gasp of excitement from the extreme right-hand side of the audience. Four or five individuals were excitedly chattering among themselves. My initial reaction was irritation. What was their problem?

After the customary question-and-answer session and book signing, I was approached by one of the disruptive group. 'Sorry about that,' he said, 'but we were stunned by what we just saw.' He introduced himself as Mick and, after shaking my hand, said, 'I have something to show you.'

He reached into his bag and pulled out a copy of a book. It was a copy of *VALIS* with an identical cover to the one in the slideshow. Interesting coincidence I thought, but nothing more. Then Mick announced, 'This book is the reason we're here.' He had been at the library picking up the copy he had ordered when he spotted a poster for the talk.

Then it got stranger. Mick leaned over and said, 'You know that Philip K. Dick predicted you, don't you?' I looked at him in surprise. 'No,' I replied. 'In *Counter-Clock World*,' came the cryptic reply. At that time I had only read two or three of Dick's books and this title was new to me.

'Anarch Peak,' Mick said.

'Who?' I replied.

'Anarch Peak,' Mick repeated as if I was hard of hearing. 'Peak is a character involved in the resurrection of the dead from a state of limbo.' He explained that, in the book, time is running backwards and people come alive in their graves and have to be dug up. They then get progressively younger until they are un-born. Peak is the leader of a religious group who is about to be re-born and, for differing reasons, some groups want him to stay dead and others anticipate his birth as a version of the Second Coming.

Later I read in detail Dick's descriptions of his 'visions' during February and March 1974, and something rather peculiar struck me. In these visions PKD saw lines and lines of books, their titles and covers flashing in front of him. He took this to be some kind of message. Indeed one particular book title came to him when he was in a semi-sleep state known as hypnagogia.

Counter-Clock World was written in 1965 and by then early manifestations of the visions, which were to appear fully-fledged in 1974, had already started. Peculiar as it may seem, I have asked myself whether, in any of these precognitive states, Dick might have subliminally seen the cover of the book you now hold in your hands. If he had, he would have seen his name and underneath it a name like An*** Peak*. This may have immediately found a home in his subconscious only to appear as an idea for the name of a character associated with the state of human consciousness at the point of death, precisely the subject of my first book.

Make of this what you will, but I do find it an interesting back-drop to this book. It also helped me structure it in a way that focuses on the precognitive aspects of PKD's life.

I have organized the book in the way I think best presents the information needed to help you, the reader, come to your own conclusions regarding the enigma that was Philip K. Dick.

The first section is a fairly straightforward chronological biography. Much of this is sourced from biographies, articles and PKD's own collected letters. The second section reviews in some detail most, if not all, of PKD's unusual experiences. I believe that it is only through appreciating how these events affected PKD that we can really understand the man and his worldview. From there I review PKD's own attempts at explaining these events. Much of this material is taken from his compendium of published journals, *Exegesis*, which was published in November 2011. A lot of this had never been published before and provides a wonderful insight into the workings of PKD's mind. I suspect that this book will be the first one to analyse PKD's experiences in the light of his own writings on the subject. This second section finishes off with an evaluation of PKD's belief that he was a form of hybrid being that he called a 'homoplasmate'. Part three will attempt a neurological explanation for PKD's experiences. The final section will be my own interpretation of a personality test that PKD completed in the mid-1950s.

I apologise for taking a fairly idiosyncratic approach to the life of this great writer. However, I feel that if PKD had written his autobiography that this is the kind of route he might have taken. His *Exegesis* was an attempt to explain exactly what happened to him during March and February of 1974, which began a time of near-religious heart-searching. He questioned everything and came up with many answers, most of which he later came to reject. I would like to believe that in this book I have attempted answers to at least some of PKD's questions. Whether I have succeeded or not is for you to decide.

Anthony Peake
July 2013

PART ONE
THE BIOGRAPHY

'My God, my life is exactly like the plot of any one of 10 of my novels or stories. Even down to fake memories and identity.

I'm a protagonist from one of PKD's books.'

Philip K. Dick

Chapter One

The End (1982)

Santa Ana, California, 18 February 1982. Alone in his small apartment in the Mexican quarter, the tallish, stocky, balding, bearded figure of Philip K. Dick lay unconscious on the living room floor, sandwiched between his broken couch and the coffee table that his two cats, Harvey and Mrs Mabel M. Tubbs, used as a scratching post. He had suffered a stroke. It would be some hours yet before help arrived.

The rundown apartment had clearly seen better days, as had the unconscious figure on the floor, clad in the casual clothes he favoured and who did not have a single suit to his name. These were the hallmarks of a writer down on his luck, and yet nothing could be further from the truth. At the age of fifty-three, PKD had achieved more as a writer in his relatively short life than many such artists might do in the space of several lifetimes. His output totalled one hundred and twenty short stories and forty-four novels. His other achievements – apart from an annual salary running into six figures – included top book awards, international recognition and a devoted worldwide fan base (affectionately calling themselves 'Dickheads'), not to mention five marriages, three children and a large and loyal circle of close friends and literary colleagues. His works are even set books on the English syllabus at Harvard University and have featured in countless doctoral dissertations and theses.

Sci-fi's Dali

Lauded by the American literary critic and political philosopher Frederick Jameson as 'the greatest of all science fiction writers', the 'ghastly humour' of PKD's novels has been compared with Dickens and Kafka and his 'paradoxical plots' have cast him in the mould of the 'Salvador Dali' of the literary world. His unique style of work has even spawned a bastardized adjective, 'phildickian', to define the surreally complex worlds that he created.

If Philip K. Dick led a simple life, it was because that was how he chose to live. He had better uses for his money, including funding humanitarian causes such as the Southern Poverty Law Center. He had recently heard that his money had helped free a young black man who had gone to prison for a crime he didn't commit. Other than that, what mattered was his writing. As he explained in a letter written only the previous month:

> 'I don't have to prove anything to anyone, especially myself. Writing novels and stories is hard work, but what matters is the work itself—the work that is produced, but also the act

of work: the task itself. The fact that I'm typing on cheap paper bought at the Market Basket Supermarket—that counts neither for me nor against me on the great tote board in the sky, which is to say, in my own heart.'[1]

In four months' time, on 25 June 1982, celebrities from the cinematic and literary world would gather for the premier of the sci-fi movie classic *Blade Runner*, loosely based on PKD's novel *Do Androids Dream of Electric Sheep?* (1968). Sadly, PKD would miss basking in the reflected glow of this latest triumph; he had always enjoyed being the centre of attention. On the plus side, missing the premier meant he wouldn't need to buy a suit. In the last interview he gave, with John Boonstra, for *The Twilight Zone* magazine, he said:

'I hear the film's going to have an old-fashioned gala premier. It means I've got to buy—or rent—a black tuxedo, which I don't look forward to. That's not my style. I'm happier in a T-shirt.'[2]

But he had at least seen some of the film footage: a segment on KNBC-TV News. When he viewed the movie's futuristic depiction of Los Angeles in 2019, one of the most iconic sequences in cinema history, PKD was absolutely delighted. It seemed as if the film-makers had read his mind. It was 'exactly as I imagined it,' he said. Philip K. Dick had finally achieved the mainstream recognition he always craved, saying that his 'life and creative work are completed by *Blade Runner*'.

Despite huge pressure from the film studio, PKD turned down the chance to earn $400,000 dollars from the studio to produce a 'cheapo novelization' aimed at 12-year-olds. It would have been based solely on the screenplay and would have meant suppressing the original novel on which *Blade Runner* is based. Instead, the original novel was re-released, earning him – and the movie studio – a fraction of the money.

'They finally recognized that there was a legitimate reason for re-issuing the novel, even though it cost them money. It was a victory not just of contractual obligations but of theoretical principles.'[3]

There would be many more film adaptations of his works in the decades to come, including *Total Recall* (1990 and 2012), based on his short story *We Can Remember It for You Wholesale* (1966), *Screamers* (1995) taken from his work *Second Variety* (1953) and *Minority Report* (2002), adapted from a 1956 short story of the same name. There are even plans for a Disney animated version of one of his short stories, *The King of the Elves*, which would bring the world of Philip K. Dick to the attention of a new generation of readers.

Yet there was so much more that PKD had wanted to do, not least in preparing the world for a 'second coming'. Alas, there was now no more time – at least, not in this reality.

Past, present and future

As an eager follower of science from an early age, PKD had been ideally placed in history to carve out a name in the world of science fiction. Not only did he live at a time when the genre was in its ascendency but science itself advanced rapidly over his lifetime. In 1927, the year before PKD was born, an unknown US Air Mail pilot called Charles Lindbergh became the first person to fly solo across the Atlantic, a total of 3,600 miles, non-stop from New York's Long Island to Le Bourget in Paris, in a propeller-driven aircraft, the *Spirit of St Louis,* made of fabric-covered wood and metal.

Over the next fifty-three years, props would give way to jets, and jets would lead to rocket-launched spacecraft. As PKD lay unconscious, the Soviet *Venera 13* spacecraft was approaching the planet Venus, after a journey of twenty-six million miles. It would soon land and then beam back the first colour images of the planetary surface. Russia's Space Research Institute at first claimed the pictures showed signs of life, including something resembling a scorpion, although that was later denied. PKD could have had some fun with that in one of his novels.

In 1945, the nightmare 'doomsday' weapon of science fiction became fact when atomic bombs were dropped on two Japanese cities, Hiroshima and Nagasaki, causing previously unimaginable levels of death and destruction. PKD would consider the consequences of a post-apocalyptic world ravaged by nuclear explosions in his 1965 novel *Dr Bloodmoney: or How We Got Along After the Bomb*.

The electronic 'brains' that science fiction writers had imagined were also realized, although today we call them computers. Even the gulf between the natural and the artificial has narrowed. The first mechanical heart was successfully implanted into a human being in 1953, when PKD was twenty-four and on the verge of becoming a full-time writer. Five years later, in 1958, a walking, talking robot called 'Elektro' wowed visitors to the Pacific Ocean Park amusement centre in Santa Monica, California, an easy drive from PKD's home at the time. This was all yet more grist to the mill of PKD's imagination.

Not only did science fiction become science fact over this period but fact and fantasy seemed to be merging. In the 1950s, sci-fi movie classics such as *The Day the Earth Stood Still* and *War of the Worlds* caught the public's imagination with their terrifying tales of alien landings. In parallel with the movie images, real US Air Force jets were being scrambled to intercept unidentified 'saucer-like' flying objects in the sky, their pilots' highly descriptive flight reports stoking the fevered minds of newspaper headline writers. As PKD would later explain:

'. . .This is why I love SF. I love to read it; I love to write it. The SF writer sees not just possibilities but wild possibilities. It's not just "What if"—it's "My God; what if"—in frenzy and hysteria. The Martians are always coming.'[4]

Soup of ideas

And not just Martians. . . Few writers would think to make a hero out of an intelligent slime mould called 'Lord Running Clam', a native of the Jovian moon Ganymede. Ideas gleaned from science and science fiction, plus a wide knowledge of music, literature, philosophy and theology, jostled for position in PKD's mind. Humans and androids, aliens and Earthlings, Spinoza and Sophocles, God and Beelzebub, all got stirred into the 'phil-dickian' soup swirling inside his head. In a celebrated talk given to a science fiction convention in 1972, PKD explored some of the themes he had made his own, such as the dissolving boundary between the artificial and the natural:

'So we and our elaborately evolving computers may meet each other halfway. Some day a human being, named perhaps Fred White, may shoot a robot named Pete Something-or-other, which has come out of a General Electrics factory, and to his surprise see it weep and bleed. And the dying robot may shoot back and, to its surprise, see a wisp of gray smoke arise from the electric pump that it supposed was Mr White's beating heart. It would be rather a great moment of truth for both of them.'[5]

PKD's ideas ranged from the fantastical, but bedded in science, to the theological and the metaphysical, drawing from sources as diverse as Plato, the *Gnostic Gospels*, the *I Ching* and the *Tibetan Book of the Dead*. He would later say that many of his works, especially the last one he completed, *The Transmigration of Timothy Archer* (1982), shouldn't be regarded as science fiction.

PKD's stories not only explored unusual ideas but also pioneered unconventional writing styles, such as switching the perspective of the first-person narrative between different characters in a novel so that the reader is initially confused about who is actually speaking. This device creates an unsettling effect, especially when the gender changes along with the character, from male to female to male again. This technique was first explored in PKD's semi-autobiographical work *Confessions of a Crap Artist* (1975), the only one of his mainstream novels to be published in his lifetime. Science fiction writer and illustrator A.L. Sirois has described him as:

> '. . .the first SF writer to really get into playing with the heads
> of his readers, and getting them to think about the nature of
> reality and their perceptions. For this reason, his books never
> really grow stale—you can come back to them years after the
> first reading and find new signposts directing you into previ-
> ously obscure pathways of your own personality.'[6]

Sounds of distant voices

PKD's own life was a fantasy as rich as many of his stories and he would
often incorporate his own experiences into his work. Fact and fiction, the
mysterious and the mystical, the paranoid and the paranormal, extrasensory
perception and precognition, conspiracy and confusion, it all found expres-
sion in his writing. Night after night, he would sit at his battered manual
typewriter, drawing on this vast mental storehouse of thoughts and ideas;
the only way of exorcizing his demons was in a frenzy of typing as he
worked hour after hour – often going without sleep for days on end – so
that his otherworldly imagination could come tumbling down on to the
copy paper and into print. To maintain this prodigious workload, he would
take copious quantities of amphetamine – a new take on the phrase 'speed
typing'. It has also been claimed that his nocturnal notions were aided by
other mind-and-mood-altering substances, including marijuana and LSD,
although he would later deny that they helped his writing in any way. He
later campaigned vociferously against drug misuse. Working late at night
also allowed PKD to 'tune in' to the 'voices'. As he explained in the introduction to an anthology of his works, these stories are. . .

> '. . .attempts at reception—at listening to voices from another
> place, very far off, sounds quite faint but important. They
> only come late at night, when the background din and gabble
> of our world have faded out. Then, faintly, I hear voices from
> another star. Of course, I don't usually tell people this when
> they ask, "Say, where do you get your ideas?" I just say, "I
> don't know". It's safer.'

In a 1974 interview for *Vortex* magazine, while defending another sci-fi
author, A. E. van Vogt, from a savaging by writer and critic Damon Knight,
PKD gave an insight into his own approach to writing.

> 'Damon feels that it's bad artistry when you build those funky
> universes where people fall through the floor. It's like he's
> viewing a story the way a building inspector would when he's

building your house. But reality really is a mess, and yet it's exciting. The basic thing is, how frightened are you of chaos? And how happy are you with order?'[7]

For PKD, 'Reality is that which, when you stop believing in it, doesn't go away.'

Dark-haired girls

Aside from his writing, PKD's other great passion was women. His turbulent relationships, especially with the 'dark-haired girls' who he found so irresistible, were a recurring theme in his life and in his literature. There is little clue in his teenage years that he would become a sexual magnet to the opposite sex.

Yet, over the course of a few years, he turned from gawky adolescent, who felt awkward around women and was even unsure of his own sexuality, to the consummate ladies' man, who could captivate female hearts with ease and who was 'in love with falling in love'.

It is difficult at this remove for those of us who have never met him to understand the hold he seemed to have over women, with only his photograph and the stories of his many affairs and failed marriages to go by. But many women clearly found this 'almost handsome man' irresistible too and have variously described him as 'powerfully charismatic', 'graceful and attractive', 'funny', 'romantic, exciting, fascinating', but also 'lost and helpless'. In addition to his five wives, he had many female friends and lovers, some of them 'live-in'.

These relationships could be, by turn, romantic, affectionate, devoted, loving, tempestuous and even violent. Other relationships with women were purely platonic or avuncular, and sometimes conducted solely by telephone. Yet they were all important to him – and he to them! And, despite everything, he would later claim, with some justification, that he was able to remain on friendly terms with all of his wives and most of the other women in his life, too. That, in itself, is a remarkable achievement.

A journal and a journey

Much of PKD's later creativity was devoted to an 8,000-page journal in which he described and explored his visionary experiences and spiritual ideas. This journal came to be known as his *Exegesis*, a Greek word meaning 'to lead out' and used to describe the critical interpretation of a text, often a religious work such as the Bible. Like many of his novels, PKD wrote his *Exegesis* in marathon sessions that could last well into the small hours.

His first visions included a beam of light that 'appeared—in vivid fire, with shining colours and balanced patterns—and released me from every thrall, inner and outer'. The initial visionary events occurred in February and March 1974 and so '2-3-74' came to be used as a shorthand term to denote these and other such experiences. The first of these visions may have been triggered by a flash of light, reflecting from a pendant depicting the Christian 'fish' symbol. The pendant was worn by a young girl from the pharmacy who had delivered his medication and who was standing in the doorway. The *Exegesis* describes the effect this first visionary experience had on him.

> 'In that instant, as I stared at the gleaming fish sign and heard her words, I suddenly experienced what I later learned is called *anamnesis*—a Greek word meaning, literally, "loss of forgetfulness." I remembered who I was and where I was. In an instant, in the twinkling of an eye, it all came back to me. And not only could I remember it but I could see it.'[8]

His 20th century suburban environment would melt into the background to reveal another reality, that of 1st century Rome. PKD came to believe that he was one of a group of secret Christians (as was the girl), and that their mission was to prepare the world for the return of the Saviour. He 'realized' that the Roman Empire had never ended but continued to rule the world and to persecute Christians, and so PKD and other members of the group had to remain in hiding, communicating by a secret code. He also became aware of another being inside him viewing the world through his eyes.

PKD believed a flash of light from another of his '2-3-74' experiences may have emanated from a spiritual or possibly alien entity and was imparting important information to him. In his *Exegesis*, PKD drew on his extensive scientific, religious and philosophical knowledge to try to explain the nature of this entity, variously called God, Zebra and Vast Active Living Intelligence System, or 'VALIS' for short. Many of its ideas are explored in other published works, including *VALIS* (1981), *The Divine Invasion* (1981), *Radio Free Albemuth* (1985) and *The Transmigration of Timothy Archer* (1982).

Lines on the Universe

Another interpretation of the source of his visions was that he was accessing a higher consciousness, possibly the right hemisphere of his brain – suddenly unleashed. But, as his biographer, Laurence Sutin, points out, PKD always bore in mind the 'minimum hypothesis' – that all he had undergone was merely 'self-delusion'. PKD's long-time friend and fellow science fiction writer Tim Powers goes further. The image of PKD as some sort of tortured genius is not one he recognizes. He told Chris Ziegler of *OC Weekly*, 'This is not a crazy guy. He was the funniest guy I ever knew.' He remembers long conversations going late into the night when PKD would propound his latest theories. When Powers reminded him about them the next day, however, PKD would often reply, dismissively, 'That's a bunch of nonsense!' Yet 'they sounded good last night,' Powers would tell him.

Another time, PKD phoned Powers to say he'd 'figured out the universe'. Powers suggested he write it out as a limerick. 'No I can't write it out as a limerick,' said PKD, 'it's the secret of the universe!' But when Powers called on him later that day, he had done it anyway.

> *The determinist forces are wrong*
> *But irresistibly strong*
> *While of God there's a dearth*
> *For he visits the earth*
> *But not for sufficiently long.'*[9]

PKD's name will live on in the Philip K. Dick Award, presented each year at the science fiction and fantasy convention Norwescon, held in the city of SeaTec, Washington State. It is awarded for the best original paperback novel published the previous year without first appearing in hardback. The award was first present in 1984 to, appropriately enough, PKD's friend Powers, for *The Anubis Gates*.

The nature of time

PKD was convinced of one point, however, that information not only flowed from the past into the future but also from the future into the past. He claimed to have been drawing on experiences that occurred in his later life as source material for stories that he wrote earlier on in his career.

Predictably, in all senses of the word, PKD's death was as curious as his life. PKD had known his end was imminent. He had had several premonitions. More remarkably, he had foreseen the manner of his departure in some detail. He knew exactly how he would appear to the first people to find his unconscious body. A letter to a friend, composed seven years before, included the following:

> 'A sort of dream-like period passed, then. . . a stark single horrifying scene, inert but not still; a man lay dead, on his face, in a living room between the coffee table and the couch.'

That is exactly how the paramedics found him. He was not actually dead, though. In fact, by the time an ambulance rushed him to the hospital, PKD had regained consciousness and was said to be 'communicative'. However, sometime after arrival, he suffered a second stroke that shut off the blood supply to the remaining functioning areas of his brain. PKD was to exist for twelve more days in the hospital's intensive care room, his life functions taken over by the latest medical equipment. Finally, after monitoring his brain for signs of activity and finding none, the doctors switched off his life-support. Those hyperactive neurons had finally stopped firing.

So, during his final days as a physical entity on Earth, PKD's bodily processes were being maintained solely by technology. He was being controlled by a machine. The author of *Do Androids Dream of Electric Sheep?* would have enjoyed the irony in that.

Twins re-united

After his funeral service, PKD's body was cremated and his ashes taken to his father's home town of Fort Morgan to be interred in the same grave as those of his twin sister, Jane, who had died when only six weeks old. They would also share a headstone, his inscription already having been carved and awaiting him for over half a century, with only the date of death to be entered. Although they were separated so cruelly soon after birth, their mortal remains would now share eternity together.

Today, the *Prophets of Science Fiction* website describes PKD as a 'literary genius', 'celebrated visionary' and 'paranoid outcast'. PKD regarded himself as a 'fictionalizing philosopher'. Friend and fellow science fiction writer Normal Spinrad provided this tribute in the introduction to PKD's work *Dr Bloodmoney* (1965): 'Fifty or one hundred years from now, [Philip K. Dick] may well be recognized in retrospect as the greatest American novelist of the second half of the twentieth century.'

As another uniquely bizarre tribute, in 2011 fans built a remote-controlled robot head called 'Phil the Android' for the annual San Diego comic book convention, Comic-Con International. It was a remarkable likeness including grey beard, receding hairline and piercing blue eyes. It then took part in a lively discussion about the film adaptation of PKD's book *A Scanner Darkly* (1977). The head was subsequently misplaced by American West Airlines and has not yet been found. Bearing in mind where airline luggage sometimes ends up, who knows where PKD's android head will surface one day. Clearly, there is comic potential there for a Philip K. Dick-style storyline. Sadly, he is no longer around to write it.

And the final inevitable phildickian twist? PKD was born in '28 and died in '82 – the same numbers reversed, just how he would have wanted it. This was, is and ever will be the confusingly fascinating world of Philip K. Dick: 'The man who remembered the future'. Welcome to it . . .

Chapter Two
The Beginning (1928–46)

Chicago. December 1928. The ban on the sale and distribution of alcohol, known colloquially as 'Prohibition', had been in force for eight years. The streets of Chicago were now a battleground of drive-by shootings, back-street stabbings and bomb outrages, as rival mobsters fought for control of the trade in illicit 'bootleg' liquor. The most powerful of the Chicago gang bosses, Al 'Scarface' Capone, was reeling from the killing of his former adviser, Antonio Lombardo, gunned down in North Street, Chicago, during the rush hour. Capone's bloody revenge would come a few months later in the 'St Valentine's Day Massacre'. In a 'sting' orchestrated by Capone, seven members of George 'Bugsy' Moran's gang gathered in a garage in Clark Street, Chicago, awaiting the arrival of a consignment of liquor. Instead of the expected booze, they were machine-gunned to death by some of Capone's gang. The killers were not what they appeared to be. They were dressed as policemen. It was a bizarre plot twist that PKD himself might have created. But Philip K. Dick the writer would not appear for some years yet. First he had to be born and then survive and that would not be easy. . .

A cold start

Philip Kindred Dick entered this world of fear and bloody mayhem at noon on 16 December 1928* in a poorly heated apartment in Emerald Avenue, Chicago. His parents were Dorothy and Edgar Dick. Dorothy was a slim, delicate yet intense-looking woman of twenty-seven whose sharp features were softened by a halo of thick, wavy hair and large, intelligent, piercing eyes. PKD's father, who was always known as 'Ted,' was slim, tallish – around six feet in height – with a high forehead, easy smile and boyish, curly hair kept relatively short and business-like. He favoured double-breasted business suits, as befitted a middle-ranking official in a government department.

At Dorothy's insistence, they had decided – reluctantly in Ted's case – that their new child would be born at home. The reason for this was that the strong-willed Dorothy was an ardent feminist (relative to the time) and had demanded that a female doctor, living in the same street, should be the person to deliver her child. What they had not expected was that the baby would arrive a full six weeks early. The doctor was there only minutes after Dorothy went into labour and yet even this short delay irritated Ted, as he felt that had there been a male doctor in attendance or, even better,

* In her book *The Search for Philip K. Dick*, his third wife Anne Dick states that the time of Phil's birth was 8 am.

that the delivery had taken place in hospital, the later tragedy might have been avoided.

As Ted was wiping mucus from the face of his first and, as it turned out, only son, Dorothy's labour pains started again. Another baby was on the way. This came as a huge surprise to both of them as, unknown even to her doctor, Dorothy had been carrying twins. Twenty minutes later, a tiny blonde girl arrived to join her darker-haired brother. It was soon evident why Dorothy and Ted had not realized that she had been carrying two babies. Both infants together weighed no more than a single normal baby. PKD weighed 4lb 4oz (1.93 kg) and Jane weighed 3lb 8oz (1.6kg)

Ted was immediately concerned that Dorothy, always thin and frail, would have insufficient milk for two babies, even such tiny ones. He immediately asked that the twins be taken to a local hospital. Dorothy's doctor disagreed and the new parents were left with two very underweight, unhealthy newborns. Dorothy now found herself in an impossible position. She was dealing with two sickly infants in sub-zero temperatures in this great metropolis of Chicago – the 'Windy City' – in the depths of a bleak Illinois winter.

A home town girl

Cold, impersonal and crime-ridden, Chicago must have seemed a huge contrast to the small, neighbourly Midwestern town of Greeley, Colorado, where she grew up. Greeley, built in the heart of former 'Cherokee Indian' country, had been founded in 1869 as a 'Utopian' and strictly teetotal religious community. Dorothy's maiden name of Kindred, from which Philip's middle name was taken, marks her out as from 'English stock', many of them Quakers, who had migrated to the United States in the 19th century. She would raise her son as a Quaker initially, instilling an interest in religion and philosophy that would never leave him. Her father was Earl Kindred, who appears in photographs as a very tall, distinguished-looking man with a kindly smile, and smart three-piece suit and tie. Her mother, Edna Matilda Archer Kindred (later known to PKD as 'Meemaw'), was tiny in comparison to her husband, her hair tied back in a prim bun and wearing simple wire-framed spectacles. Her middle name of 'Archer' would fascinate PKD and he would later use it for some of his fictional characters. Dorothy's pretty younger sister, Marion, was dark haired with a winning smile and an easy-going personality. Marion would be only the first of many attractive 'dark-haired girls' who would play an important part in PKD's life.

Ted and his family came from Pennsylvania. But, in 1915, when Ted was a teenager, they moved to the tiny rural community of Cedarwood, Colorado, not far from Greeley. It was there, one year later, the couple first met. Ted's family then moved to Fort Morgan, the largest city in Morgan County, Colorado, a pioneering town built in the 1800s to safeguard wagon trains bringing supplies to the mining community of Denver from attack by marauding Indians. Fort Morgan was later briefly famous as the boyhood home of band leader Glen Miller. To the fans of Philip K. Dick, however, it would become better known as the final resting place of this most idiosyncratic of writers.

On 6 April 1917, the United States entered World War I, a conflict that had already been raging in Europe for three years. Ted enlisted and set off for France to fight in the trenches. He was to experience the nightmare of 20th-century warfare at first hand, including the use of poison gas and the terrible toll it took on soldiers caught out in the open without a gas mask. Ted brought his own gas mask home with him and would later show it to PKD as a graphic illustration of the horrors of war. The mask had a disturbing psychological effect on PKD that would become apparent in a terrifying incident that occurred in his adult life.

The war finally ended on 11 November 1918. On Ted's return from the battlefront, the couple were able to re-kindle their interrupted love affair. They were married on 29 September 1920 when Dorothy was 19 years old. Not exactly a whirlwind romance. Almost immediately, they moved to Washington DC so that Ted could attend Georgetown University before realizing his ambition to join the Foreign Service. To finance his studies, he worked as a clerk with the Department of Agriculture. Meanwhile, Dorothy secured a secretarial post at the *Journal of Home Economics*.

Disappointingly for Ted, there were no vacancies in the Foreign Service and so he stayed with the Department of Agriculture, soon being assigned a job in the livestock and meat research programme. On graduation in 1927, he was offered a post in Chicago, working in the Department's livestock market news service. Dorothy and Ted had always wanted a family but they had so far waited over seven years. Finally, the longed-for event happened – Dorothy became pregnant.

Infant starvation

So now, at the age of twenty-eight, Dorothy found herself in this cold, violent city, friendless and far removed from her family. She was in desperate need of help and advice and so her mother, Edna, was sent for. But she would not arrive for another two weeks. The first major problem was to find a substitute for Dorothy's limited supply of milk. Other mothers in this situation would be able to supplement their babies' feed with artificial formula milk, which is derived from cow's milk. But Dorothy's babies were allergic to this. In desperation, Dorothy sought advice from any quarter, including the janitor, who suggested goat's milk.[10]

The weather worsened, plunging to sub-zero temperatures. Dorothy was desperate to keep her ailing infants warm and, according to one version of events, decided to use a hot water bottle to heat the crib.[11] This caused a severe burn to baby Jane's leg. However, PKD heard a different version. He was later to tell his psychiatrist, Barry Spatz, that:

> '[his] mother gave his sister a bath in scalding hot water resulting in severe burns, but never called a doctor.'[12]

It was the lack of milk both babies were receiving that was of most pressing concern, however. According to Dorothy, the babies were literally starving to death because her doctor simply could not find the right milk formula that the twins could tolerate. One bright light in an otherwise bleak January 1929 was Dorothy's chance discovery of an insurance policy devised by the Metropolitan Life Assurance Company that could help pay for medical aid, including a nurse to help out. The insurance could be taken out after a baby's birth. So, for the sum of $50 per child, the young couple were able to get the assistance they needed.

To add to Chicago's problems, it was in the grip of a flu epidemic. It would be another two days after the policy had become active before medical help was available. When a doctor and nurse arrived they brought with them a much-needed heated crib. Both babies were badly malnourished and close to death but baby Jane's condition, in particular, was cause for increasing concern. It is not known just how seriously the burn had affected her, but it clearly did not help her weakened state. The doctor quickly assessed the situation and decided no time could be lost; both babies were in need of urgent specialist treatment. An ambulance was called but, sadly, little Jane Charlotte Dick died on the way to Chicago's Michael Reece Hospital. The date was 26 January 1929. Jane had lived for just six weeks. PKD survived the journey and, just in time, was placed in an incubator and given special formula milk. In a letter to PKD in 1975, Dorothy told him:

> 'You were within a day or so of death, but you began to gain at once, and when you weighed 5 pounds I was allowed to take you home. I could visit you every day in the incubator, and during the periods I was there I was given instruction in making up the very complicated formula.'[13]

Jane's tiny body was taken to Colorado for cremation and her ashes interred in the Dick family plot at a cemetery in Fort Morgan. As if in keeping with the sadness of the occasion, the whole ceremony was conducted in a blinding snowstorm. Carved on the headstone, alongside their daughter's name, Dorothy and Ted had added 'Philip Kindred Dick', in readiness. Perhaps they feared that, like Jane, the tiny infant would not survive the winter. Whatever the reason, PKD always knew where his mortal remains would one day lie.

The young PKD was continually reminded of his dead sister by his still-grieving mother. So it is not surprising that, as PKD grew older, Jane would play a greater role in his inner life, taking on a personality and a reality all of her own. PKD was to build up an image of Jane, if she had survived, as living out her life as a 'wheel-chair bound cripple'. Neither Ted nor Dorothy ever mentioned the incident of the burn in any letters and, according to biographer Gregg Rickman, even Dorothy's step-daughter, Lynne Aalan, knew nothing of it.

It is clear that Jane's death bore heavily on Dorothy, too. PKD's third wife, Anne, wrote her own biography entitled *The Search for Philip K. Dick* (2010). In this she says that Dorothy always spoke of Jane as if her long-departed daughter 'had died only yesterday'.[14] Anne hints that it may have been PKD's memories of his mother's sense of loss that added greatly to his own psychological relationship with his dead sister. Anne certainly considered that the baby's death was of profound significance to PKD. He once confessed to her:

> 'I heard about Jane a lot and it wasn't good for me. I felt guilty—somehow I got all the milk.'[15]

In 1929, Dorothy, Ted and baby PKD returned to Fort Morgan, in Colorado, to visit Ted's family. But then Ted had to return to Chicago because of work commitments, and so he left PKD and Dorothy with relatives in Johnstown, just a few miles from her parent's home in Greeley. From these very earliest months, Dorothy engendered in PKD a love of music that was not only to endure throughout his life but was to become a central theme in much of his writing. In her journal Dorothy wrote:

> 'I take him on my lap at the piano while I labor over the Missouri Waltz. He watches and listens, ducking from one side to the other suddenly, and leaning forward to try to hit the keyboard with his own hands, and then all at once he leans back with his little hand against my breast and looks at me wonderingly with such a funny little grin—as if he wants to be sure it is a game for his amusement. As if he's now suddenly suspicious that I might be, after all, doing it for my own amusement. . .'[16]

Despite the happy, loving and contented picture that Dorothy paints in her journal, she was something of a recluse. Not only did the death of her daughter Jane weigh heavily on her, but she was becoming increasingly unhappy in her marriage. Dorothy slowly became a rather cold and aloof mother, at least according to Lynne Aalan, who lived with Dorothy for many years. Lynne thought Dorothy must have seemed 'overpowering to Phil as a small child'.[17] She described Dorothy as:

'. . .a restrained person, relating outwardly mainly on an intellectual level, not given to expressions of affection—not open with her feelings.'

This is not evident in family pictures of the young Philip, who appears as a happy, contented tot lying in his cot or sitting in his pram, smiling and waving at the camera. In the background can be seen his father's proudest possession, a smart Buick two-passenger business coupé. Other pictures show PKD at the age of two, still smiling happily outside his house, or sitting on his father's knee while Ted looks down on his youngest son with obvious pride. However, pictures of PKD taken a few years later, when his parents' marriage was coming to an end, tell a different story.

The United States had been going through an unprecedented economic boom. That, too, was about to end. On 24 October 1929, the country was gripped by financial panic as millions of dollars were wiped off share prices on the New York Stock Exchange. Within a year, the USA and the wider world would be mired in the economic slump that become known as the 'Great Depression'. One of the few highlights of this grim period was the work of the writer James T. Farrell, who would later become an important influence on PKD's writing.

A move to the sunshine

Around this time Ted, Dorothy and baby Phil moved to Sausalito, a city in the beautiful San Francisco Bay area of California, soon moving on again to Alameda on the eastern side of the Bay. The family then settled in Berkeley, an attractive and historic city also located on the eastern shoreline. Like everywhere in the US, California would suffer during the depression but Berkeley fared better than most thanks to the University of California at Berkeley, the oldest campus in the state. PKD was to be closely tied to Berkeley and the Bay area for much of his adult life. As an established government officer, his father Ted was relatively safe from the economic gloom, but not the trials of domestic discord.

In the summer of 1930, Ted was promoted to director of the western division of the National Recovery Association, established by President Franklin D. Roosevelt to help boost the economy by bringing government, industry and labour together to eliminate competition and set fair prices. Ted was given the task of setting up a new office in the city of Reno, Nevada. Dorothy was happy for Ted to go but did not want to move there herself. She was not sure whether the job would last that long and, anyway, she liked Berkeley. Her mother Edna, known from this time onwards by PKD's pet name for her, 'Meemaw', and father, were now living nearby with Dorothy's younger sister Marion and husband Joe Hudner. So Ted would now have to get up on a Monday morning and set off in his Buick on the two-hundred-mile journey to Reno, where he would stay all week, not returning until late the following Friday. This weekly forced separation would take its toll on the marriage. Finally, Dorothy asked Ted for a divorce. Many years afterwards, Ted was still unclear exactly how this had come about. He said:

> '. . . it just seemed to be one of those things that was done. She thought she had more freedom than when we were married. I think it was that simple. We parted very well, good friends. When we decided we were going to get a divorce I used to come down weekends, like nothing happened.'

As Ted indicated, the couple did everything to ensure the split was as amicable as possible to cause minimum disruption to young Philip. Ted would slowly spend more and more time in Reno and less and less time in Berkeley. From now on, young PKD would exist in a world with little emotional or physical contact from his parents. As Dorothy was a very non-tactile mother, PKD became closer to his more affectionate grandmother, Meemaw.

The effect that the marriage break-up had on PKD is reflected in the family album. Gone is the happy and contented infant and toddler. The five-year-old PKD who looks out at the camera has a sad and withdrawn air – even when dressed in a smart and clearly expensive cowboy suit, complete with Stetson, chaps and holster, possibly a sign his father showered gifts on his son to make up for the lack of personal attention he could provide. In one of the few photographs from this period that show a happy PKD, the boy is standing in front of his Aunt Marion with his maternal grandmother and grandfather on either side. All are smiling and PKD is beaming delightedly. Clearly, this was where he preferred to be.

PKD now enrolled at the Quaker-run Bruce Tatlock Kindergarten, which he was later to describe as a 'communist school'. PKD has claimed that his babysitter at the time, Olive Holt, was also a communist. He described how she lectured him on the merits of the Soviet Union, clearly superior to the United States in her eyes. Her name was to turn up again many years later in the most bizarre circumstances. Although separated, both parents tried to remain an important part of PKD's life as he settled into the regime of the kindergarten school.

It was around this time that he began to show a precocious gift for writing. Dorothy typed out a poem of his entitled 'A Song of Philip – Five years old' that may well have been PKD's first literary effort. Much later, as a successful middle-aged novelist, PKD would tell an interviewer that it was his mother's ambition to be a professional writer. Although she never achieved the success she craved, she passed on her love of writing to her son. 'It was from her that I got the idea that writing was a very important thing,' he said. [18]

This short period of security and stability was not to last long. By the time PKD was six, in early 1935, the divorce was finalized. Now, PKD was on the move again. The divorce proceedings had begun and turned into a custody battle for the young boy. So Dorothy and her son took off for Washington DC, on the other side of the US, where Dorothy had secured a job at the Federal Children's Bureau. She was concerned that, if she stayed in relatively close proximity to Ted, her ex-husband may, in due course, gain custody of Philip. By putting such a vast distance between them, she made this threat seem much less likely.

Berkeley is home to the California Golden Bears, at the time, one of the most successful teams in college football, and based at the California Memorial Stadium, on the UC Berkeley campus. A visit to a football game there would be the last PKD was to see of his father for another three years.

It was during his time in Washington that PKD first started having psychological problems. These manifested in physical symptoms that included periods in which he simply could not swallow. This was hugely distressing for him and Dorothy. PKD was taken to see a psychiatrist whose diagnosis, PKD claimed later, was that he was a 'hysteric'. For a time, PKD was removed from his mother and placed in a special boarding school for problem children called the Countryside School, located in Silver Spring, Maryland. PKD's swallowing problems continued, however, and he quickly lost weight.

PKD did not settle in well at the school and his deep unhappiness there was to inspire another piece of writing, a poem about a little bird being eaten by a cat. Despite the morbid subject matter, it seems that this piece of work was well received at the school's Parent's Day and, as PKD was later to write, 'My future was assured.'

PKD continued to feel unsettled at the Countryside School and so, for the next academic year, 1936/1937, he was transferred to the John Eaton Elementary School, in Washington. It is unclear if this transfer was approved by the authorities, who had initially placed PKD in the more controlled environment of the Countryside School, or that Dorothy was alone in making this decision. Whatever the reason, PKD was now back in the state school system. He bore a deep resentment towards his mother for the time he spent at the Countryside School and for keeping him away from her and home. This resentment was compounded by the fact that, even on his return, he did not get the level of maternal attention and affection he craved. He was placed in the care of a series of housekeepers who looked after him while his mother was at work. PKD also blamed Dorothy for separating him from his father, and his grandmother Meemaw, and for the move to Washington, whose cold damp climate compared unfavourably with the blue skies and balmy weather of the 'Golden State' he had left behind.

PKD rebelled by inventing a series of 'illnesses' that ensured his regular absence from school at this time and which would also become a frequent issue throughout his school life. However, he was continuing to show promise as a writer. In a school report, his fourth-grade teacher commented that 'Philip shows interest and ability in story-telling'.

In June 1938, Dorothy and PKD, now aged nine, returned to her family in California. Dorothy had arranged a transfer from the Federal Children's Bureau to the US Forestry Department, which conveniently had offices in Berkeley. This meant PKD could be close to 'Meemaw' and also see his Aunt Marion, with whom he was to develop a very close relationship over the next few years. Ted had now relocated to Pasadena, some distance to the south of Berkeley. Although Dorothy was still worried that Ted may attempt to claim custody of young PKD, the distance separating father and son may have made this threat seem far less likely. Nevertheless, they were now in the same state, close enough for PKD, on occasion, to spend time with his father. As we shall see, a father–son visit to the 1938 World's Fair in San Francisco may have stimulated PKD's lifelong fascination with science and technology and prompted his interest in the concept of simulacra, in the form of artificial humans. His father also took him on fishing trips and other outings that gave him back the feeling he craved of having two parents who loved and wanted him.

In the autumn of 1938, PKD started at the Hillside School in Berkeley. For some reason, PKD decided at this time that he would prefer to be called 'Jim'. Everybody seems to have gone along with this and even his school reports refer to this new name. It was also at this time that young 'Jim' started experiencing recurring bouts of tachycardia – a sudden and rapid increase in heart rate that can be extremely frightening. It is possible that he inherited this problem from his father. It was a complaint that was to continue throughout his life. At this time, PKD was also prone to bouts of asthma and eczema, both of which can be related to extreme anxiety. Yet it seems that his time at Hillside was a reasonably happy one. His teachers recorded that he fitted in well with fellow pupils.

For the 1939/40 academic year, he moved to the Oxford Elementary School where he reverted to being known as Phil. Again, he settled in well. However, his regular, and occasionally prolonged, absences due to illness, sometimes genuine and at other times not, had an effect on his overall performance. Dorothy was later to state that PKD found schoolwork boring and was much more at ease following up on his own interests.

A reflection of this was the production of his own newspaper, *The Daily Dick*, which he published in December 1938 when he was just turning 10 years old. Two issues of the newspaper survive and show PKD to be not only a very advanced writer for his age, but also to have a talent for art.

Discovering the land of Oz

It was around this time that young Philip first encountered the novels of L. Frank Baum, the author of *The Wonderful Wizard of Oz*. That original 'Oz' book was published in 1900 and was an immediate success, becoming the best-selling children's book for two years following its publication. Baum wrote a further thirteen novels, all about a young girl called Dorothy and the amazing characters she meets in the land of Oz. Two movie versions of the story had been made in 1910 and 1925 but it was the release of the Judy Garland musical version in 1939 that made 'Oz' the iconic worldwide phenomenon it has remained. However, it was in Baum's books that PKD first encountered the 'wonderful world of Oz' and, in doing so, began a long-lasting love of fantasy. In 1968 he wrote:

> 'I discovered the Oz books (in about 1939). It seemed like a small matter, my utter avidity to read each Oz book. Librarians haughtily told me that they "did not stock such fantastic material," their reasoning being that books of fantasy led a child into a dreamworld and made it difficult for him to adjust properly to the "real" world. But my interest in the Oz books was, in point of fact, the beginning of my love for fantasy.'[19]

It is interesting to note that in *The Wizard of Oz* there is a series of themes that feature heavily in PKD's later writing; the idea of empathy (the Tin Man needing a 'heart'), simulacra (the Tin Man and the Scarecrow as fake human beings) and, of course, the 'reality' behind 'reality' (the Land of Oz coexisting with the 'reality' of Kansas). There is even a direct reference to it in PKD's semi-autobiographical novel *Confessions of a Crap Artist* (1975). Jack Isidore, one of the main characters in the novel, had grown up in California and bears many similarities to the young PKD. In the novel, 'Jack' describes a former Japanese neighbour as looking like 'Jack Pumpkinhead', one of the Oz characters created by Baum, because of 'his skinny neck and round head'. Jack goes on:

> 'The notion that Mr. Watanaba looked like Jack Pumpkinhead could never have occurred to me if I hadn't read the Baum books in my younger years; in fact I still had a few of them around my room as late as World War II. I kept them with

> my science fiction magazines, my old microscope and rock
> collection, and the model of the solar system that I had built
> in junior school for science class.'

It was also around this time that PKD developed a close relationship with
his Aunt Marion. It may well have been Marion's positive encouragement of
PKD's burgeoning writing talents that led him to write *The Daily Dick*.
Tragically, this much-loved aunt spent much of her short life suffering periods
of catatonic schizophrenia. Her life would soon be brought to a premature
end as a consequence of complications of this condition. Her mental illness
and resulting death were to have a significant effect on PKD's attitude towards
psychological disorders, a frequent theme in his later writing.

There was soon to be another focus to PKD's life. In 1940, Ted moved
to the Los Angeles office of the Department of Commerce. He had regularly
acted as spokesman for his department and it soon became apparent that
he had a natural talent as a broadcaster. He became a regular presenter on
a radio programme called *This Is Your Government*. This gave Ted some
unexpected fame locally and PKD was understandably proud of him. By
this time, Ted had remarried. He and his new wife, Dorothea, were living
in South Pasadena and so PKD was now able to see more of his father.

By the late 1930s, the United States was beginning to shake off the
depression doldrums and had become the most vibrant and go-ahead
country in the world. For a young boy growing up in America at this time,
California was one of the most exciting places to be. In an interview with
Gregg Rickman, Ted recalled that he and his son made many visits to
Treasure Island, a huge artificial island built in San Francisco Bay to host
the 1939 San Francisco World Fair, known as the Golden Gate International
Exposition.[20] This fair was originally organized to commemorate the
opening of the San Francisco-Oakland Bay Bridge and the Golden Gate
Bridge, both completed in a frenzy of construction work only a few years
before. The event also showcased some of the most remarkable technological innovations of the time. For a bright and imaginative boy like PKD,
the event would have been a scientific wonderland providing a fascinating
glimpse of what the future might hold.

During one of these visits, PKD saw an amazing device known as 'Pedro
the Voder', designed and built by The Bell Telephone Company, which had
been one of the most popular exhibits at the Fair. This machine was an
early attempt at synthesizing the human voice by combining a buzzing
sound, created by an electrical oscillator, with a hissing sound, produced
by a gas discharge tube. An operator controlled the device using keys and
foot pedals. It is clear that this machine had a profound effect on PKD's
young mind and probably first sparked the idea of the human simulacra

that featured in many of his novels and short stories. Indeed, in his novel *We Can Build You* (1972), 'Pedro' itself is referenced.[21]

Philip K. Dick scholar Samuel J. Umland reinforces the idea that the author was working from personal memory and not from research when he points out, on a posting on his blogsite, that PKD gets the automaton's name slightly wrong in the book, spelling it 'Vodor' not 'Voder'.[22]

By this time, PKD was developing a whole series of 'phobias'. This may have triggered his later interest in psychology, both as a tool for the study of personality and abilities, and as an insight into the wider extremes of human experience. In her book *Philip K. Dick: Remembering Firebright* (2013), PKD's fifth and last wife Tessa describes a meeting she had with his father Ted, after PKD's death in 1982. Tessa was amazed by the similarities she noticed between father and son. She states that they both used the same gestures and spoke with a very similar voice. She also discovered that Ted may have had similar phobias to those of his son. Tessa had taken her son by PKD, Christopher, to meet his grandfather. For no clear reason, Ted had shown great anxiety about his grandson and even told Tessa that he felt that something terrible would happen to the little boy. Ted then went on to warn Tessa that his neighbour's pine tree was dangerous:

> '"Some day", he said, "the wind is going to knock that tree down and kill me." The tree did seem to be leaning a little but it was quite healthy and in no danger of falling.'[23]

Tessa then added the following comment:

> 'Phil had told me that, when he was a little boy, his father used to get him up in the middle of the night, put him into the car and drive as fast as he could to the east because a big earthquake was about to hit – it always turned out to be a false alarm.'[24]

Clearly this was, if true, evidence of an extreme form of phobic behaviour. But was it an actual series of events or just an example of PKD embroidering his past?

In her biography, PKD's third wife Anne managed to trace one of PKD's close friends from this period, Leon Rimov. Perhaps influenced by the technological innovations on display at the San Francisco World Fair, Leon said PKD had made a lie detector box and enjoyed fooling people with this machine. A similar machine, called the Voight–Kampff Empathy Test, appeared in PKD's most famous novel *Do Androids Dream of Electric Sheep?* (1968).[25] Leon also recalled something that contradicts other reports about PKD at that time. Anne writes that, according to Leon,

> 'Phil was sick and pale and out of school from time to time.
> He also was hyperactive. He ate a lot of cookies and chocolate
> and was overweight. For lunch he would eat several candy
> bars and some ice cream.'[26]

All other reports about PKD at that age describe him as having a phobia about eating in public and stated that, when he did, he ate only very small amounts. Here we have one of his closest friends at the time describing him as eating a great deal. Perhaps he made up for his public fasting by binging in private. PKD told Anne that when he was young he had a form of diabetes but that this cleared up as he grew older.

Fire and water

In the summer of 1940, perhaps arranged by his music-loving mother, eleven-year-old PKD attended Cazadero Music Camp, located in the heart of the beautiful redwood forest in the Russian River Valley of Sonoma County, in Northern California. He would later describe himself as being a 'tortured outsider' at this camp. And yet the PKD that attended this popular location was very much a part of the social scene. He involved himself in many of the cultural activities staged there, even acting in some of the plays. As a total non-sportsman, he did not throw himself into all the open-air activities available in this rural idyll, but otherwise he was, in general, no different from any of the other kids. However, two events that occurred there were to have a profound effect on him.

On one occasion, he got into trouble while swimming in the Russian River and nearly drowned. This brought about a fear of water that was to last the rest of his life. For someone who spent so much of his life in the San Francisco Bay area, this would cause a problem as even viewing the sea from the safety of land sometimes proved too much to cope with. The second traumatic event was that PKD saw another child burned to death. A group of boys had been playing cowboys and Indians and one boy draped himself in crepe paper. Unfortunately, he ventured too close to a log fire and was engulfed in flames. PKD was to tell Tessa, many years later, that he had attempted to rip the burning paper off the skin of the dying child, receiving painful burns to his own hands in the process.

A few years after this incident, at the height of World War II with battle raging in the South Pacific between the United States and Japan, the emotional impact that this fire tragedy had caused was to come to the surface. PKD and Dorothy were sitting in a movie theatre watching the news pro-gramme being shown before the main feature. The programme was about the latest events in the South Pacific theatre of war and included a sequence showing American GIs using flamethrowers on entrenched Japanese troops.

One of the Japanese soldiers was engulfed in flames, becoming a human torch. The horror of this image was too much for PKD and he ran out of the theatre.[27]

By now, PKD had left the Oz books behind and was developing a new literary interest. It was science fiction that stimulated his imagination. This style of literature was to bring him worldwide renown and yet he discovered it purely by chance. He had always been interested in science and at this time had his heart set on being a palaeontologist. He went into his local candy store to buy a science magazine but found instead a mind-expanding gateway to a world he never knew existed.

> 'I was twelve [in 1940] when I read my first sf [*science fiction*] magazine. . .it was called *Stirring Science Stories* and ran, I think, for four issues. . . I came across the magazine quite by accident; I was actually looking for *Popular Science*. I was most amazed. Stories about science? At once I recognized the magic which I had found, in earlier times, in the Oz books – this magic now coupled not with magic wands but with science. . . In any case my view became magic equals science. . . and science (of the future) equals magic.'[28]

'Boy! There were some really great stories in there!' he would later explain to Joe Vitale. People went back in time or travelled to the centre of the universe. One of the stories featured 'a wall that only had one side'.[29] If you fell over it you found yourself back where you started. The editor of *Stirring Science Stories* was Don Wollheim. Many years later, Wollheim would set PKD on the road to fame, if not fortune, by buying his first novel. PKD's encounter with science fiction was to change his life and, from then on, he was hooked. By the time he entered junior high school, he had already started accumulating science fiction magazines, a collection he would add to throughout his life.

In the spring of 1941, PKD, now 12, entered the seventh grade at Garfield Junior High. His friends at the time recalled that he was a slightly over-weight child with no interest in sports. Both PKD's parents had been from the conservative Midwest of America and their attitudes may have influenced the way he dressed and behaved. Compared to other boys, born to the outdoor sea-and-sunshine culture of California, PKD was, as his friend George Kohler recalled, 'somewhat old-fashioned'. However, he was far from insecure. With the natural charm, easy wit, infectious enthusiasm and captivating personality that were to be his hallmarks in adult life, PKD found friendships came easily. He was able to choose his circle of friends carefully and then, within this group, become the dominant one.

By December 1941, war in Europe had been raging for more than two years. PKD was keen to know about events in the wider world and took a keen interest in current affairs. On 7 December, military aircraft operating from aircraft carriers of the Japanese Imperial Navy carried out a surprise attack on the US Naval Base at Pearl Harbor, on the Hawaiian Island of Oahu, finally bringing the United States into World War II. PKD was shocked by the lack of interest that his mother showed in these events. When he phoned Dorothy to tell her that the USA was at war, she simply dismissed him and went back to her gardening. In his novel *Confessions of a Crap Artist* (1975), PKD paints a vivid picture of the feelings of anger and suspicion felt towards the Japanese in California at this time.

> 'It wasn't long after December 7 that the military authorities put up notices on the telephone poles, telling Japs they had to be out of California by such and such a date. . . they had to get out whether they liked it or not. In my estimation it was for their own good anyhow, because a lot of us were stirred up about Japs sabotaging and spying. . . a bunch of us chased a Jap kid and kicked him around a little, to show how we felt. His father was a dentist as I recall.'

Despite the friendships he seemed to form so effortlessly, PKD always maintained that his time at school was far from easy. He was later to write that he felt very ill at ease in class and continually had to suppress the urge to run out of the classroom. These fears and phobias may have contributed to his health problems, such as asthma, eczema and outbreaks of acne. He would later write a letter to his ex-wife Nancy and his daughter Isa in which he made the following comment:

> 'When I was in school I was ugly and dumb and other kids threw rocks at me and jeered. I used to hide under parked cars and growl at them, where they couldn't reach me. . . but later I got too fat to get under parked cars.'[30]

This does not seem to be a true reflection of his relationship with other children. As this section of the letter was addressed to Isa, it may be that he was being somewhat tongue-in-cheek. Perhaps his daughter had been having a hard time at school and he wanted to reassure her by suggesting it is something all children go through. He may also have been empathizing with the Japanese children he had seen being bullied after Pearl Harbor.

The imagery is so strong that one can reasonably assume that it influenced his 1968 novel *Do Androids Dream of Electric Sheep?*, which features an elderly religious leader called Wilbur Mercer. Mercer appears on television where he is shown attempting to climb a hill as people off screen throw stones at him. Watching the events on television while wired up to their empathy boxes, his followers – disciples of a cult known as Mercerism – can share his pain and distress. This is an example of how PKD's inward view of his childhood influenced his writing, even if it did not necessarily reflect reality.

The theme was a powerful one for PKD. The Mercer character first appeared in the original version of PKD's collaborative novel *The Ganymede Takeover*, co-written with his friend Ray Nelson in 1965, but removed from the final version, only to reappear three years later in *Do Androids Dream. . .*[31]

Dorothy was clearly concerned about the poor progress PKD was making at school and, in the autumn of 1942, when he was thirteen, she decided to take him out of Garfield and enrol him at a military-style boarding school in Ojai, sixty-six miles north-west of Los Angeles. Known as the California Preparatory School, or 'Cal Prep' for short, this school was quite different from the one he had been attending at Garfield. In 1981, PKD was to claim that he 'went nuts' at Cal Prep and started to mix with the 'tough kids'. Why Dorothy made the decision to enrol him there is shrouded in mystery. However, her step-daughter Lynne Aalan told Gregg Rickman that Dorothy 'was sending him there because it had been recommended, I believe, by therapists'.[32]

As Cal Prep was located in Southern California, it gave PKD another opportunity to stay with his father in South Pasadena before starting the new school year in September. This was only a fleeting visit as Ted was heavily involved in the war effort and was coordinating different industrial committees under the overall control of the Department of Commerce. Ted's career was to take him away from California, first to Cleveland, Ohio, and then to Richmond, Virginia. He would not see his father again until 1948, when PKD was nineteen. The absent, or distant, father figure was a recurring theme in many of PKD's stories. For example, *Martian Time-Slip* (1965) and *Eye in the Sky* (1957) both feature contentious father-son relationships that had their origins in this period in PKD's life.

PKD was to go through a period of confusion over his feelings regarding his new school, which was more than three hundred miles away from his home in Berkeley. However, one thing was for sure, as far as PKD was concerned, his mother was to blame for his exile. His anger with her and emotional turmoil is evident in his letters to her over his short time at Cal Prep:

> 'I am perfectly miserable. . . . I'm so used to having all my things private and not to be touched. . . I am getting sick and tired of knowing that the second I leave my room it will be messed up. . . I just don't fit into the group here. I am afraid that I may decide to leave. . .'[33]

Only to write again a few days later:

> 'Gee whiz, I guess that I had just better not write unless everything I say is strictly cheerful. I AM NOT COMING HOME. I have no wish to, and I don't think that what I said in that letter could be interpreted to mean that I wished to come home. . . I think that you and Meemaw are too ready to have me come home. . . For goodness sake, don't tell me that I can come home, because it is just like when you would say, 'All right, you don't have to go to school today.' . . . When I get a letter like you sent me it REALLY makes me home-sick. . .. You have hurt my feelings by suggesting that I am such a sissy that I can't stand a little work!'[34]

First sci-fi character

In a later letter, he acknowledged that he was 'very changeable' in his opinions. He stayed at Cal Prep for one year, returning to Garfield in September 1943 at the start of the ninth grade. In August 1943, aged fourteen, he launched another self-published newspaper, this time with his friend Pat Flannery. Unlike *The Daily Dick*, this was a startlingly mature attempt at popular journalism and creative writing and featured PKD's first authentic science fiction creation, a superhero by the name of *Future-Human*. This being lives in the year 3869 and uses his 'super science' to protect humanity from criminals and other anti-social elements.

It was also around the age of thirteen or fourteen when PKD made his first attempt at writing a short story with a science fiction theme. It was called *Return to Lilliput* and was an updating of the famous Jonathan Swift novel, *Gulliver's Travels*. There seems to be a degree of confusion as to when this long-lost first story was written. In a 1978 interview with Joe Vitale for the *Aquarian,* he said he was 13 and claimed it was his first attempt at a novel, although unsuccessful. In the biography *Divine Invasions – A Life of Philip K. Dick*, the writer Lawrence Sutin claims it was written when PKD was 14 years old, which suggests sometime between December 1942 and December 1943. However, in *The Pocket Essential Philip K. Dick*, Andrew M. Butler dates it as being between 1941 and 1942.[35] The Philip K. Dick 'fans' website says it was started when PKD was at Cal Prep and completed on his return to Berkeley in October 1943.[36] As the manuscript is lost there is no way of really knowing the exact dates. But we do know that from 1942 PKD had been regularly contributing stories to the Berkeley Gazette's 'Young Author's Club' with works appearing fifteen times between 1942 and 1944. The club was run by a journalist who wrote her comments under the name 'Aunt Flo'.

As well as writing, PKD's great love was music, nurtured by his mother and perhaps inspired by those early occasions when, as a baby, he had sat on Dorothy's lap while she played the piano. His prized possession was now his Magnavox record player. Thanks to his mother's influence, he developed an enthusiastic and knowledgeable interest in classical music that was to provide a useful moneymaking opportunity when he started working at a record store. In particular, PKD was passionate about the works of Franz Schubert, Offenbach and especially Richard Wagner, and would one day name one of his daughters Isolde, after the tragic heroine in the Wagner opera *Tristan and Isolde*.

Behind the counter

During the summer of 1943, aged fifteen, PKD had begun a part-time job at University Radio and Electronics, in Central Berkeley, essentially a sales and repair facility that sold refrigerators, phonographs and other domestic electrical goods, and repaired goods when requested. PKD would later tell his friend, the science fiction writer Kevin ('K.W.') Jetter that he had warned the owner of the store, Herb Hollis, that a group from school was planning a shop-lifting spree at one of his premises. Hollis was so impressed by PKD's behaviour that he offered him a part-time job sweeping the floors and being a general 'gofer'. Hollis himself was to become a huge influence on PKD emotionally and creatively. Hollis and his philosophy are said to have inspired the following inter-office memo, to 'Pre-Fash' consultants at Perky Pat Layouts, Inc, dictated by Leo Bulero in *The Three Stigmata of Palmer Eldritch*.

> 'I mean, after all, you have to consider we're only made out of dust. That's admittedly not much to go on and we shouldn't forget that. But even considering, I mean it's a sort of bad beginning, we're not doing too bad. So I personally have faith that even in this lousy situation we're faced with we can make it. You get me?'

Hollis also owned a record store called the Art Music Company, on the corner of Telegraph Street and Channing Street, Berkeley. All the staff, with the exception of the service engineers, alternated between the two shops. Over time it became obvious that PKD's almost encyclopaedic knowledge of classical music could be put to use at Art Music, which specialized in classical and jazz recordings. PKD subsequently became a sales clerk at the shop. However, in his time working with the engineers and technicians, he developed a love of high-end equipment together with a working knowledge of how musical reproduction systems worked. Pictures of this time show a fresh-faced, if rather serious, young man in a smart suit and wide, flamboyant floral tie. It was within this seemingly happy environment that PKD encountered the first of his 'experiences'. He describes it in this way:

> 'One day I was standing in the record store when my old bogey hit me. My old globus hysteria and I thought I was choking. I was strangling to death. And it takes the form of claustrophobia. I got choked, strangled, the confusion of inner and outer space. I can't explain it. You've got to have it. You have to have the phobia to know what it feels like. It is *hell*.'[37]

What is intriguing about this incident is that PKD goes on to explain that it was like space itself collapsed in and closed around him. 'The walls seem to crush you and then all of a sudden the walls open out like a bellow and suddenly you have nothing to stand up against and support yourself and hold on to.' And then he makes what seems to be a very telling statement:

> 'My special sense would get impaired. So I experienced first spaces too small and then spaces too large.'[38]

It is clear that, for PKD, reality was not as solid and consistent as it was for other people. As we shall discover, it was this subjective interpretation of 'reality as an illusion' that was to allow his imagination to flourish and create a series of fictional worlds where nothing can be taken for granted.

PKD's time at Garfield came to an end in the autumn of 1943 and in February 1944 he moved up to Berkeley High School. After the summer recess, PKD returned to school in September 1944. But PKD's problems at school continued, and after his eighteenth birthday (December 1946) he never went back. He completed his senior high school year at home with private tuition, graduating in June 1947.

The world was changing dramatically. On 6 August 1945, a US Air Force Superfortress bomber dropped an atomic weapon on the Japanese city of Hiroshima, killing an estimated 50,000–80,000 people in the first twenty-four hours. A similar number would die from radiation burns and radiation sickness over the following two months. The horrific potential that science can unleash now became only too apparent to PKD.

It was around this time that PKD revisited short story writing. It is unclear whether he was still at High School when he wrote these stories. If so, then an incident described in his story *Stability* may have been influenced by his attacks of 'agoraphobia'. PKD describes how the main character, Benton, experiences a sensation in which 'the room began to waver and give way (like) a quality of jelly.' Could this have been PKD incorporating into an early short story, unpublished at the time, an event that had actually happened to him?

Whatever took place at the store that day, it had been building up for quite a few years and it was to manifest at least three more times in his life. In a celebrated 1974 interview with rock journalist Paul Williams, PKD acknowledged that he had experienced three 'breakdowns' in his life. He said these occurred at the ages of nineteen, twenty-four and thirty-three. He did not consider the disorientation he felt in the store to be anything other than one of his unusual phobias causing him problems. His first 'real' breakdown, we can reasonably assume, took place after his nineteenth birthday, which suggests it was sometime after December 1947, six months after he graduated. However, he was later to inform his psychiatrist, Barry Spatz, that the treatment took place when he was eighteen and involved a series of visits to the Langley Porter Clinic in San Francisco. It was here that PKD first encountered the work of the psychologist Carl Jung. PKD was later to incorporate Jung's ideas on the nature of personality into many of his short stories and novels.

According to Spatz, PKD thrived on the attention he received at the clinic. It may have provided a replacement for the emotional support he believed he was not receiving from his mother and school teachers. It made him feel special and different. It was also at this time that he encountered various psychometric and personality tests, again a theme that can be found in some of his later novels, such as the Voight–Kampff Empathy Test in *Do Androids Dream of Electric Sheep?*.

The loss of his final months at school put paid to any ambitions PKD may have had with regard to a career in music, despite the great talent he had shown, nurtured by Dorothy. His time at Art Music helped him through the trauma of his last few years at Berkeley High School and was a source of great support, both from fellow workers and the manager, PKD's 'replacement father', Herb Hollis.

On leaving Berkeley High School, PKD began to work full time for Hollis and, over the years, he became very close to this 'mentor figure'. Indeed, in many of PKD's future novels and short stories, the relationship between the 'Patriarch-Boss' and the central character was used many times. Examples of these are Leo Bulero in *The Three Stigmata of Palmer Eldritch* (1965), Gino Molanari in *Now Wait For Next Year* (1966) and Glen Runciter in *UBIK* (1969). PKD also became friends with the older clerks in the store, men who would help PKD through the painful journey from teenager to adult. The next step was to seek his independence by moving out of the maternal home.

Chapter Three

The Young Writer (1947–53)

In the autumn of 1947, Jerry Ackerman, a second-year student at UC Berkeley, was looking for premises near the campus when he heard about a vacant room in the top floor of a warehouse in McKinley Street. Although still a working building, the top floor had been converted into rooms that were available to rent. At that time, there was a mixture of students and working men living there. After a short period of time, the workers tended to move out, probably deterred by Jerry's loud music and noisy parties, leaving more rooms available for his friends. These new arrivals included writers, poets and artists. Like Jerry, many were gay. A few weeks later, another new arrival turned up to take a room there, Philip K. Dick.

PKD and Jerry had been friends at high school and, when Jerry informed PKD that a room was available, he jumped at the opportunity. PKD could now attain a degree of independence from Dorothy and strike out on his own. The warehouse was close to his workplace at Art Records and his mother's house, so the maternal ties had not actually been cut, merely stretched a little.

PKD moved into one of the small rooms opposite Jerry's. He brought with him his precious Magnavox record player and little else. Up to this time, PKD had not dated girls, partly because of his shyness, and possibly his unusual dress sense. His move seems to have been an act of rebellion against his mother and an opportunity to 'find himself'. However, his mother regularly castigated him for the move, saying that without her guidance he would become a 'queer'. She may not have known that Jerry and his associates were homosexual, but PKD almost certainly did. After all, Jerry had been his friend for some time and it is unlikely that PKD would have been unaware of the 'gay scene' at the building in McKinley Street.

Initially, PKD kept himself to himself. Unlike the other residents, PKD worked normal business hours. But with his natural gift for making friends he soon attracted a small group who, like him, were interested in music. One of his co-workers at the store, Norman Mini, would remain a friend and would later marry PKD's second wife, Kleo. However, the arrival of a new manager at the Hollis store, Vince Lusby, was to open up a whole new social scene for PKD and lead to his first serious relationship with the opposite sex. PKD and Vince soon struck up a close friendship.

Vince introduced PKD to some of his friends and they would occasionally visit local jazz clubs. These visits had to be quite rare as PKD still suffered from attacks of agoraphobia. He would try to select a table tucked away in a corner and close to the toilets. With his new circle of friends, he now decided he was ready to move out of McKinley Street. He had confided in Vincent that he feared he might be gay, like Jerry Ackerman. Vincent pointed out to PKD how different his tastes in most things were to those of Jerry and his gay associates. When this didn't have the desired effect, Vince decided on a more practical solution:

> 'At that time we had some rather peculiar ideas about homosexuality. Philip, who was a virgin, thought he might be one. I thought it was a curable condition. A good piece of ass and it would all be over. So I availed him of a good piece of ass.'[39]

Marriage to Jeanette Marlin

As Vince had hoped, this 'good piece of ass' soon appeared. There was also a readily available location for PKD's initiation into manhood. A basement room at the store housed a collection of very expensive music reproduction equipment. As this room was rarely used for anything else, it was the perfect place for PKD to assuage his worries regarding his sexuality. But who was the female who took PKD's virginity in the basement? According to Anne Dick, it was the woman who was to be PKD's first wife. Whoever it was, from that moment onwards, PKD's interest in women was to become a driving force in his life.

For a short period of time, PKD played the role of 'young man about town' and, according to Vince, had a few short relationships. But soon afterwards he was to meet a young woman called Jeanette Marlin, marry her, and then divorce her within a period of just seven months. This relationship has long been a mystery. PKD rarely talked about Jeanette so who exactly she was and what became of her remained, until very recently, an unknown part of his life story.

According to Anne Dick, however, Jeanette Marlin came into the store one day to buy a record and was served by Vince. As Vince has taken credit for helping PKD lose his virginity, he must have arranged a date between them. In Anne's version of events, 'Phil and his future wife cohabited in the basement of University Radio one night and he established his masculinity. They married shortly afterwards.'[40] Anne said that in those days it was common to marry the first person one slept with and that PKD was no exception. In his early mainstream novel, *Mary and the Giant* (written between 1953 and 1955 but not published until 1987), PKD fictionalizes some aspects of this first sexual encounter. In the novel, his main female character is seduced in a similar set of circumstances by her much older boss.

PKD and Jeanette were married on 14 May 1948 when PKD was just nineteen. Because PKD was not yet twenty-one, the age of majority under Californian law, Dorothy had to sign her agreement to the marriage on the wedding certificate. Dorothy may have had her reservations over this sudden turn of events but one can at least assume that she would have been delighted to have PKD taken away from his hedonistic lifestyle in McKinley Street and by this proof that he was not a 'queer'.

The newly-weds found an apartment on Addison Way. It was small and cramped with old furniture and unpacked boxes. This was not an ideal start to married life.

Vince Lusby says he witnessed fights between PKD, Jeanette and her brother, who had soon appeared on the scene, and that threats were made with regard to the destruction of PKD's writing and, especially, his records.[41] When the inevitable divorce proceedings took place, this threat to PKD's musical collection was cited as one of the grounds for divorce. PKD was to tell his second wife, Kleo, that the judge found this to be the most ridiculous reason for divorce he had ever encountered. He said it was the first case he had ever presided over in which a phonograph record was 'cited as co-respondent'.[42] However, the judge still agreed to grant the divorce. The couple's six-and-a-half-month marriage ended on 30 November 1948 after one month's formal separation. The official grounds, a charge of 'extreme cruelty' made by Jeanette against PKD, was not contested.

The search for Jeanette

So who was Jeanette Marlin? Fortunately a recent article by Frank Hollander in the Philip K. Dick online fanzine *PKD-OTAKO* has helped shed a little light on this woman from PKD's early life. Hollander used the written material I sourced for this biography and followed it up with some painstaking detective work.

As his starting point, Hollander used the 1940 census, which was only released to the public in early 2012. He found in that a family called Marlin who were living in Byron Street, Berkeley, at the time. The eldest was a girl called Jeanette and there was a younger boy called Wendell. In 1940 Jeanette was thirteen years old and Wendell was twelve. If this is indeed the same Jeanette Marlin, then she was either 21 or 22 when she married PKD. This contradicts all the biographies which state that she was much older than PKD. For example PKD's stepsister, Lynne Aalan, is quoted by Rickman as stating that she was at least 25.[43] Anne Dick, in her biography *The Search for Philip K. Dick*, puts Jeanette's age at 26.[44] Lawrence Sutin makes her even older, stating that Jeanette was 'in her late twenties' with no caveat of doubt.[45]

Hollander then went to Berkeley Public Library and ploughed his way through the local high school yearbooks. He found Wendell in the 1943

Garfield Gleaner but there was no reference to Jeanette. He now knew that Wendell had attended Garfield so there was a chance that Jeanette may have attended the same school. On checking the on-line facilities for the Berkeley Daily Gazette he spotted an item dated 19 January 1942. This was a list of upcoming junior high-school graduates. As he scanned down it he found what he was looking for. There was a reference to a Jeanette Marlin. He went back to the library and checked out the other local schools' yearbooks. There he found a photograph of Jeanette Marlin at the age of fourteen. The 'California Birth Index' showed that 'Jeannette' Julia Marlin had been born on 1 January 1927 to Arthur and Lydia Marlin. The 1930 census had already told Hollander that Lydia had been born in Finland and that Arthur, who was born in Detroit, was the son of Finnish immigrants. A further internet enquiry brought up the information that Wendell died on 24 November 2009 in Pleasanton, California.

Thanks to Frank Hollander's meticulous research, we now know that Jeanette was just over twenty-one when she married PKD. Far from the 'much older woman' of legend

When the divorce finally came through, PKD returned to his old lifestyle. He roomed with Vince Lusby for a time before Vince married his fourth wife, Monica. Vince and Monica had an autistic child and, according to Anne, PKD was later to base the character Manfred in his novel *Martian Time Slip* on this boy.[46]

PKD then found his own apartment on Bancroft. Here he moved his precious collection of science fiction magazines, his record collection and, of course, his trusty Magnavox. It was as if the six months with Jeanette had never happened. He was soon in love again, this time with a beautiful Italian girl. She was soon followed by another of PKD's 'dark-haired girls', this time a pretty Jewish girl. PKD's taste was not restricted to petite Mediterranean types, however.

In April 1949, at the age of twenty, he fell in love again, this time with a vivacious blonde called Betty Jo Rivers. She was totally in keeping with PKD's interests at that time. He was going through a profound Germanic phase in which the music of Wagner and the writings of the German Romantics kept him company in his new apartment and so her fair 'Aryan' looks fitted the theme perfectly.

The relationship blossomed over that spring and summer. Evidence of PKD's eclectic reading at this time came when he gave Betty Jo a copy of William James' *The Varieties of Religious Experience*. Betty Jo completed her master's degree and was awarded a grant to continue her studies in France. PKD asked her to choose. It was him or France. Sadly for PKD, Betty Jo was too young to think about settling down to a life of domestic bliss and the romance of France won out.

Writing for radio

It was also at this time that PKD rediscovered his interest in writing: not short stories or poems but sales patter for the disc jockeys on the local FM radio station KSMO at San Mateo, in the San Francisco Bay area. One of the programmes on this station was sponsored by his boss Herb Hollis, who also supplied the records. As part of the sponsorship arrangement, they played on-air adverts for Hollis's shops. Somebody had to write these and PKD soon discovered his forte.

He would carry this ability through into his later fiction writing. He had a great deal of fun in his novel *UBIK* (1969) in which each chapter starts with an advertising slogan, clearly harking back to the skills he acquired in the late 1940s. For example:

> 'My hair is so dry, so unmanageable. What's a girl to do? Simply rub in creamy Ubik hair conditioner. In just five days you'll discover new body in your hair, no glossiness. And Ubik hairspray, used as directed, is absolutely safe.'[47]

Each one of these strap-lines shows that PKD had an eye for snappy advertising copy. Had things worked out differently, perhaps he would have ended in an advertising agency in New York's Madison Avenue, rather than working as a writer in the San Francisco Bay area.

The groves of academe

This re-stimulation of his creative side may have helped PKD decide that he needed to take his intellectual studies more seriously. He enrolled at UC Berkeley to study Philosophy and German, with additional classes in history, psychology and zoology. Rickman uses PKD's application form to give us an excellent snap-shot of PKD at this stage in his life. He was 5ft 11ins (1.8m) tall and weighed 176lb (12st 8lb/80kg). He had a place in Delaware Street, Berkeley. His mother, who is cited as his legal guardian, lived in El Cerrito, a small city located just to the north of Berkeley.[48]

Although his time at university was brief, his studies in philosophy, and the metaphysical works of Plato in particular, had a major influence on his later writing. He came to believe that the world is not truly 'real' but merely a projection of one's internally based perception. He would refine this concept by saying the universe was an extension of God, and describing himself as an 'acosmic panentheist'. The idea that what we think of as reality did not actually exist, a recurring theme in many of his works, has its origins in this period of PKD's life.

In the late 1940s, universities such as UC Berkeley still had an active military recruitment campaign, a legacy of World War II and the Cold War that followed. It would not be until the 1960s that Berkeley would gain a reputation for student activism, anti-war protests and opposition to the Vietnam conflict. PKD has claimed, however, that he was already opposed to war at this time and that his university career came to a shuddering halt due to a conflict between his social conscience and something called 'ROTC training'. He said that, at the time, enrolment in the Reserve Officer Training Corp was compulsory for male students at many of the major universities and so he left. This may have been because he was not physically capable of military training but PKD has suggested that it was to do with the strong anti-war sentiments that he was developing.

In a 1974 interview given to the London *Daily Telegraph*, he made the following comment:

> 'At Berkeley my anti-war convictions were actually the reason why I had to drop out. It was just before Korea, you had to belong to the military training corps. I disassembled my M1 rifle and refused to reassemble it – it's probably in pieces to this day because I dropped one small piece inside another so no one could get it out. I was very left wing. I also had a very personal feeling about the use of fire in war – we'd see those newsreel shots of flaming Japanese, you know – because as a child I saw another child burned to death.'[49]

Having dropped out of college, PKD continued his own education. He began devouring the works of the great philosophers, including Bergson, Spinoza, Plotinus, Leibnitz and Whitehead. But he also became interested in poets including Wordsworth, Yeats and Goethe. He then developed a passionate interest in theology, however, later claiming that he had studied enough to take it to degree level. He said of all the philosophical ideas, he was most in tune with Spinoza's *Deus sive substantia sive natura* – 'God that is reality that is nature'.

On PKD's twenty-first birthday, on 16 December 1949, he wrote a letter to Herb Hollis thanking him for all his help and support since 1944. In this curiously emotional letter, PKD reflects on the past years and especially on how Hollis had overseen his transition from boy to man. He described himself as a fifteen-year-old who was:

> '. . .just out of Junior high school, I had not started at Berkeley High yet. I had never kissed a girl. I did not shave, I read *Astounding Stories* for entertainment. At 21, I have been married and divorced, shave every day, and read James Joyce, & Herodotus' "Persian Wars", and the "Anabasis" of Xenophon for entertainment.'[50]

In many ways, this is a reflection of PKD's great need to be accepted as an intellectual rather than a simple sales clerk. He clearly needed something to give him focus. Soon he would be married and settled again, this time with a woman who would nurture his fledgling writing talents and help him soar.

Serious-minded Kleo

PKD was still aching over his loss of Betty Jo when he met seventeen-year-old Kleo Apostolides, a student at UC Berkeley. The record store had, by then, become a popular place to simply 'hang out'. One day Kleo walked into the store to buy a record. Later pictures of Kleo show a stunning-looking young woman, her Greek ancestry evident in dark, wavy, luxuriant shoulder-length hair, high cheekbones, and dark, deep-set eyes. They began seeing each other outside the shop on a regular basis and romance soon blossomed. It was a relationship that would last over ten years during an important period that saw the transition from PKD the shopworker and dreamer to PKD the professional writer.

Not only was there an instant physical attraction between the two, but PKD and Kleo also shared similar musical interests, including a love of Italian and German opera. Kleo was on PKD's intellectual level, with an interest in literature, philosophy and, to a certain extent, politics. She was a budding writer with firmly held left-wing political convictions and would later become a successful copy-editor. Despite the fact that PKD would later describe himself to the London *Daily Telegraph* as 'very left wing', PKD's political views were actually more liberal than socialist, but under her influence he would become more radical in his views.

One day PKD suggested that he and Kleo get married and Kleo agreed. They were wed on 14 June 1950 when Kleo was nineteen. It was then a question of where the newlywed couple were to live. They began married life in a rented apartment in Sausalito, near San Francisco Bay. But this was a bad decision. PKD had not overcome the fear of water he had developed when he nearly drowned in the Russian River at music camp and he only needed one look out of the window to decide that this was not the place for him. Within the day they were back in Berkeley. They then bought a small house in Francisco Street. PKD's third wife, Anne, said he told her this cost $2,000 and was financed by Kleo's father, Dr Apostolides. But Kleo told Anne that PKD had already put a down payment on the house when the couple started dating and that from then on both PKD and Kleo contributed to the payments. This house was infested with mice when the couple moved in and so they bought a couple of cats to deal with the problem. Cats would be PKD's constant companions from then on.[51]

The published writer

PKD now focused all his attentions on his goal of becoming a published writer. He decided his best option was to find a local professional who could act as his mentor. One day, while going through a billing list of the shop's customers, PKD came across the name Anthony Boucher, which he recognized as the pen-name of an Oakland-based mystery writer William White. In 1946, Boucher had helped found the organization Mystery Writers of America and in the same year had won the Edgar Award for his mystery reviews in the *San Francisco Chronicle*. But Boucher had been turning towards science fiction and in 1949 founded a publication called *The Magazine of Fantasy and Science Fiction*.

Boucher is credited with raising the standard of science fiction writing and his publication would later win the prestigious Hugo Award for Best Professional Science Fiction Magazine two years running. As an avid reader of science fiction, PKD was fully aware of Boucher's influence on the genre and tried to engineer a meeting. The next time Boucher entered the store, PKD told him how much he admired his writing, especially the novelette *We Print the Truth*. Boucher would soon provide the guiding hand that PKD needed to make a career of writing.

In his spare time, Boucher ran writing classes at his home in Dana Street. By an amazing stroke of luck, PKD's mother, Dorothy, had started attending these meetings. She suggested that PKD come with her. This seemed an ideal opportunity to learn at the feet of a master. PKD managed to attend a few times and even built up a good relationship with Boucher until his fear of group meetings slowly came to the fore. For a time, Kleo attended in his place, delivering PKD's work for his assessment and reporting back on what had been discussed in the meeting. In commenting on PKD's work, Boucher did not pull any punches, but overall the criticism was positive and PKD made use of the advice he was given. He proved to be a good student. PKD has always given Boucher full credit for starting him off on his writing career, saying, 'Without his help I'd still be in the record business.'

Boucher was particularly impressed with a short story called *Friday Morning*, which he thought had true potential. In PKD's initial draft, this story was around 'eight or nine thousand words'. But Boucher helped PKD hone it down to a much sharper story of around two thousand words. Boucher got PKD to re-write the story over and over again until he was happy with it. The new story was also given a new title, *Roog*. In this final format, Boucher was willing to accept it for publication in his *Magazine of Fantasy and Science Fiction*. From this, PKD received not only his first letter of acceptance for a written work, but also something of even greater significance, a payment of $75. At long last PKD had finally become a professional writer.

Roog was an example of how PKD could weave stories out of his own observations and experiences, even the most mundane of them. The idea for *Roog* came from a dog called Snooper who had belonged to a neighbour. Every time the garbage men came down the street on their weekly collection round, Snooper would start barking in a frenzy of fear and excitement at the noise they made. PKD thought about what might be going through Snooper's mind, and from this *Roog* was born. In PKD's story, Snooper becomes 'Boris', who is convinced that his master is storing food in large containers outside the house. 'Boris' does not know that these containers are trash cans and so is convinced that the 'food' is being stolen by the garbage men, who the dog believes to be alien predators, called 'Roogs'. His attempts to alert his master with cries of 'Roog!' 'Roog!' are interpreted as the dog's excited barking. What makes the story stand out is the care with which PKD describes everything from the dog's perspective. Although the story is humorous, PKD maintained there was a serious underlying message about 'loyalty', 'fear' and 'menace'.

PKD continued to work at the music store during the day and carry on his writing when he got home. Every evening PKD would sit at his typewriter and generate, at blistering speed, page after page of material, sometimes novels and sometimes short stories. He would work into the early hours of the morning and then get up a few hours later to go to work. Kleo was fully supportive. They had set aside a corner of their small dining room for PKD's writing studio. Surrounded by his records and his book collection, PKD hammered away at his old $65 portable typewriter, made in Hong Kong, in which the 'e' key frequently got stuck, hoping that one day he would get a positive response to some of the many manuscripts that he and Kleo posted off to publishing houses. PKD taped the publishers' rejection slips on the wall as an incentive to keep on writing. Kleo said that he once had seventeen manuscripts returned in one day. Kleo was a college student during the day but she, too, was writing articles and sending them to magazines.

There was a long delay before *Roog* appeared in print. So PKD's first published story was *Beyond Lies the Wub*, which appeared in the July 1952 issue of *Planet Stories*. In this story, the 'Wub' of the title is a huge pig-like creature from the planet Mars that has the ability to read and control minds. The Wub is acquired by the crew of a spaceship during a stopover on the planet. After they depart, the crew discover the creature to be highly intelligent and sensitive with an interest in mythology. Wub and crew are soon enjoying long intellectual discussions. The captain of the spaceship is scared of the Wub, however, and has it killed so he can eat it. The twist in the tale is that the crew suddenly realize that their captain has now been taken over by the Wub.

By the time *Roog* finally appeared in the *Magazine of Fantasy and Science Fiction*, in February 1953, PKD had already had another six short stories published in a variety of magazines, including *Astounding* and *Galaxy*. PKD had started as he meant to go on, a writer with almost limitless imagination and a work-ethic that turned this creativity into a production line of finished articles.

One of the most intriguing of these early stories is one entitled *The Skull*. It was accepted by *Worlds of If* magazine in March 1952 and was published in September 1952. As with all writers, PKD was influenced by what he had read and heard. However, being the complex individual that he was, his influences were probably far more literary than his competitors. He had long held a fascination for German culture, specifically German music. As such he had been attracted to the songs of Franz Schubert and the works of Offenbach. From the former he would have encountered the song *Der Doppelgänger*, based on a poem of the same name by Heinrich Heine:

> You double of mine, you pallid other!
> Why do you mimic my love's wild woe
> Which tortured me, your wretched brother,
> So many a night here long ago?

In *The Skull*, a man is sent back in time to kill the leader of a religious cult before he can later become a problem. On eventually tracing the religious leader, he discovers that the man is himself. From these early beginnings, the concept of the 'double' becomes a theme that frequently recurs in PKD's writing. At this time, writing was still a part-time pursuit for PKD. But within a few weeks of these early successes, PKD's writing was to become, by necessity, a full-time career.

PKD gets the sack

The staff at both of Herb Hollis' establishments had grown into a close-knit team sharing many interests and often socializing outside work. Although a kind and supportive owner, Hollis kept his distance from his staff and maintained a strict code of conduct. He would not tolerate any behaviour he thought was out of keeping with the way he liked his business to be run. Just before Christmas 1951, one of the sales clerks, PKD's friend Norman Mini, made a risqué joke to a female customer who was so upset she stormed out of the store.

This was observed by the bookkeeper and deputy manager, Eldon Nichols, a 'hunchback', who had worked for Hollis for many years. Nichols was intensely loyal to his boss, a man who had given him a career opportunity that others might have refused him. He thought that such an incident could damage the store's reputation and so he fired Mini on the spot. Hollis subsequently stood by his deputy's decision. Mini then applied for unemployment benefit. Hollis took a strong line on this, insisting that he had fired Mini because of his conduct. This led to a hearing that Mini won. This soured the atmosphere in the shop. A few weeks later, Mini walked into the store and was greeted warmly by PKD and another clerk who worked there. Nichols fired them both.

PKD made just one attempt to hold down a regular job after the sacking. Tupper and Reed, a record shop located in Shattuck Avenue, Berkeley, agreed to take PKD on as a manager. This appointment did not last long, however. According to Kleo, PKD felt extremely restricted in this new environment and it brought about a recurrence of his 'agoraphobia'. PKD was used to the free-and-easy atmosphere in the Hollis shops. Tupper and Reed were far more formal with an older, wealthier clientele. PKD simply could not settle into the new role and he quit.

PKD was twenty-three, married, and now unemployed for a second time. He signed on for unemployment benefit and registered his occupation as 'writer'. As it was difficult for the benefits office to force PKD into a job that was not related to his 'career', he was in the fortunate position of being able to receive a small amount of money each week and have the time to focus on his writing.

The best option for somebody with agoraphobia was to stay at home. This is exactly what a writer does and, from then on, writing was his only career and, more importantly, his only personal source of income. When PKD wasn't writing he was reading, voraciously. His very wide-ranging tastes now encompassed Flaubert, James Joyce, Maupassant and Stendahl, all the way through the literary alphabet to Xenophon.

PKD did not neglect home-grown writers, however. He was greatly influenced by the works of the Irish-American novelist and poet James T. Farrell, now regarded as one of the most important literary figures to appear during the Depression era.

Farrell, too, was born in Chicago, twenty-four years before PKD, and although Farrell's parents were much poorer than Ted and Dorothy, there were parallels between the two writers. Several of Farrell's siblings died at birth or shortly after. And because Farrell's parents were so poor, Farrell was brought up mainly by his grandparents and so, like PKD, had a far closer relationship with his grandmother than with his mother. Farrell, too, became associated with left-wing politics, although because of his impoverished background his political beliefs were much more firmly rooted.

Farrell's most successful work was the 'Studs Lonigan' trilogy. Farrell had drawn on his own experiences of living in the poor Irish-American community of Chicago to chart the life of Studs, a fundamentally decent teenager who is slowly broken by the spiritual poverty of his environment, ending his life as a hopeless alcoholic. In reading the Studs Lonigan books, PKD found Farrell's descriptive skills and naturalistic style helped him to develop his own unique way of writing.

PKD was now regularly selling stories to various magazines. However, what he needed now was a literary agent, somebody who could help him get the best price. The question was who? PKD was delighted to discover that a science fiction writer called Scott Meredith had recently set up a literary agency in New York and was now actively looking for young science fiction writers to represent. PKD wrote to Meredith and, in May 1952, was taken on as a client. At that time the agency was very small, consisting of just Scott and his brother Sydney.

As PKD lived in California and the agency was in New York, there was little, if any, personal contact between writer and agent. But the agency was keen, and able, to sell anything that PKD could produce. And produce he did. It was the perfect time to be a science fiction writer. There seemed almost unlimited demand from the public and new magazines were appearing all the time to take advantage of this ever-expanding market. According to statistics collected by Lester del Ray in his *World of Science Fiction*, in the twelve months of 1950 alone there were twenty-five magazines producing one hundred and ten separate editions. The peak came in 1953 with thirty-six magazines accounting for one hundred and seventy-four issues.[52] With the help of the agency, PKD's output reflected this trend. From 1952, when he published just four stories, PKD had by 1953 had thirty-one stories accepted. His success rate the following year was only slightly less at twenty-eight stories.

In November 1952, PKD received some very sad news. His much-loved aunt, Marion, had died suddenly. Not only were they very close but they shared many traits and had many interests in common. One of these was spiritualism. Aunt Marion was a 'spiritualist medium' who regularly went into 'trance states' in which she would communicate with disincarnate entities. In 1944, she married a sculptor called Joe Hudner and they had two children, twins Lynne and Neal. In the late 1940s, the family was devastated by the news that Marion had been diagnosed with catatonic schizophrenia – the likely cause of her trance states. On 11 November 1952, she collapsed. Her family thought it was one of her catatonic/trance states but it was, in fact, a massive stroke. By the time medical help arrived Marion was dead. As we shall discover later, there were eerie echoes of her illness, experiences and untimely death in the life of her nephew PKD.

In late 1953, Herb Hollis died. PKD had been sorely missed at the record store and he was approached by Hollis's wife, Pat, and asked to return to his old job. PKD accepted the job but he only stuck at it for a few days as he simply could not settle back into his old life. The writing bug had bitten and this was to be his future. He left the store for the second time, and this time there was no going back. From now on his occupation, and only source of income, was to be writing.

That same year, much to PKD's discomfort, Dorothy married Aunt Marion's widower, Joe Hudner. The twins, PKD's first cousins Neil and Lynne, now became his step-brother and step-sister. Soon afterwards, Dorothy took early retirement from the US Forestry Department. Officially, this was due to ill health but it is clear that Dorothy also wished to involve herself totally with her new family. PKD, who was not happy about the new family relationships, became even more concerned when his mother started to dabble in non-traditional approaches to physical and mental health such as Wilhelm Reich's 'orgone energy' theories and science fiction writer L. Ron Hubbard's 'Dianetics'.

Reich believed orgone energy to be a universal life force that coalesced to form living organisms, clouds and even entire galaxies. Dianetics was the belief system created by Hubbard relating to the metaphysical relationship between mind and body. It is the basis of the worldwide movement known as Scientology.

PKD was particularly concerned about Dianetics. He was well aware of Hubbard's previous career as a science fiction writer and, although he had admired some of Hubbard's earlier work, had become very dismissive of his later writings, and regarded the overall concept of Dianetics as being slightly ridiculous and possibly dangerous. PKD was to use this as the plot for a short story called *The Turning Wheel*. This was submitted to PKD's literary agency in July 1953 and published in *Science Fiction Stories* in 1954. The story tells of a mystical philosophy promulgated by an elite group known as The Bards. The senior member of this group is a Bard known as Elron Hu. This is obviously a play on the name L. Ron Hubbard.

In this early short story, PKD combines eastern philosophy with a western social system. As we shall discover later, one particular eastern philosophy, *I Ching*, ('Book of Changes') stimulated PKD to write one of his greatest novels, *The Man in the High Castle* (1962).

One of the most intriguing short stories of this period was *Adjustment Team* (1954). This was submitted to the Scott Meredith Literary Agency on 11 February 1953 and was eventually published in the October 1954 edition of *Orbit Science Fiction* magazine.

The central theme of *Adjustment Team* is that reality is malleable and changeable and that there is a team of bureaucrats whose role it is to make small 'adjustments' to ensure that this reality runs smoothly and to plan. This involves 'de-energizing' sections of 'reality' when necessary. On one such occasion, a man accidently wanders into a section where this process is taking place. He notices a building in front of him becoming an indistinct grey colour. Suddenly the de-energizing process begins in earnest and the man sees an entire section of the building fall away before the whole structure disappears from view.

Later, PKD was to discover a similar lack of permanence in his own reality. In his 1958 novel *Time Out of Joint*, a character called Vic Nelson discovers that a light cord he had used many, many times had suddenly changed to a light switch. This event, PKD claimed, had actually happened to him and so he decided to incorporate it into his novel. PKD was entering his Francisco Street bathroom one dark evening and, reaching up to pull the light cord, he found himself grasping at thin air. The cord had been 'replaced' by a light switch.

Chapter Four

The Novelist (1954–58)

By 1954, PKD's reputation as a writer had come to the attention of a British publisher, Rich and Cowan. They included fifteen of PKD's stories in an anthology entitled *A Handful of Darkness*. That year, from 3-6 September, the 12th World Science Fiction Convention, 'SFCon', was to be held virtually on PKD's 'doorstep', at the Sir Francis Drake Hotel, in San Francisco. It was too good an opportunity for the fledgling sci-fi writer to miss. Guest of honour was John W. Campbell, editor of the pioneering *Astounding Science Fiction magazine*. It was the chance for PKD to meet some of the people who had already made a name for themselves in the world of science fiction, including a personal hero of PKD's, the Canadian-born author Alfred Elton (A.E.) van Vogt, who now lived in Hollywood.

The van Vogt novel that most influenced PKD was *The World of Null-A* (1948), the story of an apparent utopia where some members of society have advanced mental powers and are in charge of everyone else. One of these superior beings decides to test the extent of his mental abilities but discovers that his memories are false. He then sets out to discover his true identity and in the process realizes the true nature of reality. This novel explores many of the themes that would later be hallmarks of a Philip K. Dick work. Van Vogt's novel had poor reviews on its release but for PKD it was a revelation. He would later say:

> 'I started reading sf when I was about 12 and I read all I could, so any author who was writing about that time, I read. But there's no doubt who got me off originally and that was A. E. van Vogt. There was in van Vogt's writing a mysterious quality, and this was especially true in *The World of Null-A*. All the parts of that book did not add up; all the ingredients did not make a coherency. Now some people are put off by that. They think that's "sloppy" or just "plain wrong", but the thing that fascinated me so much was that this resembled reality more than anybody else's writing inside or outside science fiction.'

Meeting van Vogt at the convention was to set PKD's career in a new direction. Like PKD, van Vogt had started out as a short-story writer but by the 1950s had successfully branched out into novels, some of these serialized in Campbell's *Astounding* magazine. Initially, some of van Vogt's novels were expanded versions of his short stories or – like *The World of Null-A* – they were 'fixups', a term he coined for a novel created by joining together several previously published short stories, which are then shortened and revised. During a friendly chat at the convention, van Vogt warned PKD that the great days of the science fiction magazine were effectively over and the market for short stories was drying up. He urged PKD to become a novelist, especially as there was much more money to be made than from short stories – even when published in magazines as well regarded as *Astounding*.

PKD didn't need much persuading. Even though he could churn out short stories in large numbers, he could not earn a living by this work. Kleo worked tirelessly during this period, attending college and holding down a job, as well as helping PKD sell his stories. PKD and Kleo had been mainly getting by on her income. As PKD was fond of mentioning in letters and articles, they were so 'very poor' he was once forced to buy horse meat at a pet store for their dinner.

Around this time, PKD and Kleo met science fiction writer Poul Anderson and his wife Karen, who lived less than 10 miles away in Orinda, Contra Costa County. The two couples were to become close friends. PKD immediately began work on what would be the first of four novels that he would write between 1954 and 1955. The first to be published was *Solar Lottery* (1955), also released, in revised form, as *World of Chance*. It was accepted by the legendary science fiction editor Donald 'Don' Wollheim. Wollheim had moved to the Ace Magazine Company in 1952 where he started up the paperback imprint Ace Books. In 1953, he began publishing science fiction books for the first time and over the next twenty years would debut several sci-fi novelists, including John Brunner, Leigh Bracket, Samuel R. Delaney and Ursula K. Le Guin. Many of these novels, including PKD's *Solar Lottery*, were released as 'Ace Doubles' – two novels by different authors bound together.

Solar Lottery tells of a world dominated by numbers and chance. Even the head of the World Government, called the Quizmaster, is selected by computerized lottery. A TV programme regularly selects an assassin to try to kill the Quizmaster. Evading such attempts on his life helps the Quizmaster earn the people's respect. If the assassin succeeds, however, a new Quizmaster is selected.

The beat goes on

The San Francisco Bay area in the mid-fifties was closely associated with the 'beat movement', which had begun in New York in the late 1940s. The term 'beat' came from underworld slang for 'beaten down' and originally referred to the world of New York petty crooks, conmen and drug addicts. But the movement itself attracted mainly poets, artists, writers and those with left-wing and anti-establishment views. The term 'beatnik' (coined in an article in the *San Francisco Chronicle* by adding '*beat*' to *-nik* from the

Russian satellite *Sputnik*) was used to describe members of this group. PKD and Kleo's home inevitably became a place where Berkeley's 'beatnik' writers, artists and left-wing intellectuals would chat about the local art scene and politics and smoke marijuana.

Around this time, PKD got to know many of the avant-garde poets living in the Bay area, including Philip Lamantia, Jack Spicer and Robert

1954 – The World Jones Made

'The irony was that my second novel, THE WORLD JONES MADE, was about a precognitive. And it didn't do him a damn bit of good. He couldn't avert the event. It was hell for him. He had precognition for one year ahead. And when he got within the last year of his life, he had a precognition of being dead, so it really was not a talent that gave him any options.'

– Philip K. Dick, *Martian Time-Slip*

This was PKD's second novel. His first was *Solar Lottery* which had been published in May 1955. He wrote this in late 1954 with the original title of *Womb for Another*. It was received at his agency, the Scott Meredith Literary Agency (SMLA), on 28 December 1954. Ace bought the book in 1955 and, after making the title change, published it as part of an 'Ace Double' in March 1956.

In this novel we see many of the themes that carried through PKD's writing career. We have a central character, Floyd Jones, who can 'precognize' events a year in the future. He uses this ability to become a form of religious leader. 'Precogs' and 'religious leaders' appear time and time again in PKD's writing. He was already investigating the implications that time does not flow but simply 'is' and as such the future already exists. For PKD the issue here is one of Free-Will. By knowing the future Jones was trapped by it. He had no other course of action but to follow what was pre-ordained. In his later novels Phil introduces the idea of alternate futures and as such escapes this problem.

At this stage in his writing career Phil was consciously applying the technique of James Joyce to his work. PKD had ambitions to be a mainstream novelist and as such he was keen to apply the techniques of the great writers to his own work.

This novel showed its own form of precognition. Twenty years later, another religious leader called Jones brought tragedy to his followers. But what is more intriguing is that at one stage Phil's ex-wife Nancy had been involved in the Jim Jones Ministry and was considering taking herself and little Isa off to one of Jones's communities.

Duncan. It was the linguist Spicer who would trigger PKD's idea of developing an alien language for his novel *Martian Time-Slip* (1965). For PKD, though, writing was not just an artistic pursuit. He expected to make a living from it. He said, 'They all encouraged me to write, but there was no encouragement to sell anything.'[53]

The obligatory 'uniform' of beatnik girls was black leotard and long hair, kept simple and unadorned as a reaction against the heavily coiffured 'Hollywood style' of the glossy magazines. Kleo adopted the beatnik look enthusiastically. The 'typical' male beatnik wore a goatee beard and beret. PKD didn't go quite that far. Pictures from this period show a serious twenty-five-year-old with the high, intelligent-looking forehead he inherited from his father, gazing intensely out at the camera, his chin cupped in his hand to give him a thoughtful air. His hair is short – but not too short – and he is wearing a jacket and the obligatory round-neck sweater then favoured by writers, poets and artists on both sides of the Atlantic. He is still clean-shaven, at this stage. The bearded 'wild man' of science fiction the world would later come to know had yet to make his appearance.

The men from the Bureau

During the late 1940s and early 1950s, Cold War tensions began to escalate, giving rise to a fear bordering on paranoia that the United States was riddled with Communist infiltrators. When, in 1951, Ethel and Julius Rosenberg were found guilty of passing US nuclear secrets to the Soviet Union and subsequently executed, these fears seemed justified, especially by those in the Republican Party with the most extreme right-wing views. The most vociferous of these was Senator Joseph McCarthy, who would instigate a campaign to root out all 'subversives' as he saw them.

Anyone with perceived left-wing sympathies was viewed with suspicion. It would lead to a series of FBI investigations and political hearings, such as the House Un-American Activities Committee, in which the patriotism of anyone with left-wing, and especially 'socialist', views could be brought into question. In 1950, the *Washington Post* cartoonist Herbert Block coined the term 'McCarthyism' to describe those who took this extreme line and the investigations themselves became known as the 'McCarthy witch-hunt'. People from all walks of life, but especially writers, artists, actors and academics, were likely to be investigated. Thousands would be unjustly accused of being communists or communist-sympathizers. Some would face imprisonment, and many others would be 'blacklisted' and unable to find work in their own field.

Always a middle-of-the-road liberal at heart, PKD was too independent a thinker to follow any party line but he did share many of Kleo's left-wing sympathies. Kleo was closely involved in left-wing activism at her University.

1957 – The Cosmic Puppets

'"*Get it!*" *Peter ordered sharply. He snatched up the first one, jumped quickly to his feet and hurried after the other one. It ran desperately – straight toward Doctor Meade's station wagon.*

As the station wagon started up, the tiny clay figure made a frantic leap. Its tiny arms groped wildly as it tried to find purchase on the smooth metal fender. Unconcerned, the station wagon moved out into traffic, and the tiny figure was left behind, still waving its arms futilely, trying to climb and catch hold of a surface already gone.

Peter caught up with it. His foot came down and the clay man was squashed into a shapeless blob of moist clay.

Walter and Dave and Noaks came slowly over; they approached in a wide, cautious circle. "You got him?" Noaks demanded hoarsely.

"Sure," Peter said. He was already scraping the clay off his shoe, his small face calm and smooth. "Of course I got him. He belonged to me, didn't he?"'

– Philip K. Dick, *The Cosmic Puppets*

This originally appeared as a novelette entitled *A Glass of Darkness* in the December 1956 edition of *Satellite* Science Fiction magazine. PKD finished the manuscript by 19 August 1953. In October 1957, after some minor changes, it appeared as part of an 'Ace Double' under the title *The Cosmic Puppets*. Unusually for Phil's novels this was not to be published again until after his death in 1983. It seems that the problem with *The Cosmic Puppets* was that it was a fantasy rather than a Sci-Fi novel.

Ted Barton is travelling across the country and decides to visit the small town he grew up in, Millgate in Virginia. Barton finds that the town has changed and has a run-down feel. He then discovers that in this version of Millgate he died of scarlet fever at the age of nine. What is more disturbing is that when he tries to leave town he discovers the way out is blocked by a maze-like pile of timber.

Although this is PKD's first published novel, we have many themes he is to develop throughout his career: the idea of reality as an illusion, of time being manipulated and the central concept of Gnostic mythology, that this world is under the control of a negative deity and that there is a greater god – the true creator – who is suffering from a form of amnesia.

The theme of a 'socialist' wife compromizing a 'liberal' husband can be found in PKD's 1957 novel *Eye in the Sky*. Unsurprisingly, the combination of Kleo's university connections and political views, and the couple's eclectic mix of friends inevitably drew them to the attention of the FBI.

One day, PKD and Kleo were visited by two mysterious men wearing dark suits and grey fedora hats. They introduced themselves as Mr Smith and Mr Jones. The visitors took out a photograph of a recent meeting of the Socialist Workers' Party in San Francisco and asked PKD and Kleo to identify people in it. They soon discovered that 'Smith and Jones' were, in fact, FBI agents called George Smith and George Scruggs. PKD would later claim they were members of the 'Red Squad', specialist police units whose aim was to tackle labour unions, anarchists, communist sympathizers and anyone deemed a 'dissident'. This was the first of a series of visits by the two agents and the four of them became quite friendly. Scruggs even taught PKD how to drive. In a 1978 interview with Joe Vitale for *The Aquarian*, PKD said:

1957 – Eye in the Sky

'All eight of us dropped into the proton beam of the Bevatron. During the interval there was only one consciousness, one frame of reference, for the eight of us. Silvester never lost consciousness.'

– Philip K. Dick, *Eye in the Sky*

PKD submitted a manuscript entitled *With Open Mind* to the Scott Meredith Agency on 15 February 1955. He had written the whole novel in a two-week period of intense creativity, a creative fugue. In 1970 he wrote, 'I don't know where I got the dialogue from, it just rolled out of me.' Unfortunately it was only after extensive re-writing that the novel was eventually published by Ace Books in March 1957. The title was also changed to the far more descriptive *Eye in the Sky*. This was the first of PKD's novels to be published as a stand-alone title rather than part of an 'Ace Double'. It was well received and given a 'best novel of the year' rating by Sci-fi author and editor Tony Boucher. PKD was so pleased by this that he decided that novel writing was the way forward.

This novel reflects Phil's concerns at the time. The central character, Jack Hamilton, has a wife who is dabbling in left-wing politics (shades of Kleo's political position), which compromises his position vis a vis his employers.

The plot involves alternate worlds but this time they are the creation of the characters. In this way Phil questions the true nature of perception. Can we be influenced by the thoughts of others? Is the external world simply a creation of the mind? This idea of a form of 'group mind' that can be accessed under certain circumstances may have been influenced by PKD's admiration for Fredric Brown's 1949 story *What Mad Universe*. This Gnostic theme was to develop in his later novels and was discussed endlessly in his *Exegesis*.

'They asked many questions about my life and my writings and my philosophy. This, of course, made me very angry and very frightened. They asked me all about my wife, about her political philosophy, about what student groups she belonged to. I mean, I honestly expected to be called before the House Un-American Activities Committee. But I guess they didn't consider science fiction writers important enough.'[54]

Physically, PKD seemed to be in reasonably good health during his marriage to Kleo. But one day while playing tennis PKD developed a hernia. He was concerned that this may, in some way, affect his ability to have children and spent a good deal of time reading up about the inguinal region of the body. In 1974, his baby son Christopher (by his fifth wife) suffered a life-threatening inguinal hernia. On that occasion, PKD claimed to have had no knowledge about this part of the body when this was clearly not the case. Perhaps he just forgot.[55]

North by north-west

PKD was keen to break into the literary mainstream but, whereas there was a ready market for his science fiction material, SMLA could not sell PKD's other efforts. PKD and Kleo felt that a change of location was needed. They had already visited Point Reyes Station, a small community in western Marin County, about thirty-five miles north-west of San Francisco, and decided it would be the ideal location for a new start. Bearing in mind PKD's phobia of water, this seems an unusual choice as Point Reyes is located close to the Pacific coast and marks the entranceway to an area of rugged natural beauty called the Point Reyes National Seashore. The area also includes an important historical site, Drake's Landing, on the Port Reyes peninsular, where the English explorer and adventurer Sir Frances Drake is said to have made landfall in the 16th century. Drake's Landing and Port Reyes Station would both feature in PKD's semi-autobiographical work *Confessions of a Crap Artist*, which was written in the summer of 1959.

PKD and Kleo really loved this area of countryside and the feeling they got from being outside the big city. PKD's mother Dorothy and her husband Joe had bought a cabin just a few miles to the north-west, in the town of Inverness, on the edge of Tomales Bay. The couple had stayed at the cabin a few times and so knew the area reasonably well. Although sparsely populated, it was still only a ninety-minute drive from Berkeley, close enough for Kleo to commute three days a week to the university Treasurer's office where she worked. The couple had already found a small house for sale. They sold their old one and, in September 1959, moved into their new home in Lorraine Avenue, Point Reyes Station.

Apocalyptic cults and flying saucers

Soon after arriving in Point Reyes Station, PKD and Kleo made friends with their neighbours, June and Jerry Kresy. The Kresys suggested the newcomers join a small group of locals who regularly met up in Inverness to discuss philosophy and other allied topics. This was very much in keeping with the intellectual atmosphere that the Dicks had left behind in Berkeley, and they were keen to involve themselves. It soon became clear that this seemingly innocent set had an unusual agenda. The group was dominated by a formid-able woman, whose powerful personality had steered them away from a general discussion group towards becoming an apocalyptic cult that believed the world was about to end. This sect believed they would be saved by a group of 'space brothers' who would arrive on the day of reckoning and fly them to safety in their flying saucer. The woman announced that the day of reckoning would be 22 April 1959.

This group and its oddly charismatic leader also feature in *Confessions of a Crap Artist*. It was the only one of PKD's mainstream novels to be published in his lifetime, eventually appearing in print in 1975. Even so, it still shows many of the hallmarks of later Philip K. Dick stories, including the quest for spiritual salvation, psychic powers, regression to past lives, precognition and the blurred distinction between reality and unreality. The story is told in the first person but the perspective switches between all the main characters so readers are not immediately aware through whose eyes they are seeing the world.

The book effectively deals with the lives of three main characters: Jack Isidore, his sister Fay Hume, and her husband Charley. Jack is a simple character who becomes involved in a flying saucer group with a similarly powerful female leader. In the novel, PKD calls her 'Claudia Hambro'. She is described as 'breathtakingly beautiful' and yet very strange, with strong chin, sharp teeth 'like a savage', and 'large brown eyes that stared at me so hard and fixedly that I became nervous'.

> 'The strength of her gaze made my head hum. I have never met a person to this day who affected me as much as Claudia Hambro. The sunlight, when it reached her eyes, didn't reflect in the usual way but was broken up into splinters. That fascinated me.'

The non-fictional 'Claudia' certainly disturbed PKD. He was worried that this dominant and slightly creepy woman would brainwash him and make him part of her cult. He was later to describe how he would hide in his house hoping that she would not call by to see him. Fortunately for PKD, this cult was living on borrowed time. Once 22 April 1959 had passed with none of her predictions coming true, 'Claudia' cut off her long hair and moved away from the area with her two daughters.

Straight-talking Anne

By that time things had changed dramatically for PKD and Kleo. It all started with an innocent-sounding knock on the front door one afternoon in late October 1959. Kleo answered it and standing in front of her was a slim blonde with high cheekbones, her hair cut in a fringe, wearing studious-looking spectacles. She introduced herself as Anne Rubenstein. Anne, her late husband Richard, and their three daughters had moved to Point Reyes around four years before. Richard, a poet from a wealthy New York family, had died only recently, leaving her a widow at the comparatively young age of thirty. Being from a literary background herself, Anne was keen to meet this writer who had moved into the area from San Francisco. In part, she was looking for a way to take her mind off her recent loss and thought this new couple might be the ideal distraction. She asked her eldest daughter, Hatte, to babysit the two younger ones, Jayne and Tandy, and

1959 – Time Out of Joint

'The scarecrows lolled forward, back, forward, back. Ahead of him he saw the driver; the driver had not changed. The red neck. Strong, wide back. Driving a hollow bus.

The hollow men, he thought. We should have looked up poetry.'
– Philip K. Dick, *Time Out of Joint*

Phil submitted the manuscript of *Time Out of Joint* to his agency on 7 April 1958. It was immediately accepted by Ace Books, but with a request that certain changes be made. However, Lippincott were keen to take the book for their new science fiction line and published it in 1959.

The central character, Ragle Gumm, lives in small town America in 1959. Ragle keeps winning a newspaper competition known as 'Find the Little Green Man'. This involves guessing the location of the green man on a chart of small squares. The strange thing is he keeps seeing objects disappear to be replaced by slips of paper. With the help of his brother-in-law Vic, he discovers that he is living in a fake town created by the government and that the year is 1998.

Here again we have the Gnostic idea that the world we perceive is an illusion in which a 'real world' exists beyond, and outside, our senses. We also have the precognitive, aware of the future before it has happened.

drove over to Lorraine Street. She found the gate to PKD and Kleo's house too stiff to open and so, not one to stand on ceremony, she hitched up her skirt and climbed over the fence.

Kleo invited Anne in and introduced her to PKD who was in the kitchen. This is how Anne describes her first impression of PKD, who was to be her next husband:

> 'I still have in my mind a vivid picture of Phil standing with his hands in his back jean pockets, rocking on his heels, frowning slightly and staring at the floor. He was twenty-nine years old, just under six feet tall, and on the slender side. He had dark hair above a high forehead and intense gray-green eyes. An almost-handsome man, he wore an old brown leather jacket with knitted cuffs and knitted waist, a cheap plaid flannel shirt, stiff jeans, and clunky, brown Army boots. Nevertheless, he managed to look graceful and attractive—like someone wearing a disguise.'[56]

She then describes a sensation that sounds more like a section from PKD's more esoteric speculations of the late 1970s than something experienced by a pragmatic, down-to-earth individual like Anne:

> 'He looked up at me as we came in, and I looked up into his eyes, and, as I was beginning to say, "How nice to meet you," I had an odd experience unlike anything that had ever happened to me before. A voice from the depths of my mind said, "I already know this person. I've known him for eons." But my practical conscious mind, astonished, answered itself, "Ridiculous, how can that be? You just met him."'[57]

After a short time, Anne announced that she had to get back to her children. As she left, PKD insisted on loaning her some of his books: Franz Kafka's *The Castle*, Herman Hesse's *Siddhartha*, and James Joyce's *Portrait of the Artist as a Young Man*. The loaning of books sometimes leads to more than just a meeting of minds, and so it was with PKD and Anne.

The books were a symbol of an immediate attraction between the two. Within three weeks, PKD had pledged his love for Anne. By January 1959, PKD's second marriage was over. PKD got the house in Port Reyes Station and Kleo took the car. PKD was to enter a totally new stage in his life. No longer the beatnik, he would now become bourgeois.

Chapter Five

The Bourgeois Idyll (1959–64)

Considering the sudden change in her circumstances, Kleo was surprisingly relaxed about this turn of events. She returned to Berkeley, allowing PKD to move in with Anne and the girls. With him came his trusty Magnavox record player, his collection of records, books and magazines, his current cat Tumpey and his second-hand typewriter. But most important was his two-drawer filing cabinet. This contained a carbon copy of every letter he had written.

Living in California, PKD and Kleo were relatively well placed to apply for a divorce under Mexican law, which meant it went through very quickly. Kleo would later marry Norman Mini, PKD's friend and co-worker from University Radio and Art Music. They would all remain good friends for the rest of their respective lives.

Now single again, on 1 April 1959 PKD married Anne, also under Mexican law, making the long drive down to Ensenada, in Baja California, seventy-eight miles south of San Diego – far enough inside Mexico to make the marriage official. Anne's house and grounds were far more palatial than PKD had been used to. The house was surrounded by a five-acre field, containing a variety of animals, including a small flock of Suffolk sheep. A picture taken by Anne shows PKD holding one of the sheep, suggesting that he may have helped out with the care of the flock on occasion. To make the rural idyll complete, there was even a rose garden.

In late Spring, PKD took Anne to meet Dorothy and Joe at their main house in Hearst Street, San Francisco. Here, Anne was introduced to Dorothy's step-children, the twins Lynne and Neal. Although the atmosphere was cordial, PKD had never really forgiven his mother for marrying Joe and even intimated to his new wife that the death of Marion had been 'suspicious'. Soon, PKD would be voicing similar suspicions about the death of Anne's husband, Richard. For the time being, though, their marriage was a happy one. PKD threw himself into his new family life and settled down to a nine-to-five routine of writing.

He was keen to write a novel about the West Marin community that he now felt a part of, and from this period came his mainstream novel *Confessions*. Although it incorporated some of his experiences with the Inverness flying saucer group, the main theme of the book was relationships, specifically a fictionalized account of his own life with Anne. This was completed by the end of their first summer together and PKD proudly presented Anne with the fruits of his labour.

1959 – Confessions of a Crap Artist

'I did not attend the services, because it seems to me, as Pythagoras says, the body is the tomb of the soul and that by being born a person has already begun to die.'

– Philip K. Dick, *Confessions of a Crap Artist*

PKD wrote this 'mainstream' novel in 1959. No publisher showed interest in it. However, in 1975 Entwhistle Press published a limited hardback edition of 500 copies, with 90 numbered and signed by the author. In August 1982, soon after Phil's death, Timescape published a paperback edition followed by a trade paperback from Vintage in August 1992. Sadly this was the only one of PKD's 'mainstream' novels to be published in his lifetime.

Jack Isidore is a 'crap artist' who lives with his sister, Fay, and her husband, Charley Hume, in Seville, California in the late 1950s. He collects worthless objects and is prone to unusual beliefs such as the existence of telepathy, flying saucers and the idea that the world will end on 23 April 1959. However, the main narrative concerns the deteriorating relationship between Fay and Charley.

The character of Fay was based on Anne Dick and many elements of PKD's life with Anne can be found in the novel. Was the killing of Fay's animals a way of PKD showing his frustration with the bucolic life and mundane domesticity of rural Marin County? According to Anne Dick, the massacre was based upon an incident in Dorothy Kindred's life when her father, Earl Grant Kindred, announced that there was not enough money to feed both the family and the animals. He went outside and summarily despatched the family pets along with their other domestic animals.

We have already met Jack Isidore, the 'crap artist' of the title, Jack's sister Fay and brother-in-law Charley. Jack almost certainly reflects aspects of PKD's younger, adolescent self, who is something of a dreamer with aspirations to be an artist and who feels unsure and even intimidated around women. Charley represents aspects of the older PKD. But it is clearly not intended to be an exact likeness, as the character is described as 'a paunchy, beer-drinking ignorant mid-westerner who never got through high school'.

It was clear that the character of Fay was based on Anne, and Fay's relationship with Charley was a mirror image of PKD and Anne's marriage. Fay is described as a 'tomboy' who has 'never gotten much of a figure, even now she is more than 30 years old'. However, he says Fay has 'nice long legs and a springy walk'. She is depicted as a strong-willed, blunt-speaking and independent woman who has a turbulent and sometimes violent relationship with her husband. Anne was very disturbed by the message she got from the book as she revealed in her biography of PKD.

> 'When I finished it I sat for a while with the book on my lap, feeling puzzled and uneasy. "What a strange, uncomfortable novel," I thought, "so close to reality in some ways, so far in others. Was I really like Fay? I hoped not, because I didn't like her at all. No I wasn't like Fay. I guess this is what fiction writers do." I swept any problems the novel hinted at out of my mind. I had tremendous faith in Phil as a writer and tremendous faith in our relationship. Call it denial if you will, but perhaps faith is the other side of the denial coin and faith can move mountains.'

Although the book was said to draw heavily on his relationship with Anne, by the time it was published in 1975, PKD had dedicated it to his fifth wife, Tessa, 'the dark-haired girl who cared about me when it mattered most, that is, all the time'.

Soon after moving in with Anne, PKD began to grow the trademark beard that would stay with him for the rest of his life and, along with his piercing blue eyes, would make his image so distinctive on the jackets of his books. Not for PKD the neatly trimmed Van Dyke of the artistic set. Photographs taken at the time show a man with a beard that is bushy and unkempt, with hair to match, like a wild woodsman, perhaps emulating one of his literary heroes, Ernest Hemingway. It was the very image of an avant-garde writer, pounding the keys in his coastal hideaway and pushing the boundaries of fiction.

At some point in the late 1950s, if not earlier, PKD had begun using amphetamine, a powerful stimulant drug also known as 'speed' to help him cope with the punishing output of writing he had set himself, completing anything up to sixty pages a day. As amphetamine can help suppress fatigue and sleepiness, it enabled PKD to carry on working all day and late into the night.

Initially, amphetamine can also aid mental focus but that can decline over time. Unfortunately, there are serious side effects associated with prolonged and excessive use of amphetamine including delusions, hallucinations and psychosis. As he began to tolerate its effects, PKD's amphetamine intake steadily increased – with inevitable psychological consequences.

To PKD and Anne – a daughter

At around the time PKD completed *Confessions*, Anne discovered she was pregnant. They had both wanted a child and were delighted with this news. Anne put the implications of the novel to the back of her mind and prepared for the arrival of her fourth child and PKD's first. As soon as *Confessions* was finished, PKD started on another mainstream novel, *The Man Whose Teeth Were All Exactly Alike* (eventually published in 1984). He finished this one quickly and then began work on a series of new novels or re-worked ones he had written over the previous decade. PKD was desperate to put his science fiction writing behind him and to be seen as a serious mainstream novelist. In the meantime, fatherhood now loomed large in his life. On 25 February 1960, Anne gave birth to an 8lb (3.6kg) baby girl they named Laura. PKD's first words on seeing his new daughter were 'now my sister is made up for'.[58]

The following autumn, Anne became pregnant again. But this baby had not been planned and was certainly not expected as PKD and Anne had been using birth control. Anne did not feel ready for a fifth child. Nor did she feel that they had the financial security to support such a large family. Despite strong opposition from PKD, Anne had an abortion. She had to travel north all the way to Seattle, in Washington State, for the termination as it was illegal under Californian law. PKD never really recovered from this. In October 1962, he delivered his novel *We Can Build You* to his literary agent. In this, the central character, a woman called 'Pris Frauenzimmer' (German for 'Sprinkle Women's Room'), kills a little robot with her high-heeled shoe. Anne acknowledges that the character Pris is based on her. In the novel, Pris even tiles her bathroom in exactly the same way that Anne was doing when PKD was writing it.

> 'About the same time I began to tile the master bathroom in our house. I bought different colored small tiles and made a mermaid, several fish, a cosmic eye right over the toilet, a boat, and a large sea serpent. It felt like you were under water when you were taking a bath.'[59]

This is how PKD describes Pris' bathroom mural:

> 'On the bathroom walls she had sketched all sorts of sea monsters and fish, even a mermaid; she had already partially tiled them with every color imaginable.'[60]

PKD would later write a short story called *The Pre-Persons* (1974) that alienated a section of his readership with its strident condemnation of abortion.

The abortion had soured the marriage and they were steadily growing apart. They both had separate interests to keep them occupied. PKD had his writing and Anne was developing a jewellery business. Anne became increasingly irritated with PKD, especially whenever he disturbed her by reading a section of his latest work to her while she was busy. She suggested that PKD find another place to work, well away from the house. According to Anne, PKD thought this was a good idea. They found an old wooden cabin nearby owned by their friend Sherriff Bill Christensen. They paid Christensen $30 a month for PKD's isolation and Anne's peace of mind. They named this building 'The Hovel' and it was here that PKD was to work on his novel *The Man in the High Castle* (1962).

The man in the high hovel

Vulcan's Hammer, written in 1953, was finally published in February 1960 and PKD went on to complete another two 'mainstream' novels that year, *The Man Whose Teeth Were All Exactly Alike* and *Humpty Dumpty in Oakland*. Like his other attempts at 'serious' fiction, with the exception of *Confessions*, these novels were ignored in his lifetime. *Teeth* was eventually published in 1984 and *Oakland* in 1986. PKD seemed to have run out of ideas. He was later to claim in a 1976 interview that he decided to pretend to be writing a new novel to avoid spending time with Anne.

> 'And to make the fabrication convincing, I actually had to start typing. And I had no notes, I had nothing in mind, except for years I had wanted to write the idea, about Germany and Japan actually having beaten the United States. And without any notes, I simply sat down and began to write, simply to get out of the jewelry business.'[61]

This is not how the events are described by Anne. She says that PKD became fascinated by the trial of an important Nazi, Adolf Eichmann, a senior SS officer and one of the engineers of the Holocaust. In the final months of World War II, Eichmann had managed to escape justice by fleeing to Argentina. But he was kidnapped by agents of Mossad, the Israeli intelligence service, and brought back to Israel to be tried for war crimes and crimes against humanity. This trial, which was being held in Israel, started on 11 April.

The following day marked the centenary of the start of the American Civil War. Anne had shown interest in the build-up to the commemorations and PKD, having a long-time interest in the Civil War, suggested Anne read a book by science fiction writer Ward Moore entitled *Bring the Jubilee*. Anne took herself down to the local library and found a copy of this 1953 classic. In the novel, the South wins the war after a decisive victory at the Battle of Gettysburg. In this alternative history, Confederate forces invade Mexico and then take over the whole of Latin America. Later, 'The German Union' defeats France and Great Britain in a shortened version of World War I. And so, by the time in which the novel is set, the world is effectively divided into two spheres of influence, German and Confederate America.

In his interview with Gregg Rickman, in 1981, PKD states that the idea for an alternative history novel in which the Axis Powers won World War II had 'been in the back of my mind for years. I had already done all the research when I was still at Berkeley'.[62] It is possible that although PKD had long had the idea for such a novel, it was the Ward Moore novel that gave him the initial structure he needed, particularly when Anne spotted an obscure footnote in Moore's work. This footnote drew attention to a literary device of a 'book within a book'. Moore brings the reader's attention to a novel that had been written describing a Northern victory in the Civil War. Anne thought this was an intriguing premise; a novel within a novel with the 'fiction' representing our actuality. She said to PKD:

> 'I wish Ward Moore had developed that fascinating idea further. I wonder what that world was like?'[63]

According to Anne, this was the stimulus PKD needed. The Eichmann trial had revived his interest in Nazi Germany and the alternative-world scenario, as presented by Moore's novel, was an ideal starting point. But what really must have interested him was the idea of a novel within a novel. Anne said that he started work immediately. He was using his old thirties typewriter with its sticking 'e' key.

High Castle not only has the idea of a novel within a novel but, as literary critic N.B. Hayles observes in his essay *Metaphysics and Metafiction in 'High Castle'*, the realization by a central character (Mr Tagomi) that he is a fictional character.[64] This powerful literary technique has become a staple of much post-modernist fiction, but here we have Philip K. Dick using such a device in the early 1960s suggesting influences of Latin American 'magical realism' writers such as Jorge Borges and Gabriel García Márquez.

But *High Castle* was regarded as a revolutionary science fiction novel in other ways, too. PKD again employs the narrative device he first used in *Confessions of a Crap Artist*, in which the viewpoint is switched from character to character. But as *Confessions* will not appear in print until 1975, the device is first seen in *High Tower*. Hayles suggests that PKD's unusual writing style is a reflection of the 'acausality' of an Eastern work called the *I Ching* or 'Book of Changes'.[65]

The *I Ching* is thought to date back around 3,000 years. Many in the West regard it as a system for divining the future, but in the East it is seen as an important book of spiritual wisdom. Unlike other forms of divination, the *I Ching* does not regard the past and future as fixed, but as a dynamic, ever-changing flow. As such, it offers possibilities rather than specific advice. The book features sixty-four line arrangements known as hexagrams. Each hexagram consists of six lines that are either unbroken (*yang*) or broken with a gap in the middle (*yin*). Each line is decided upon by using yarrow stalks, but in the West this has often been replaced by the throwing of three coins on to a flat surface six times in a row. Each combination of heads and tails creates a *yin* or *yang* line. In an interview in 1974, PKD described how he used the coin method to decide what actions his *High Castle* characters took when faced with a decision:

> 'In each case when they asked a question, I threw the coins and wrote the hexagram lines they got. That governed the direction of the book. Like in the end when Juliana Frink is deciding whether or not to tell Hawthorne Abensen that he is the target of assassins, the answer indicated that she should. Now if it had said not to tell him, I would have had her not go there. But I would not do that in any other book.'[66]

It may be that PKD was drawing up information from his subconscious to develop his storylines. Methods of divination such as the *I Ching* are designed to facilitate communication with rarely accessed areas of the human mind. They open up portals that are usually denied to everyday consciousness. It is as if once these portals have been opened all kinds of thoughts can spill over into our mundane, 'consensual' reality. This includes the Jungian archetypes, the idea proposed by the psychologist Carl Jung of ancient images derived from a collective consciousness, in which our deepest fears are suddenly manifest. While accessing these areas of his subconscious, PKD was to experience something that was to have a profound influence on him, both psychologically and creatively, and to act as a signpost to greater things to come. It was as if PKD's alternative universe was to come crashing into his bucolic isolation.

The Eldritch vision

On Good Friday 1961, Anne was working just inside the house while PKD was close by tending the flowerbeds around the patio. (PKD was later to joke that he had absolutely no gardening skills and that his tending was more likely to kill plants than allow them to thrive!) On this particular mid-April day, PKD was to shatter the peace of the household by running into the building and announcing that he had experienced a terrifying vision. He described to Anne what he had seen.

> 'A great streak of black sweeping across the sky. For a moment there was utter nothingness dividing the sky in half.'[67]

In an interview he gave to the London *Daily Telegraph*, in July 1974, he adds more detail:

> 'There flooded in the perception of something in the sky. I wasn't on LSD or any other drug, not at the time; just this deprivation of the sense of other living things about me. What I saw was some form of evil deity. . . not living but functioning; not looking so much as scanning, like a machine or monitor. It had slotted eyes and always hung over one particular spot. I've used it for the title of my next-but-one story, *A Scanner Darkly*.'[68]

Many years later (in 1981), PKD discussed with Gregg Rickman an incident that took place when he was four years old. PKD described how his father was keen to inculcate in his son a proper understanding of the horrors of war. Ted had seen action on the Western Front in World War I and had experienced, at first hand, poison gas attacks and the effects this had on soldiers. He showed his son the gas mask that he had brought back from France. This clearly had a powerful effect on PKD's young mind. Even over forty-five years later, PKD could describe, in detail, what the mask looked like:

> 'The canister worked down into an entire filtration, diaphragm system. It looked like a mask like a catcher wears in a baseball game. A huge chamber with a charcoal filtration system.'[69]

'I remember it to this day.' Could this memory have contributed to the horror he saw in the sky that Good Friday and for days afterwards?

Just before this event, real or imagined, took place, PKD had started writing his novel *The Man in the High Castle* in April of that year (1961), as we have already discovered, his creative faculties being stimulated by the TV coverage of the Eichmann trial taking place in Jerusalem and by the commemorative events surrounding the centenary of the start of the American Civil War. In her book *The Search for Philip K. Dick*, Anne says: 'By 1961, my small inheritance and the money from the sale of PKD's house were gone.'[70] She then goes on to write:

> 'That spring, Mamie Eisenhower – that was the name we had given our oldest Suffolk ewe, she had bangs like Mamie's – had triplets. On Good Friday afternoon Phil played the Dublin version of Handel's Messiah on the record player while working just outside on the flowerbeds around the patio. He came running back into the house. . .'[71]

PKD then described to Anne what he had seen in the sky. We know that PKD worked through that summer writing *The Man in the High Castle* (1962). Anne describes how in the late summer he proudly presented her with the manuscript to read. She told him it was the best thing he had ever written and urged him to send it off to his agent. PKD made a few small changes and then posted it. It was accepted by publisher Putnam's on 10 December 1961.[72]

In the headnote for a reprint of the short story *The Days of Perky Pat*, cited by Patricia Warrick in *Minds in Motion*, PKD presents a very different set of circumstances that led to the 'vision':

> 'There I went one day, walking down the country road to my shack, looking forward to eight hours of writing, in total isolation from all other humans, and I looked up at the sky and saw a face. I didn't really see it but the face was there, and it was not a human face; it was a vast visage of perfect evil. It had empty slots for eyes – it was metal and cruel and, worst of all, it was God.'[73]

The Days of Perky Pat was the short-story from which many of the ideas that appear in PKD's 'post-vision' influenced novel *The Three Stigmata of Palmer Eldritch* (1965).

A marriage in freefall

Anne states that 'as the spring of 1963 approached, we were arguing more and more'.[74] Indeed PKD started to make some damaging accusations. Anne was told, many years later by her eldest daughter, Hatte, that on one occasion PKD shouted, 'You killed Richard and now you're trying to kill me.'[75] This accusation is an interesting echo of PKD's lifelong belief that his mother was responsible for the death of his sister, Jane. The relationship became progressively worse and the arguments turned violent.

The main arguments were about money. By this time Anne had set up a fairly successful jewellery business that PKD occasionally helped out with. In the last interview he gave, with John Boonstra, for *The Twilight Zone* magazine, PKD said:

> 'I had gone to work making jewelry with my wife. I wasn't happy. I didn't enjoy making jewelry. I had no talent whatsoever. She had the talent. She is still a jeweler and a very fine one, making gorgeous stuff. . . It's great art. But I couldn't do anything except polish what she made.'[76]

It was clear that PKD resented the fact that his wife was the major breadwinner. He started telling friends that Anne was out of control. The couple had been attending therapy in order to resolve their problems. Initially, they shared the same female psychiatrist, Dr 'J'. PKD discussed his wife with their therapist and managed to convince her that Anne was so dangerous she needed to be confined to a psychiatric hospital for observation. One evening Bill Christensen, the local police sheriff, who had become a family friend, turned up at their door with legal papers requiring Anne to go to nearby Ross Psychiatric Hospital, Kentfield, near San Rafael, for seventy-two hours of observation.

Anne was then transferred to the Langley Porter Clinic, in San Francisco, for two weeks. She was released with instructions to continue with her medication for a further two to three months. Whatever PKD's motivations for this action, relations within the marriage did not improve. In his novel *Now Wait for Next Year* (1966), written in the autumn of 1963, PKD creates a monstrous female character called Kathy Sweetscent. Anne has no doubts that this character, who is 'sadistic, self-destructive, and makes more money than her husband – dear, earnest Dr Eric Sweetscent',[77] is based on her. The reference to money echoes the fact that by this time Anne's small cottage industry of jewellery making was bringing in more money than PKD's writing. What was clearly most disturbing for Anne was that by the end of the novel her character has deteriorated into a mentally unstable, violent psychopath who has to be forcibly committed to a mental institution. Was this a form of wish-fulfilment by PKD, after his failure to have Anne similarly confined? In what may be a telling aside, Anne states that PKD never showed her this novel. She only read it after his death.

At a party at a friend's house in the nearby hills in the autumn of 1963, PKD's secret thoughts became manifest. Although he had drunk a number of martinis and was slightly inebriated he insisted on driving the car home. On the way, he failed to negotiate a turn and ended up with the car hanging precariously over a cliff edge. The neighbours turned up in a truck with a tow rope. As they were attaching the rope to pull the car to safety, Anne says PKD grabbed her arm and forced her towards the car saying, 'Get in and I'll push.' She understood this to be a form of suicide attempt.

> 'If he had pushed the car it could have gone over the side of the mountain. Of course, there were trees to stop it from going terribly far—I think. I pulled away from him, annoyed—and as usual, immediately put this incident out of my mind. I was very good at denial—or was it faith—or bourgeois family values—or an excess of loyalty?'[78]

As far as PKD's science fiction writing was concerned, at least, things were starting to look up. In September 1963, PKD heard that he had won the Hugo Award for Best Novel for his *The Man in the High Castle* (1962). The Hugo is named in honour of Hugo Gernsback, an American inventor, writer-editor and magazine publisher who is known as 'the father of science fiction' as he is credited with producing the first magazine in the genre. The Hugo Awards are presented at the annual world science fiction conference, 'Worldcon', which is hosted by a different North American city each year.

In 1963, the 21st World Science Fiction Convention, 'Discon I', was held at the prestigious Statler-Hilton Hotel, in Washington DC. The event attracted six hundred members of the World Science Fiction Society and included many of the greats of sci-fi including writers Isaac Asimov, creator of the classic *'Foundation'* series, and William Fitzgerald Jenkins, author of the sci-fi novelette *First Contact*, who wrote under the penname Murray Leinster. The winners of the Hugo Awards are decided in a ballot of members of the society, so writers are judged by their peers and supporters. Other Hugo awards presented at the convention included Best Fiction, awarded to Jack Vance for *Dragon Masters*. Asimov received a special award for the science articles he wrote for *Science and Fantasy Magazine*, which itself won the Hugo for Best Sci-fi magazine.

A mind in freefall

So, PKD was in distinguished company. He should have been elated. Unfortunately, he also craved recognition as a 'mainstream' writer but his non-science fiction novels failed to attract any interest. A few weeks after the announcement of the award came more bad news. His literary agent sent all his manuscripts for 'mainstream' novels back to him, explaining in an accompanying note that they simply could not sell them and, from that point on, they would only be interested in his science fiction novels and short stories, nothing else.

This was a huge blow for PKD and he took it badly. He started to withdraw from the family and spent more and more time in the 'Hovel' and less and less time with his wife and children. When he did join them, arguments would soon erupt. Anne describes how he regularly stormed off back to his mother's house, only to return a few days later. Things did not improve. Anne was finding dealing with PKD's instability and unpredictability an ongoing strain. During one argument, Anne describes PKD as 'pummeling' her. She reacted by clenching her fists and for a few seconds the situation could have turned very violent but PKD then ran out of the room.

On 22 November 1963, President John F. Kennedy was shot dead as his presidential motorcade passed along Dealey Plaza in Houston, Texas. The man accused of the killing, Lee Harvey Oswald, was then shot by Jack Ruby before he could stand trial. The assassination had a profound effect on PKD. Anne describes how PKD, on hearing the news, fell to the floor with shock. He was depressed for many weeks afterwards.

A whole series of sad events, including the deaths of their dog and two kittens, added to PKD's mood of despair. Soon after the death of the kittens, PKD stormed out of the house and went back to Berkeley to stay with his mother. He only returned after Anne and the girls drove down to find him and brought him back. There clearly were problems with the marriage. Anne's solution was to enrol the whole family in the local Episcopal Church in Inverness. The family started confirmation classes and became part of the small community that took an active interest in the church.

In January 1964, in a final attempt to bring the family closer together again, PKD, Anne and the children were baptised into the Episcopal Church. A month later they were confirmed. However, things remained difficult between Anne and PKD. Their therapist felt that the relationship would benefit from having separate councillors and PKD was allocated a new, male psychiatrist. Many years later, in 1982, Anne met up with her psychiatrist, Dr 'J', who informed her that there had been genuine concerns for Anne's safety. It seems that PKD's psychiatrist had contacted her to inform her of his worries that PKD might actually try to kill his wife.

The Three Stigmata

It was in this atmosphere of dread and depression that PKD began writing *The Three Stigmata of Palmer Eldritch* (1965). By this time, PKD was finding it difficult not to imbue into his writing his emotions with regard to the break-up of his third marriage.

The Three Stigmata of Palmer Eldritch is one of his first novels to have a religious theme. PKD set the novel in a future in which Earth is rendered almost uninhabitable by global warming. This showed remarkable foresight as, at the time he wrote it, scientists were more concerned about a possible return to the ice age. In the novel, colonists are drafted to other planetary bodies in the Solar System. To escape from their bleak existence, they take an illegal drug called 'Can-D' in order to enter an artificial reality and experience the fictitious life of a character called 'Perky Pat'.

The corporation that owns 'Perky Pat' and 'Can-D' discover their monopoly is at risk from a rival product, 'Chew-Z', offered by Palmer Eldritch, a bionic interstellar trader with electronic eyes, steel teeth and an artificial arm (his three stigmata). The novel's central question is: who exactly is Palmer Eldritch – God? Satan? All of us? And if so, can we resist him or is free will merely an illusion? Many commentators assumed that PKD wrote *The Three Stigmata* while under the influence of LSD. But, in an interview with Joe Vitale, PKD denied these claims, saying, 'I wrote that after reading a magazine article on hallucinogenics by Aldous Huxley.'[79]

1964 – The Three Stigmata of Palmer Eldritch

'"You learn to get by from day to day," Sam Regan said sympathetically to him. "You never think in longer terms. Just until dinner or until time for bed; very finite intervals and tasks and pleasures. Escapes."'
– Philip K. Dick, *The Three Stigmata of Palmer Eldritch*

There is a degree of confusion as to when this was actually written. The general consensus is early 1964, but some date it back to 1963. Andrew Butler states that it was completed on 18 March 1964. It was published in hardback by Doubleday on 17 November 1964.

The original story was taken from the short story 'The Days of Perky Pat'. This was written the year before, being submitted to SMLA on 18 April 1963 and published in December 1963 in *Amazing*. According to Patricia Warrick, the idea for the short story occurred when PKD saw his daughters playing with their Barbie dolls. He noted how closely the child who plays with these dolls relates to the world of Barbie and how Barbie perceives her own world.

Central to this complex novel is the practical applications of precognition in business. Precogs are employed to predict future market trends. Woven within this is the idea that reality can be warped by the taking of powerful hallucinogens such as 'Can-D' and its replacement, the even more powerful 'Chew-Z', which is about to be brought to Earth by the eponymous Eldritch.

The name 'Palmer Eldritch' literally means 'horrible pilgrim' and the novel contains many religious allusions. This may reflect the fact that at the time of writing Phil had become a member of the Episcopal Church and, as part of his confirmation classes, he had been reading a great deal of theological material.

The idea that illusory worlds can be created by the mind of somebody else was first investigated by PKD in *Eye in the Sky*, but it is here that it develops into a true Gnostic nightmare in which the Demiurge controls everything.

The Three Stigmata of Palmer Eldritch was nominated for 'Best Novel' in the 1965 Nebula Awards.

In early 1964, PKD was finishing the final sections of the *Clans of the Alphane Moon* and it is clear from this novel that much of his personal life was spilling over into his fiction. The story is set in a former psychiatric institution built to provide mental care for colonists living on worlds orbiting the star Alpha Centauri and who were finding it difficult to cope with the stresses of colonization. Within a fascinating story about various forms of mental illness, the book also focuses on the relationship between two central characters, Chuck and Mary Rittersdorf, who are going through a bitter divorce. Chuck and Mary become reconciled at the end of the novel. Sadly, PKD could not create the same happy ending for his own marriage.

PKD was now spending more and more time at Dorothy and Joe's home in Berkeley. So it came as no surprise when PKD filed for a divorce on 9 March 1964. He was not only leaving Anne and his step-daughters but also his own daughter, Laura. The state of the relationship was not the only factor in the divorce. He also felt he needed to leave the sedate 'bourgeois' country life he had been leading in Reyes Point Station and revert to being a single man once more, enjoying the hurly burly and excitement of the big city. Initially, PKD moved in with Dorothy and Joe but he soon began renting accommodation nearby.

1964 – Martian Time-Slip

'I'm not much but I'm all I have.'

– Philip K. Dick, *Martian Time-Slip*

PKD sent the completed manuscript of a novel entitled *Goodmember Archie Kott of Mars* to his literary agency on 31 October 1962. The story was then serialized in the magazine *Worlds of Tomorrow* under the title of 'All We Marsmen'. By the time it had appeared in this format it had been sold to Ballantine who published it under the title *Martian Time-Slip* in April 1964. It was rejected by Pyramid, Ace and Berkley.

In this curious novel PKD focuses in on the nature of autism and schizophrenia. It is set on Mars in August 1994. A young boy by the name of Manfred Steiner has powerful precognitive abilities facilitated by his autism. The central character, Jack Bohlen, has bouts of schizophrenia.

Some see schizophrenia and autism as a danger, whereas others, such as Arnie Kott, the leader of the powerful Water Workers' Union, feel that precognitives such as Manfred can be used to gain political power and financial advantage.

The novel focuses on fake psychotic realities and was greatly influenced by the writings of Swiss existentialist psychiatrist Ludwig Binswanger. PKD presents a universe in multiple layers of 'reality', where autism/schizophrenia allows access to alternate time-streams. He was later to call this concept 'Orthogonal Time' and discusses its potential existence in great detail in his *Exegesis*.

Ten days later, on 18 March 1964, he sent the manuscript of *The Three Stigmata of Palmer Eldritch* to his literary agent. In a period of days he had divested himself of a novel that he feared and a life that he found suffocating. As a certain Bob Dylan wrote that year, 'The times they are a changin'. . .

Chapter Six

The Hackett Years (1965–70)

The previous year, PKD had started a correspondence with Grania Davidson, the wife of fellow science fiction writer Avram Davidson, after she wrote praising his novel *The Man in the High Castle* (1962). By the time PKD had left Anne, Grania's own marriage to Avram was coming to an end – though an amicable one. When Grania heard that PKD was now single, too, she and her son moved to Berkeley. PKD had found a new soul mate.

Humpty Dick in Oakland

In June 1964, the three of them settled down in a small rented cottage in Lyon Avenue, Oakland, a port city on the east coast of San Francisco Bay. Like PKD, Grania was fascinated by the *I Ching*. In one of her earlier letters to PKD, she said she had asked the oracle 'what would happen between us' and received the answer 'hexagram 45' – meaning 'Gathering Together', which she took to be a positive sign.[80] The relationship got off to an unfortunate start, however. When PKD and Grania were in the process of moving their possessions into the Lyon Avenue house, PKD took a corner too fast in his Volkswagen and badly dislocated his right shoulder. He was encased in body plaster for some time and so was unable to write. He tried to put on a brave face for Grania and her son but this did not help his overall mood. Indeed, he informed a new friend, fellow science fiction writer Ray Nelson, that he had secretly tried to commit suicide. The motoring injury never fully healed and he was to suffer with repeated dislocations for the rest of his life.

But his mood did improve. PKD and Grania had a good relationship at first, with PKD delighting in his role as father to her son. When he was in a good mood it was easy to see why so many women fell for him. Ray Nelson's wife Kirsten told Anne she found him:

> '. . .romantic, exciting, fascinating, as did several other ladies there. He had fantastic charisma. He proposed to every woman he met. The jokes he would crack were so funny. Phil loved to fall in love; he was in love with falling in love.'[81]

Love and paranoia

Indeed, he was in love again, with Grania, and so it is not surprising that PKD soon proposed. But this was not what Grania was looking for. Although she found him to be wonderful company he was also 'beset by inner demons'[82] such as his paranoia towards Anne, which became so strong that he bought a .22 Colt Derringer to protect himself. He painted a picture of his ex-wife as a dangerous psychopath. When researching her biography of PKD, Anne spoke to his old friend from Art Music, Vince Lusby. What Lusby told her she found hugely upsetting.

> 'Phil told Vince that the reason he was getting divorced was that I would buy every new car that came along and that he had to stop me before I lost the house. He told Vince that I had attacked him with a carving knife, that I had chased him around the yard with the white Jaguar (which we hadn't owned for years), and that I had murdered my first husband. Vince was surprised at all this since he knew me. Then Phil told Vince seriously, "Anne has wired up my old Magnavox so that she can listen and spy on me here".'[83]

Vince also said that PKD claimed Anne was planning to break into his office and steal his financial records. He not only thought that Anne had 'murdered' her ex-husband, but that his good friend Ray Nelson was planning to kill his wife, Kirsten. Grania became very concerned about his 'self destructive moods', fearing that PKD might turn the gun on himself. Grania managed to steal the pistol and gave it to Ray for safekeeping. But it seems that PKD had more than one gun.

From 4 to 7 September 1964, The Leamington Hotel in Oakland hosted the 22nd National Science Fiction Convention, known that year as 'Pacificon II'. The 1964 Hugo-Award-winning novel was Clifford D. Simak's *Way Station*. For reasons that are unclear, PKD phoned Anne and invited her down to attend the last day of the convention with him and Ray Nelson. She agreed and travelled down from Point Reyes Station for the occasion. But the day did not go well. In the early hours of the morning, PKD left Anne to make her own way home through the potentially hazardous Oakland streets. It is unclear why this happened or, indeed, how Anne managed to get home that night.

One clue to PKD's odd behaviour may be found in Sutin's interview with a science fiction fan called Dick Ellington. Ellington describes how PKD was wearing a three-piece suit with lots of waistcoat pockets.

> 'I swear to God Phil had enough foreign and exotic substances in those pockets to stock a large drugstore and enough left over for a voodoo shop.'[84]

The next day, Anne decided to drive back to Oakland to find out why PKD had behaved in such a manner, bringing with her their daughter, Laura, then four years old. Anne said she knocked on the door of PKD's house in Lyon Avenue. A few seconds later, PKD opened the door still wearing his pyjamas and began brandishing a revolver. Anne grabbed Laura and left the scene as quickly as she could. She was both puzzled and frightened by this dangerous mood-swing. She has since described how this turn of events made her contemplate suicide, but she changed her mind for the sake of her children.[85]

Emmanuel Carrere gives a different version of events in his off-beat and slightly fictionalized biography, *I Am Alive And You Are Dead: A Journey Inside The Mind Of Philip K. Dick* (2005). According to Carrere, on seeing Anne approaching the house, PKD ran from room to room brandishing the revolver before shoving Grania into a closet. He then let Anne and Laura come in. In Carrere's account, Anne and her daughter stayed for several hours, with PKD cooking bacon and eggs and singing 'some Schubert lieder in his fine deep voice, then the sounds of a peaceful family get-together round an amply laden dining room table.'[86]

Anne heard nothing from PKD for a few weeks. Then, in October 1964, he rang her to ask if he could come home. She agreed and he arrived later that day carrying his typewriter and a single suitcase, which he took into his study. Anne was working in her studio that day making jewellery. She decided not to make a big issue of her ex-husband's return and just continued with what she was doing. PKD obviously felt that he was being shunned because, an hour later, when Anne came out of the studio for a glass of water, she saw PKD getting back into his car with the suitcase and typewriter. She watched him drive away, knowing that it was for the last time.

Grania moved out of the Lyon Avenue property on 31 October 1964. It is not known what brought this about. PKD felt that he had been abandoned again. Within a few days, another friend, Jack Newkom and his wife, Margo, had moved into the house but this arrangement didn't last long with both of his new lodgers moving out within a month.

PKD's musical tastes began to broaden during this time. He would never lose his interest in classical music but during the sixties he got into rock music, including the Rolling Stones, Jefferson Airplane, The Grateful Dead and Country Joe and the Fish. In California in the 1960s, hand in hand with rock music went drugs. People were experimenting with new forms of drugs, seeking to gain an experience that transcended the mere 'high' that marijuana and amphetamines provided to something more spiritual. The best known of these was LSD, an abbreviation of lysergic acid diethylamide, or 'acid' for short. The best-known 'acid guru' was a former assistant professor at Berkeley, Timothy Leary, who championed the use of hallucinogenic drugs to achieve altered states of consciousness. In 1964, Leary had co-authored a book entitled *The Psychedelic Experience*. In the book he writes:

> 'Of course, the drug does not produce the transcendent experience. It merely acts as a chemical key — it opens the mind, frees the nervous system of its ordinary patterns and structures.'

Many people in the literary world were also experimenting with LSD in order to gain psychological and spiritual insights. PKD was no exception. On at least two occasions during December 1964, PKD began taking acid along with his old school friend, fellow science fiction author Ray Nelson, who had acquired the drug from contacts. During the first of these LSD 'trips' at PKD's house, PKD seemed to take on the personality of an Ancient Roman, possibly an early manifestation of his 'Thomas' character. From the depths of his acid trip PKD, it is regularly reported, spoke to Nelson in flawless, grammatically correct, Latin.[87]

However, as part of my research I had the opportunity to ask Ray for his recollections of this incident. In a personal correspondence to me, Ray stated:

> 'I can't be sure Phil was speaking real Latin during his LSD experiences. I wouldn't know the difference between real Latin and fake Latin.'

Many fans of PKD have assumed that the surreal and unworldly images and plots that the author has devised must have emanated from acid-induced hallucinatory visions. PKD often encouraged these ideas himself. In an interview with Joe Vitale, he said, 'Look, I'll be honest with you. There was a time in my life when I thought drugs could be useful, that maybe if you took enough psychedelics you could see beyond the illusion of the world to the nature of ultimate reality. Now I know all they put you in touch with is the rubber room at the psychiatric hospital.'[88] He later came to play down the importance of the drug in his work and also the amount of acid he had taken. In an interview with science fiction writer Arthur Byron Cover, PKD said:

> 'I wasn't getting up in the morning and dropping acid. I'm amazed when I read the things I used to say about it on the blurbs of my books. I wrote this myself: "He has been experimenting with hallucinogenic drugs to find the unchanging reality beneath our delusions." And now I say, "Good Christ!" All I ever found out about acid was that I was where I wanted to get out of fast. It didn't seem more real than anything else; it just seemed more awful.'

1965 – Dr. Bloodmoney

'I'm tired and I want to rest; I want to get out of this and go lie down somewhere, off where it's dark and no one speaks. Forever.'

– Philip K. Dick, *Dr. Bloodmoney*

On 11 February 1963 SMLA received a manuscript entitled *In Earth's Diurnal Course*, after Wordsworth. The title was changed to *Dr. Bloodmoney or How We Got Along After the Bomb* and was published by Ace on 11 June 1965. It was nominated for the Nebula Award for the Best Novel of 1965.

In 1972 a miscalculation during a nuclear test has brought about widespread fall-out across large areas of the San Franscisco Bay. Many children were born with genetic mutations. The story opens in 1981 when Dr. Bluthgeld ('Bloodmoney' in German), the scientist responsible for the error, is dealing with his paranoia and guilt by seeking psychiatric help. The second section of the book takes place seven years later after a nuclear strike on the USA. Civilisation is re-building itself and we focus on a group of survivors in a self-governing community in northern Marin County.

The character of Hoppy Harrington is based on Eldon Nichols, the hunch-backed accountant who worked at Art Music and was responsible for PKD's dismissal from the job he loved so much. Indeed the television repair shop in the novel matches exactly the Herb Hollis shop with both located at Shattuck Avenue in Berkeley.

One of the children affected by the 1972 accident is Edie Keller. She has, within her, the tiny body of her twin brother, Bill. Bill communicates telepathically with his sibling and claims to be the reincarnation of shop owner Jim Fergusson. Not only is this is a reversal of Phil's relationship with his long-lost twin sister Jane, but the idea that a 'Bill' will believe himself to be the reincarnation of a person called 'Jim' will recur in PKD's 1982 novel *The Transmigration of Timothy Archer*.

Dr. Bloodmoney also contains elements of another 'phildickian' theme, that of reality as the projection of the observer, in this case Bluthgeld himself.

He is convinced he is 'the omphalos, the center, of all this cataclysmic destruction'. From this position of supreme solipsism, he believes he has the psychic power to bring about further nuclear destruction simply by willing it to happen.

Fragile, vulnerable Nancy

First Grania and then his two lodgers had left. PKD was not happy living alone. He was looking for company, especially female and young. He suggested that the step-daughters of a family friend from Marin County move in with him. He had met the two girls, Anne and Nancy Hackett, a few times with their mother, Maren, while he was living in Point Reyes Station. He had then met the three of them again at a dinner party at Maren's house. PKD had been initially attracted to Anne but soon his affections turned to the fragile, intelligent and psychologically vulnerable younger sister, twenty-one-year-old Nancy.

By any standards, Nancy had already had a difficult time in her young life. Her mother and father divorced when she was very young. Her mother re-married for a short period but this proved to be an abusive relationship. When Nancy was aged twelve, her mother was diagnosed with an inoperable brain tumour. She fell into a coma, eventually dying in 1961 when Nancy was eighteen. By this time her father had married a bright, caring woman by the name of Maren. Nancy and her elder brother and sister moved in with them, and even though Maren and their father later divorced, Maren was happy to continue to take responsibility for the three children.

Considering the disruption in her life, Nancy did well at school and attended San Jose State University, in California. But she had been psychologically damaged by past events. She was not only very shy but also showed signs of what would now be diagnosed as bi-polar disorder but was then known as 'manic depression'. It is therefore not really surprising that this sensitive young woman found her college days difficult. She spent a short time studying at the Sorbonne in Paris, but the time she spent away from home proved problematic. Marijuana and other drugs were readily available and Nancy began to experiment with them. These drugs and her own psychological frailty proved a dangerous combination. She suffered a breakdown and had to return to the United States.

Pictures of Nancy show a slim girl with long, straight, dark hair, a wide friendly mouth but sad, deep-set eyes. This complex person was another of his 'dark-haired girls'. Nancy was one of many such young women who would accompany PKD through the ups and downs of his post-Anne life. According to Anne, PKD told his friend Kirsten Nelson that, 'I am in the Christ sweepstakes, if I don't save Nancy, no one else will.'[89]

In March 1965, Nancy moved into PKD's cottage in Lyon Avenue. They lived there for a few months before relocating to San Rafael on the opposite side of San Francisco Bay. In November, Nancy got a job at the local post office and all seemed to be going well. Just over a year later, Nancy became pregnant. The couple married in July 1966 in a civil ceremony at the house of a family friend, Judge David Batty. Also in attendance that day was James A. Pike, the Episcopalian bishop of North California. At the end of the short ceremony, Bishop Pike gave the newly married couple his blessing.

Bizarre events

The Episcopalian Church does not usually support civil marriages nor, at that time, did it look positively on divorce. However, Jim Pike was far from being a typical Episcopalian cleric. He was a radical theologian with some unusual ideas regarding the early Christian church. He was also having an affair with Nancy's mother, Maren. By this time, PKD and Jim had developed a close friendship, one that was to provide material for a novel and also mark the prelude to a train of bizarre events.

In February of the following year, Jim Pike's son, Jim Junior, committed suicide. This tragedy was followed by a series of curious poltergeist events, including the mysterious burning of Maren's hair and a series of odd occurrences involving safety pins. Pike began to believe that his son was trying to communicate with him. According to Lawrence Sutin, in October 1966 Pike went to a séance held at the home of the then-famous medium George Daisley, in Santa Barbara, California. Also in attendance were Maren, PKD and Nancy. PKD's role was to take notes and ensure that nothing that happened during the séance was missed.[90]

Pike was later to write a book called *The Other Side* (1968) in which he describes his experiences after the death of his son and his subsequent search for proof of Jim Junior's post-mortem survival. However, in this book, Pike states that on his first visit to Daisley's home he was accompanied by Maren.[91] He mentions nobody else being in attendance. He says he took Maren with him because she had previously witnessed a séance in London given by the British medium Ena Twigg and he wanted an objective evaluation of the two sessions.

Pike states that this first meeting with Daisley took place in August 1966. He then describes a second visit to Daisley's home on the 9 September 1966.[92] The impression given by his description of this meeting is that he met with Daisley alone. His third, and final, meeting took place in December 1966 and again seems to have involved just the two of them.[93] So, if Pike's account is accepted as the most accurate available there was no meeting with Daisley in October 1966 and PKD and Nancy did not attend any of them. Sutin states that Pike thanked PKD and Nancy in the foreword to *The Other Side*.[94] In my own copy of this book, published in 1975, there is no mention of PKD and Nancy in the foreword or, indeed, anywhere in the book. When I mentioned this to Tessa Dick, PKD's last wife, she checked her own first edition copy of the book, and confirmed to me that Pike's acknowledgement to PKD and Nancy was included. I have no idea why a later UK edition omitted this.

1967 – Counter-Clock World

'Just because the old-borners can't remember doesn't mean nothing happened; like a lot of times in the morning I know I've dreamed like hell all night but I can't remember a damn thing about them, not anything at all.'

– Philip K. Dick, *Counter-Clock World*

PKD submitted a short story entitled 'Your Appointment Will Be Yesterday' to SMLA on 27 August 1965 and it was published in *Amazing Stories* a year later. Clearly PKD found this story intriguing and, from late 1965, had begun turning it into a novel with the working title of *The Dead Grow Young*. It was published by Berkley Books on 7 February 1967 with the revised title of *Counter-Clock World*.

Each chapter heading has a quotation from Erigena, Boethius or St Augustine, which pointedly raises questions about the nature of reality. As the plot unfurls, the world has entered the 'Hobart Phase', which involves time running backwards with people being 'born' in a grave, growing progressively younger until they 'die' by being born. Books are 'unwritten', people greet each other with a cheery 'goodbye' and say 'hello' when they leave. One of the 'old-born', whose return to life is anxiously anticipated, is the religious leader Anarch Peak. Some see this as an event of hugely significant importance, whereas others see his return as putting social stability at risk.

The character Anarch Peak is based upon Bishop James Pike who reappears in the role of Bishop Timothy Archer in PKD's later novel, *The Transmigration of Timothy Archer*.

On 17 March 1967, Nancy gave birth to a baby girl, PKD's second daughter. They named her Isolde Freya, a reflection of PKD's love of Wagnerian opera. She would be called 'Isa' for short. The birth of the baby caused a rift between PKD and his young wife, however. He was keen to give Nancy advice on the rearing of his daughter. The death of his sister in early infancy had played on his mind for years and he didn't wish the same fate to befall little Isa. But Nancy was keen to care for her daughter in the way her instincts told her to. PKD felt he was being pushed away. He turned inwards and began taking prescription drugs in large quantities. He was registered with a number of doctors in the area and knew exactly which symptoms to present to be supplied with a specific medication.

The family were desperately short of money. PKD needed to write novel after novel to keep them fed and clothed. To keep up this punishing regime, he needed help in the form of more prescription drugs and an increasing need for amphetamine, only available from drug dealers. Worse was to follow. Nancy's step-mother, Maren, who had been successfully treated for cancer, was told that her cancer had returned. At around this time, Maren also discovered that her husband, Jim Pike, had been having affairs with other women. This was all too much for her to bear and, in June 1967, she committed suicide. PKD was later to describe this in a semi-fictional format in his book *The Transmigration of Timothy Archer* (1982).

PKD took this very badly and, in July, he experienced what he was later to describe as a return of his 'borderline psychotic symptoms'.[95] This was a recurrence of the distortions of time-sense, paranoia and memory loss that he experienced in his teens. We shall come back to this particular experience later, when we discuss a possible neurological explanation for PKD's 'breakdowns'. These events led to a downward spiral that was exacerbated when, according to Anne, PKD bought some contaminated amphetamines from a drug dealer and became seriously ill with acute pancreatitis and was forced to spend some time in hospital.[96]

Despite their parlous financial state, the new baby meant that PKD and Nancy urgently needed to find a larger property. They were helped by Dorothy and Joe who put down a deposit on a house in Hacienda Way, Santa Venetia, a town located just north of San Rafael, around fifteen miles from San Francisco. This attractive town was originally modelled on Venice, in Italy, hence the 'Venetia' of the name. Only one canal was actually built.

In June 1968, PKD, Nancy and baby Isa moved into their new home. Although his mother and step-father had provided the initial downpayment, PKD needed to find $167 a month for the mortgage. At first, the family settled in well at their new home but then PKD started to become over-possessive of Nancy who, at that time, was becoming more confident and outgoing. PKD was unhappy if she went out on her own, even if she was only visiting her sister, and would phone her constantly. This atmosphere clearly had an effect and, in 1969, Nancy suffered another nervous breakdown. She refused to allow PKD to visit her, believing that their relationship had somehow become 'evil'.[97]

One of PKD's most successful books, *UBIK* (1969), was written during this highly productive period. It has been described as a 'searing metaphysical comedy', a 'tour de force of paranoiac menace and unfettered slapstick' and also an 'existential horror story'. *UBIK* is set in a future in which psychic powers are commonplace and 'dead' people can be kept in a form of suspended animation called 'half-life' that allows limited consciousness. Glen Runciter, boss of a firm of professional 'anti-telepaths', is killed in an explosion staged by a rival that leaves his co-workers unscathed, including protagonist Jo Chip. Runciter is put in half-life but Jo and the

1968 – Do Androids Dream of Electric Sheep?

'Empathy, he once had decided, must be limited to herbivores or anyhow omnivores who could depart from a meat diet. Because, ultimately, the empathic gift blurred the boundaries between hunter and victim, between the successful and the defeated.'

– Philip K. Dick, *Do Androids Dream of Electric Sheep?*

This was based upon a short story, 'The Little Black Box', written in 1964, which introduced the religion of Mercerism and empathy boxes. Finished by 20 June 1966, the novel first appeared in a hardcover edition published by Doubleday in 1968. In its original form it had various titles, including *The Electric Toad, Do Androids Dream?* and *The Killers are Among Us Cried Rick Deckard to the Special Man.*

The action is set in California in 1992. Due to pollution and radiation fall-out most animal species have died out and the ultimate status symbol is to own a real animal rather than their mechanical replacements. Rick Deckard is a bounty hunter whose quarries are 'Nexus-6' androids who illegally return to Earth from off-planet colonies. He is licensed to 'retire' (terminate) these fabricated beings which are so convincingly human that they easily blend into society.

Again PKD picks up on the theme of entropy. The Nexus-6 androids have a restricted life-expectancy programmed into them. A small group comes to Earth to seek out their 'creator', the cybernetics genius Eldon Rose, in the hope that he can extend their existence. The novel is a meditation on exactly what it means to be alive.

Do Androids Dream of Electric Sheep? was nominated for Best Novel in the 1968 Nebula Awards.

others then get obscure messages from him and soon wonder who actually died in the blast. The only hope is a substance called 'UBIK' (from ubiquitous), which comes in a spray can and can preserve those in half-life.

Here, PKD pursues one of his favourite themes by blurring the nature of reality and unreality. The readers never know from start to finish which characters are alive and which ones are dead. But, although the book is a comedy, it carries a spiritual message. PKD's fifth wife Tessa has offered her own interpretation of the novel, saying that:

'Ubik is a metaphor for God. Ubik is all-powerful and all-knowing, and Ubik is everywhere. The spray can is only a form that Ubik takes to make it easy for people to understand it and use it. It is not the substance inside the can that helps them, but rather their faith in the promise that it will help them.'

Talking about the enigmatic ending she states, 'Actually, this is meant to tell you that we can't be sure of anything in the world that we call "reality".'

One highlight of this period was the 26th World Science Fiction Convention, 'Baycon', which was held at The Hotel, in Clairmont, Berkeley from 29 August to 2 September, 1968. Appropriately enough for an event held in California at this time, for the first time, the convention had a strong 'hippy' theme. Robert Silverberg gave a talk about using hallucinogenic drugs to attain a mystical experience, Harlan Ellison read a story set in a commune, and a psychedelic lightshow was staged in the hotel ballroom. Guest of honour was writer Philip José Farmer and the Hugo Award for best novel went to Roger Zelazny for *Lord of Light*.

PKD went along on his own, leaving Nancy at home with baby Isa. For PKD it was a great opportunity to catch up with old acquaintances, such as Ellison and Zelazny, and also make new ones, including Norman Spinrad, then a rookie science fiction writer, who would become an important friend, and rock journalist Paul Williams, who would later interview PKD for the magazine *Rolling Stone*. Williams, too, would become a life-long friend and later executor of PKD's literary estate.

In September 1969, another loss put even more pressure on PKD and Nancy's already fragile relationship. Following Maren's suicide, James Pike had married again, to a woman called Diane. He resigned as Bishop of California and immediately set off to the Holy Land to continue his biblical archaeological research. He drove into the hot, dry and very hostile Judean desert, accompanied by Diane, searching for archaeological proof of the historical Jesus. Their car broke down and Diane left James to go for help. When she returned there was no sign of her husband. Jim had wandered off. His body was found a short time later.

PKD later used the circumstances surrounding Pike's death and those earlier encounters with the spirit world for his lightly fictionalized novel *The Transmigration of Timothy Archer* (1982). In this work, PKD describes the suicides of Jim Junior and Maren in detail and weaves around these tragic events a tale that suggests not only that there is survival after death but that the dead can develop a symbiotic relationship with the living. This novel, along with *VALIS* (1981), *The Divine Invasion* (1981) and *Radio Free Albemuth* (1985), were to be PKD's final legacy.

In September 1970, Nancy left PKD, taking Isa with her. According to PKD, she ran off with a 'Black Panther'. In reality he was a man called Honor Jackson who lived just across the Street. In his biography *Divine*

Invasions, Lawrence Sutin quotes Jackson as saying that the simple reason Nancy left PKD was that 'there were too many drugs.'[98] Little did she know that this was just the beginning.

1969 – UBIK

'I am Ubik. Before the universe was, I am. I made the suns. I made the worlds. I created the lives and the places they inhabit; I move them here, I put them there. They go as I say, then do as I tell them. I am the word and my name is never spoken, the name which no one knows. I am called Ubik, but that is not my name. I am. I shall always be.'

– Philip K. Dick, *UBIK*

On December 7, 1966 PKD submitted a manuscript entitled *Death of an Anti-Watcher* to SMLA. The novel was eventually published under a revised title of *UBIK* in May 1969. The novel's plot was based upon his 1963 short-story, 'What Dead Men Say'.

It is 1992. On a visit to Luna, businessman Glen Runciter is killed in a bomb attack. His subordinate, Joe Chip, brings Runciter's body back to Earth and delivers it to a Swiss organisation that places bodies into a cryogenic state known as 'half-life'. However, the Earth that Chip returns to seems to be in a state of decay: food goes stale and technology has devolved to levels of the 1930s. Again we have the Phildickian theme of entropy. However other strange events occur which lead Chip and his associates to believe that Runciter is somehow manipulating reality from beyond the grave. His head appears on coins, his words appear on matchboxes and his voice appears on 'vidphones'. . .

This idea that the world around us may be a fake was first introduced by PKD in *Eye in the Sky* and developed in *Martian Time-Slip* and *Stigmata*. In *UBIK* this concept becomes a sophisticated mixture of Tibetan Buddhism, Hinduism and Gnosticism. To this PKD adds an amusing critique of modern advertising and consumerism.

1969 – Galactic Pot-Healer

'We peep out, but what do we see, really? Mirror reflections of our own selves, our bloodless, feeble countenances, devoted to nothing in particular, insofar as I can fathom it. Death is very close, he thought.'

– Philip K. Dick, *Galactic Pot-Healer*

On November 3 1967 PKD sent a letter to Scott Meredith describing a storyline for a new novel. This was finished by February 1968 and published by Berkley Books in June 1969.

The plot involves a central character called Joe Fernwright who mends broken pottery. The Glimmung, a god-like entity made manifest in human form, meets Joe at the Cleveland spaceport and shows him a shard. This piece of pottery is termed 'the small divine fragment' and it comes from a huge submerged cathedral located out in space on Plowman's Planet. The Glimmung informs Joe that he must assist in the raising of a cathedral. Joe travels to the planet and there he discovers that there are not one, but two, cathedrals. As well as the edifice described, there is a black version. This reflects the two aspects of the Glimmung itself.

The story's central theme is light and darkness as represented by the Glimmung. There are also elements of the 'Tomb World', the *Bardo Thödol* of the *Tibetan Book of the Dead* and the works of Jung. The 'divine shard' is a concept central to Kabbalistic and Gnostic beliefs. It is a piece of the divine that has fallen out of the 'Pleroma' into the corrupt universe of base-matter and contains the light of divinity within it.

A central question asked in the book is the true nature of this being – is it God or just a god?

Chapter Seven

The Single Life (1970–71)

According to Lawrence Sutin, within a few days of Nancy moving out of the house in Santa Venetia, Nancy's brother, Mike, and her brother-in-law, Bernie Montbriand, moved in. Bernie was then replaced by a man called Tom Schmidt. All recall that PKD was extremely paranoid, believing at different times that communists, Nazis, and the FBI were on his trail. PKD's cousin, Lynne, later told Anne Dick that PKD believed the CIA, too, was 'after' him.[99] These reports can be taken at face value to suggest that PKD was in a heightened state of paranoia. But subsequent events suggest PKD might have had good reason to expect that the police, at least, might be taking an interest in him.

The drop-in centre

Local drug users soon came to regard PKD's home in Hacienda Way as an 'open house' and more and more undesirable individuals began turning up to crash out, score drugs or just party. PKD was happy with this at first. He hung up communist posters saying things like 'Workers of the World Unite! You Have Nothing to Lose But Your Chains!' because, he said, 'I thought [they] were very beautiful aesthetically.' He liked having young people around, particularly cute, dark-haired 'chicks'. He went through a series of 'crushes' with a number of the regulars. It is a moot point whether he was taking advantage of them or they were taking advantage of him. The one who would have the most influence on PKD's literary creativity was a seventeen-year-old high school girl called Kathy Demuelle.

PKD had started to source his amphetamines from the local 'chapter' of the Hell's Angels, a motorcycle gang linked with drug dealing and violent crime. His supplier was Kathy's boyfriend, a heavily bearded character called 'John'. Kathy had taken a liking to PKD and began spending more and more time at his house in Santa Venetia. She was another of PKD's 'dark-haired girls', a theme in his life that he would discuss in detail in his book *The Dark-Haired Girl*, written in the autumn of 1972 but not published until 1988, six years after his death. In his letters, PKD describes Kathy as a 'heroin addict' and an 'edgy' character.

Kathy is referred to as 'Donna' in much of the PKD literature because the character 'Donna Hawthorne' in *A Scanner Darkly* (1977) was based on her. Indeed, Sutin suggests that 'Donna' was also the model for 'Angel Archer' in *The Transmigration of Timothy Archer* (1982).[100]

Many years later, PKD's ex-wife Anne managed to trace her. At that time Kathy (or 'Cindy', as Anne called her), was aged thirty-one, which dates the interview to around 1984.[101] In this interview, Kathy described herself as being a fairly average kid of that time.

She admitted to smoking 'a little pot' but said that was all. She told Anne that PKD was very helpful to her during that complex time in her life and even fulfilled the role of surrogate father. She claimed that she never took money from PKD but that many of the other people that hung around the house did.

Kathy says the local kids saw PKD's house as a 'sort of paradise' where music was always playing at a very high volume and various cats and dogs wandered around unrestricted. But Kathy herself saw it as a rather chaotic and confrontational environment and said there were incidents of violence, including a knifing.[102] It was clear that things were getting out of control.

In the autumn of 1971, PKD became convinced that a former housemate called Rick was planning to kill him. What happened next could have come out of a Mickey Spillane novel. British author Ian Armer would later use this event as a central incident in his Philip K. Dick-inspired book *Mad Gods and Englishmen* (2013). PKD was convinced that Rick was going to turn up and attack him one night and so he recruited three local 'contract killers' to protect him. Nothing happened and the hired heavies left the next morning.

The break-in

In November that year, PKD returned home to find that his windows had been smashed in, his doors broken and, he would claim, his fire-proof safe blown open by explosives. All his papers had been stolen. In an interview for the documentary The Gospel According to Philip K. Dick (2001), his great friend and fellow science fiction writer Ray Nelson states that he had once seen inside the safe and had noticed plastic bags full of a white powder. He confirmed this account in a personal email to me:

> 'At one point Phil showed me a bag of some sort of powder which he said was worth a fortune and which he kept in his safe. It was about the size and shape of a loaf of bread.'[103]

Ray's wife, Kirsten, had stopped visiting PKD by this time because she was worried that the house might be raided by police. Indeed, Ray informed me that PKD's relationship with the FBI and the local 'gang members' was somewhat strange:

1970 – A Maze of Death

'He still saw himself, in his mind's eye, as youthful, and when he caught sight of himself in photographs he usually collapsed . . . Somebody took my actual physical presence away and substituted this, he had thought from time to time. Oh well, so it went.'

– Philip K. Dick, *A Maze of Death*

A manuscript with the title *The Hour of the T.E.N.C.H.* was received by SMLA on 31 October 1968. The novel, with a revised title of *A Maze of Death*, was published by Doubleday in July 1970.

Seth Morley and his wife arrive at a small scientific colony on Delmak-O. They are to meet with twelve others arriving from various locations. Unfortunately, due to the fact that their briefing tape has accidently been erased the colonists have no idea what their mission involves. Soon members of the group start to die under mysterious circumstances.

In discussion, PKD and his friend William Sarrill had created the theology believed by the various protagonists of the novel. As with *The Grasshopper Lies Heavy* in *The Man in the High Castle*, a book-within-a-book is used as a literary device. In this case, it is *How I Rose From The Dead In My Spare Time And So Can You.* This book, indeed the whole 'religion' that is believed by the colonists, is a collective fabrication. However, at the end of the novel, the illusory God, the 'Intercessor', seems to manifest and give Seth Morley the chance of a re-birth away from the eternal-return scenario on Delmak-O. We are left with the suggestion that this god has been made real by belief alone.

'What really bothered Kirsten was that Phil was on social terms with an actual FBI agent he had caught parking outside his house. Phil actually invited the agent in to have lunch with him, saying that if the agent really wanted to know what was going on, he should spy on him close up. There were times when Phil and I and the agent and one or two gang members sent out for pizza – we sat around Phil's dining room table chatting and listening to classical music on the hi fi.'[104]

Ray was puzzled by this behaviour because he was sure the mysterious white powder kept under lock and key in PKD's safe was heroin. Ray was also fairly sure he knew the source of the drugs. He states that, at that time, PKD was friendly with a local poet who edited a well-received literary review magazine. This individual, called 'The Connection' by Ray, also had associations with many of the original members of the 'beat' movement such as the novelist and artist William Burroughs and the poet Allen Ginsberg. PKD had been hugely influenced by Burroughs, Ginsberg and other members of this group and so was keen to nurture the relationship with 'The Connection'.

But the poet also had a much darker side. He earned his living (as Ray states, 'a very good living') as a drug dealer and was Burroughs' supplier. PKD must have been aware of the high standard of living that 'The Connection' enjoyed and could compare it with his own at that time. Since Nancy had left, PKD had written little. Apart from the occasional royalty cheques he received from his agent, he had no income. He was heavily in debt and was in danger of losing the property in Hacienda Way.

Ray suggests that 'The Connection' must have been very aware of PKD's situation, and also aware that PKD's home had become a 'drop-in' centre for many of the local disaffected youths, who regarded it as a place 'to crash out' and where food was always available. PKD was also taking a considerable amount of amphetamine at that time in the form of Benzedrine tablets (or 'bennies') and was quite happy to share them with any kids willing to sit and listen to his stories and his philosophy of life. These youngsters were the perfect market for the 'goods' supplied by 'The Connection'. Whether the heroin in PKD's safe was supplied directly by 'The Connection' is unclear from Ray's account, but what is clear is that Ray believed that PKD had been tempted to relieve his pressing financial problems through drug dealing.

Whatever the source of the heroin, Ray is fairly sure that he knows how the break-in came about.

> 'One of those girls, the one he called the 'dark-haired girl', that he professed to be madly in love with, was, I think, in love with, or associated with, drug suppliers, and she persuaded them to give Phil some drugs on credit which he had in the safe. Later she and her friends blew the safe and took the drugs and left him owing the gangsters for the drugs.'[105]

In March 2013, Ray told me that he was 'pretty sure it was to get that bag that the gang blew PKD's safe, though he refused to believe it'.

In his September 1981 interview with Gregg Rickman, Ray states that Kathy was a dope dealer and a police informant. If this was the case then her involvement in the November 1971 break-in is a possibility.[106] Indeed this is what PKD had to say about her at that time:

> 'She was apparently into major theft, as well as drug dealing, she was probably into major rip-offs, working with a rip-off gang, to raise money for her habit.'[107]

Is this PKD's version of Ray Nelson's 'Connection'?

In his 1978 interview with Joe Vitale, PKD suggested that the break-in may have been brought about by Government concerns regarding his novel *The Penultimate Truth*.[108] In this book, PKD describes a phony war between the United States and Russia. He told Vitale that he may have represented something too close to the real truth, so close as to raise the suspicions of the security services. They decided to steal his files in order to discover whether or not PKD had access to classified material. What is intriguing is why PKD came to such a conclusion. It suggests that he believed he had a way of subliminally picking up information from sources unknown, a skill that he gives many of his characters in his stories and novels.

However, there may be a much simpler explanation. Sutin references an entry in PKD's journal in which he states that while he was in hospital in August 1971 his housemate Daniel had 'systematically and thoroughly damaged beyond repair' the file locking mechanism.[109] We know that PKD kept most of his valuable and nostalgic documentation in the cabinet. To find that it was impossible to access these pieces must have been extremely frustrating. Was the 'explosion' actually an attempt by PKD himself to regain access to his papers? There were many theories as to who was responsible, both at the time and throughout the rest of his life – and even that PKD did it himself in some form of 'fugue' state. His later novel, *A Scanner Darkly* (1977), takes as its central theme a character who has two personalities.

Intriguingly, Tom Schmidt, one of the witnesses to the aftermath of the break-in, told Sutin that as far as he could see the filing cabinet had been 'forced open'. Indeed it was only PKD who insisted that the file had been blown open using explosives. Another witness, 'Sheila', states that 'one of the drawers looked exploded – just enough to break the lock.' Probably the most telling account was what the local Sherriff's office verbally told the rock journalist Paul Williams in 1974:

> 'There was a metal cabinet, the police report said, that had been drilled or pried – the homeowner said it had been blown open but it looked to the reporting officer like it had been pried.'[110]

Whether the burglary was the work of agents of the state, his so-called 'friends' or PKD himself in some sort of 'blackout' state, the circumstances really scared him. PKD later claimed that he began getting threatening phone calls and that the police accused him of being a 'dope guru' to the 'high school kids' and had warned him to get out of Marin County or he might be 'shot in the back'. He needed to get away from Santa Venetia, Marin County and California – and maybe even the USA.

Escape to Vancouver

After the break-in, and following the collapse of yet another marriage, PKD's world fell apart and he became increasingly depressed. It was clear to him that he needed a fresh start. Fate was to lend a hand. He received an invitation to speak at the Vancouver Science Fiction Convention, 'VCON 2', to be held on 18 and 19 February 1972 at the Biltmore Hotel, Vancouver. As PKD was guest of honour, the organizers would pay all his expenses. Without hesitation, PKD agreed and immediately started working on his speech. He asked Kathy to go with him and even bought her a plane ticket. The speech, which PKD dedicated to Kathy, was to be entitled *The Android and the Human*. Kathy was not keen to accompany PKD. There are various versions of what Kathy did with the ticket. Sometimes PKD stated that she simply ripped it up and other times he claimed that she traded it in for cash. Whatever the true circumstances, PKD was forced to go to Vancouver alone.

He had a little spare time before the convention and decided to drive to Point Reyes Station to see his daughter, Laura, his three step-daughters and his ex-wife Anne. Anne thought PKD had visited simply to see Laura. However, his daughter only stayed with her father for a few minutes and then went out to play. Once alone with Anne, PKD burst into tears, apologized for upsetting her and then walked out of the door.

After PKD left for Canada, the Santa Venetia house went into foreclosure. It was left to his mother to sort out the legalities and ensure that PKD's belongings were placed in storage. In a series of letters written the following year, PKD wished it to be known that his mother had sold on much of what he owned. However, it is also clear from other letters that most of his belongings did, in fact, end up back in his possession when he moved down to Los Angeles later that year.

PKD's escape to Canada was timely. It allowed him to distance himself from the circumstances surrounding the break-in and to make a new circle of friends. PKD gave his speech, *The Android and the Human*, at the University of British Columbia first of all and then, two days later, at the science fiction convention itself. The reaction to the talk was extremely positive and he got a standing ovation. In his wide-ranging speech, PKD covered many of his favourite topics, including the suggestion that instead of studying machines to understand human behaviour, scientists should study humans to get an insight into machine behaviour. He also discussed the view – held by many people at the time – that machines would one day become all-powerful and would try to dominate mankind. PKD, however, thought they could never really gain the upper hand, as the following quotation illustrates. It also gives an insight into his award-winning novel *A Scanner Darkly* (1977).

'"We see as through a glass darkly," Paul says in First Corinthians—will this someday be rewritten as: "We see as into a passive infrared scanner darkly?" A scanner which, as in Orwell's *1984*, is watching us all the time? Our TV tube watching back at us as we watch it, as amused, or bored, or anyhow somewhat as entertained by what we do as we are by what we see on its implacable face? This, for me, is too pessimistic, too paranoid. I believe First Corinthians will be rewritten this way: "The passive infrared scanner sees into *us* darkly," that is, not well enough to really figure us out. Not that we ourselves can really figure each other out, or even our own selves. Which, perhaps, too, is good; it means we are still in for sudden surprises, and unlike authorities, who don't like that sort of thing, we may find these chance happenings acting in our behalf, to our favor.'

PKD enjoyed being the centre of attention and as the guest of honour he had plenty of opportunities to use his charm on the women he met. He soon found a replacement for Kathy, another 'dark-haired girl' by the name of Jamis. As was to be the theme of his life, PKD fell madly in love with her. At the conference, he also met Michael and Susan Walsh, who invited him to stay with them at their Vancouver apartment. So, within a few days, he had found both a new girlfriend and a place to stay.

Sliding back down again

It didn't take long for things to go downhill again. Within two weeks, he had 'hit' on Susan and then accused Michael of being a bad husband and said he would take Susan away from him and 'make her happy'.[111] Michael told him to leave, which he did. Clearly, PKD was in one of his very negative states of mind and, to make matters worse, the events he thought he had left behind in California were about to catch up with him again. According to his old friend Ray Nelson, PKD was approached in the street by a smartly dressed individual who said, in a calm but threatening voice, 'We all have to pay our dues'. Ray is sure this is evidence that PKD had in some way ripped off his drug-dealer associates and that the break-in had been either an attempt by PKD to claim the drugs had been stolen from him or that his young friends were responsible and left PKD to deal with the consequences. As we shall discover later, PKD also believed that at some time in early 1972 he was abducted by a group of mysterious men in black suits. Was this again related to the fall-out from the break-in or was there something far more sinister going on?

To add to his problems, PKD had now broken up with Jamis and was in a very dark mood. He was a long way from home and sliding into depression. On 23 March, he phoned Susan Walsh to tell her that he was going to 'turn out the lights'. According to Anne's biography, Susan was confused by what he said and simply hung up on him. In fact, he was contemplating suicide by taking a drug overdose, although it is unclear whether PKD had taken any pills at the time he phoned Susan. Anne states that PKD wrote the number of a suicide help-line on a piece of paper and placed it next to the phone in case he changed his mind. She said he did, indeed, change his mind, and called for help.

As well as calling Susan Walsh, PKD told *Vertex* magazine, in a February 1974 interview, that he had taken 700mg of potassium bromide, a sedative, and phoned the suicide help-line. He then 'talked with this guy for almost an hour and a half'.[112] At the end of the conversation, the councillor suggested that PKD check out the local heroin re-hab centre, known as the X-Kalay Foundation Society, in Vancouver. However, Anne Dick describes how, within minutes of PKD's call to the help-line, medical help arrived and they 'took him to the hospital and saved his life'.[113] So what did happen that evening? In the final analysis we will never know but it shows how difficult it is to pin down facts in the life of Philip K. Dick.

Whatever the truth of the matter, PKD was in a poor psychological state and he did indeed end up checking himself in to X-Kalay. He told his *Vertex* interviewer that he had to pretend to be a heroin addict to be accepted. This was not difficult as the effect of the sedative he had taken had left its mark:

> 'I had to pretend I was an addict. I looked in bad shape, you see, from all that potassium bromide. I did a lot of method acting, like almost attacking the staff member interviewing me, so they never doubted that I was an addict.'[114]

He did not find the regime at X-Kalay to his liking. For one thing, the rehabilitation programme involved a great deal of manual labour, including 'pitching big wooden beams into the back of trucks'. But it meant he was much fitter and put on so much muscle his sports jacket was now too tight for him. Before he could be allowed to leave, PKD had to find a sponsor. He had previously been in contact with a Professor Willis McNelly, a lecturer at California State University ('Cal State'), in Fullerton, California. They had previously met at a science fiction convention. The professor was putting together a sci-fi collection at the university and PKD was interested in archiving his manuscripts and correspondence there. The break-in at PKD's flat made him realize how vulnerable his papers might be. Now he wrote to McNelly and made an emotional plea for help. This was his route back to the 'Golden State'.

Back in the USA

Professor McNelly read PKD's letter to the students in his science fiction English class. Two female students, Joanne McMahon and Sue Hoglind, were so touched by his request for a new home away from the San Francisco area that they wrote to PKD in Canada, offering a room in their house in Fullerton. Before accepting the offer, PKD phoned a young sci-fi writer called Norman Spinrad, who he had met at the 1968 World Science Fiction Convention in Berkeley. He informed Spinrad that he had been about to kill himself, explaining that his girlfriend had left him and he was deeply depressed. Indeed, the only thing that had stopped him was that he had just read Spinrad's short story *Carcinoma Angels*. This had made him decide to speak to Spinrad before he did anything he might have regretted.

What ensued was an hour-long conversation between two individuals who had been, a few hours before, effectively strangers. The discussion became very intimate and PKD ended up asking his new friend some advice regarding his future options. This is how Spinrad describes the conversation:

> "'On the other hand," Phil said, "I've got this offer from Willis McNelly at Cal State Fullerton to come down there to Orange County to live. What's your honest opinion, would I be better off moving to Orange County, or killing myself?"
>
> "Well, Phil, personally, I can't stand Orange County," I found myself saying, "but you might as well give it a try. If you don't like it, you can always kill yourself later."'[115]

PKD took Spinrad's advice and decided to move to Fullerton, a town in the north of Orange County, reputed to be one of the most conservative locations in the United States and mainly known at the time, aside from the university, for its orange groves. Not far from Fullerton, in Anaheim, is the famous Disneyland theme park. One of the most popular attractions at Disneyland at this time was a stage show called 'Great Moments with Mr Lincoln', which featured an audio-animatronic version of the US president – in effect, a simulacrum – that had been on show at the theme park since 1965. Curiously, PKD had already written about an artificial Abe Lincoln in 1962. The story was initially rejected by several publishers and finally appeared in *Amazing Stories* magazine in November 1969 under the title *A Lincoln Simulacrum*. The story would later reappear as *We Can Build You* in 1972. In an interview, PKD commented in passing about another connection with the Disney's Lincoln:

> 'I rented an apartment in a building where one of the ladies living in the building worked at Disneyland. I said to her,

"What do you do there?" "I reapply the makeup to the Lincoln every night, so that next morning when the park is open, it looks real.'"[116]

He would later describe Orange County as 'plastic-town, USA'. However, it is likely PKD was grateful for a quieter life after the traumas he had faced in Northern California the year before. This was a new location that offered a new start. It also offered other opportunities involving his new young, female, housemates, who said they were willing to cook, keep house and provide 'fringe benefits' (unspecified) in return for a modest share of the expenses.

Professor McNelly had agreed to take some of PKD's papers and manuscripts and place them in the university library. Many years later, in late 1982, Anne Dick, as part of her research for her biography of her ex-husband, visited the library and discussed PKD's personality with Professor McNelly. It seems that McNelly considered PKD to be powerfully charismatic figure and, at one stage, was worried about PKD making a play for his wife.[117]

Lost and lonely Linda

On 7 April 1972, a student of McNelly's, twenty-one-year-old Linda Levy,* also sent a letter to PKD at X-Kalay. Evidently this was unsolicited but it is reasonable to conclude that PKD would have been delighted to receive it.[118] In her letter Linda finishes off with the comment:

> 'But please don't think that if you write to me that I will be another problem, another crazy lost and lonely girl that you will have to worry about because I do not mean to be that. It's just that dammit, I need something too, and that is a friend, somebody to think about. Will you be my friend?'[119]

After reading it, it seems that PKD asked McNelly to arrange for Linda to be part of the reception team at the airport. PKD did not respond personally to Linda's initial letter. The first she knew about his response was when McNelly informed her that PKD wanted her to pick him up from Los Angeles International Airport (LAX). She excitedly agreed and asked her friend, Tim Powers, to join her. Tim was a student at Cal State University and would later embark on his own career as a science fiction writer and also become another of PKD's close circle of friends. [120]

And so it came to pass. On arrival back in the USA, PKD was met at LAX by a small group of Cal Tech students: his two new roommates, Joanne and Sue; Tim and, of course, his classic 'dark-haired girl' correspondent,

---

* Now known as Linda Castellani. For a list of her PKD letters go to http://www.thedark-hairedgirl.com/PKDCorrespondenceModified.pdf.

Linda Levy. To those waiting to greet the famous writer, PKD was not a particularly prepossessing sight, with his long grey beard, greying tousled hair and, according to Tim Powers, a sports jacket that was now too small for him. He was also 'carrying a cardboard box tied up with an extension cord' and holding the Jehovah's Witnesses' version of the Bible, apparently to 'mollify customs'. On the drive from the airport, PKD was cheerful and talkative as he tried to find out more about his new companions. But, Powers said, was clearly still recovering from his time in Canada and seemingly 'desperate'. Many years later, Linda was to describe to Anne Dick this encounter at the airport. Her version differs from Powers' in some respects:

> 'My first impression was of a man with a long, gray beard, wearing a trench coat, carrying in one hand a box wrapped in brown paper. . . and a Bible in the other. He reminded me of a derelict rabbi. When he saw me, he stopped suddenly, eyes fixed on me. He never took his eyes off me the whole evening.'[121]

As soon as PKD set eyes on Linda it was love at first sight. A photograph that PKD took of her at the time shows an attractive young woman, with shoulder-length dark hair, full mouth and widely spaced deep-set eyes peering out from under a fringe. It is fair to conclude that a middle aged man who, a few days before, had received such a letter from a twenty-one-year-old – like many of his infatuations, a young woman half his age – would be fascinated to meet the source of the correspondence. In a letter dated 20 May 1972 and sent to Bev Davies, PKD describes his first impression of her at the airport:

> 'Linda had written to me while I was in Canada, and, when I got off the plane at LA International there she was waiting, with the others, to meet me. Destiny in a miniskirt.'[122]

PKD stayed with the students for two months, sleeping on the living room couch. According to Tim Powers, it was a traumatic time for PKD as he was still convinced that drug enforcement officers were keeping him under surveillance and he was seeing a 'narc' in every neighbour with a CB radio. In an interview that Powers gave to Chris Ziegler of *OC Weekly* in 2002, he said PKD's paranoia was fuelled by the students. 'Anyone who stayed in the bathroom more than a couple of minutes was running the risk of having the door broken down because everyone would assume you were attempting suicide.'[123]

During a talk given to the Cal State English class, PKD joked about his living arrangements. A mature student in the class, Joel Stein, had just split up from his wife and had an extra bedroom in his apartment. He offered

PKD a place. Stein was thirty-five at the time, much closer in age to PKD's than the teenagers he had been sharing with until then. PKD gratefully accepted and moved in with Stein at his home in Quartz Lane.

The 'honorary student'

His six-month stay in Quartz Lane was just as lively as living with Joanne and Sue, but along more 'grown up' lines. Finally, PKD started to relax. Despite the grey beard, he began to fit in with college social life and was even named 'honorary student', albeit at the age of forty-two. His wide knowledge of music and his conversational ability made him popular with other students. He had a considerable amount of freedom to come and go as he pleased and soon embarked upon an intense relationship with Linda Levy, as evidenced by the love letter he wrote to her on 21 April 1972.

> 'It is almost May, Linda. And we already love you. Unfold and let us watch you unfold and that'll delight us. That'll give us such great joy. Am I making you a deal you can't refuse? Right? Right. In the letter you wrote me you asked me if I would be your friend. The answer is yes! Absolutely, totally yes, without qualifications or conditions of any kind. YES, YES, YES. I feel like filling up the whole pack of typewriter paper beside me with yesses, and then typing on the table and then the floor and especially the walls, on everything I can find. But I think you know how much yes there is in that yes already; it's the biggest yes I ever yelled in my life. The greatest, loudest, most emphatic thunderclap sound I have ever made. P.S. I am very much, very deeply in love with you. So this here is what I'd like to ask you; Will you marry me?'[124]

His feelings were not reciprocated, however. According to Sutin, this letter was handed to Linda as they were driving to meet the science fiction writer Harlan Ellison for dinner at his home in Hollywood.[125] As she did not have time to read it in the car, she opened it in the restaurant. She felt extremely awkward and PKD, thinking that Linda was not taking his offer of marriage seriously, took offence. An argument ensued.

Later, PKD claimed he had calmed the situation by stating that he only made the proposal because she had told him nobody had ever asked her to marry them. It is possible that this letter was the start of Linda's change of attitude towards PKD, when fascination of the writer turned to fear. Another insight into the state of PKD's mind at this time has come to light in an unpublished interview that PKD gave around a year later to Cal State University student Nita J. Petrunio. It also reveals how relations became soured with Ellison. Nita reported PKD saying that:

'At dinner everything had been fine, but afterwards Harlan steered the group through the Hollywood boulevard throngs of tourists and cyclists to a bookstore where there was a display of Harlan's books. Harlan, according to Phil, began telling the book browsers that he was *the* Harlan Ellison. He pointed to a large sign over his book's display and to himself and repeated that he was *the* Harlan Ellison. Phil, having heard enough, picked Harlan up from behind, under the arms, carried him out of the store and in this fashion propelled him along Hollywood Boulevard. Harlan was not pleased.'[126]

When the group returned to the Ellison's house, Harlan began 'berating' Linda 'prophesying terrible things about PKD's and her relationship in the future'. As events proved, PKD said, Harlan was right. This was just one of a series of incidents in which PKD exhibited extreme behaviour. In paperwork attached to the sale of her PKD letters, Linda wrote:

'Shortly after his arrival in Fullerton, I became afraid of Phil. His intensity, his unpredictable anger, his tendency to curl up into a ball, locked away inside himself, eyes empty, cold and silent scared me. I was 21 and he was 42. I kept thinking that someone his age should be more together than he seemed to be, to not reel from passing remarks and obsess over them. I suggested that he get some help. He told me that he had never needed psychological help before, but I had destroyed him, broken down his defenses, and he would acquiesce, although reluctantly, to my wishes.'[127]

In a letter posted on-line, Linda describes an event that took place at the time that shows how PKD would take a relatively minor problem and blow it out of all proportion. Linda explains that she had received a notification from her landlord that her apartment was going to be fumigated. She was instructed to remove everything from the cupboards and drawers and cover them up. She was then told to vacate the premises for a few hours. PKD lived just down the street so when the day arrived Linda went over to his place to fill time. Unfortunately, she had forgotten to remove the marijuana she had stashed there. She describes the scene as she returned:

'When I got there, I saw that, much to my horror, they had also pulled the drawers out of my dresser, and the top one, placed in front and center of the bed had a "lid" [*1oz marijuana*] in it. I figured I was busted for sure and called Phil, looking for reassurance, and possibly help. I think that, in reality, I wasn't too scared, but, since Phil thrived on crisis, those of us who delivered crises were richly rewarded. This time was no exception.'[128]

It was clear that she was worried that her stash of marijuana had been the reason for the search. PKD moved into action. He suggested they visit every 'Carl's Junior' burger bar in Orange County and buy something. From this they could collect a large number of identical plastic bags containing receipts from various locations. In this way the owner of each bag would be impossible to trace. Then:

> 'We would put a little bit of the marijuana in each bag. Then, we would take as many cars as possible, each containing Carl's Junior bags [and leave them] in Dumpsters and trash cans all over Orange County. I loved this plan. I thought it was hilarious.'[129]

But this was no joke – PKD was deadly series. For him it was clear evidence that they were all under surveillance by 'the narcs'. This showed to Linda just how unpredictable in his behaviour PKD could be. The way he interpreted situations was so very different from most people.

Linda's fear of him proved to be justified. On one occasion, they both went to see the movie *Fiddler on the Roof*. As they were driving to the cinema, Linda mentioned that she had 'made plans' with Norman Spinrad. It is unclear what Linda means by this term but from PKD's reaction he must have taken it to mean a date. PKD suddenly withdrew into himself in what she describes as a 'solid rock of cold silence and inward focus'. After the movie there was little communication between them.

On the way home, Linda decided the car needed topping up so they stopped at a gas station. Linda suddenly realized that working at the station was a fellow student who she had also 'made plans' with. To avoid any awkwardness, she jumped out of the car and engaged her student friend in conversation. PKD was clearly annoyed by this and stormed to the Tick Tock clock shop next door. He returned with his purchase and, without a word, got back in the car. As they were driving the few remaining blocks back to Quartz Lane, PKD, without any warning, grabbed the steering wheel and turned the car into the on-coming traffic. Linda managed to wrestle control back from PKD, narrowly avoiding a collision. The whole incident had only lasted about ten seconds but Linda was, by now shaking with fear. She describes what happened next:

> 'With heart pounding and adrenaline pumping, I was so shocked and frightened I had difficulty speaking. I pulled over to the curb and said, "Get out." Phil turned and grabbed me by the windpipe with the hand that was in a sling (that's

another story) and began to squeeze, cutting off both my air and blood supply, while pummeling my face with his other hand. Furious, and disbelieving, I fought him off, and again ordered him out of my car. I somehow got him to leave and I drove off, determined to have nothing further to do with him.'[130]

She ran into him again a few months later at the World Science Fiction Convention in Anaheim and he introduced her to his companions as 'the woman I was in love with until she beat me up'. In his semi-autobiographical book *The Dark-Haired Girl*, PKD says of her:

'Linda finally dropped acid and wandered out of my life, too screwed up in her head even to leave her apartment. She is now in Europe, which is weird considering her phobias. By the time she returns, I hope Tess and I will be gone. Linda's apartment is just up the street. We walk past it every day. Linda was the cruellest girl I ever encountered.'[131]

This quotation includes a reference to the next 'dark-haired girl' to appear in his life, Leslie Tessa Busby, at eighteen years old even younger than Linda. Tessa was not only to become wife number five, but was also to bear witness to some of the most amazing events in PKD's life.

Chapter Eight

The Theophany (1972–74)

In late June 1972, PKD attended the 25th West Coast Science Fantasy Conference, 'Westcon', held at the Edgewater Hyatt House Hotel, in Long Beach, California, where he formed a friendship with a tall, slim, twenty-seven-year-old woman called Ginger Smith, a former school bus driver. Ginger soon found PKD to be somewhat 'clingy' and quickly decided to end the relationship.

Tessa – wife number five

The following month, Ginger had been invited to a Fourth of July party and knew that PKD would be there. She asked her friend, Nita Busby, if she would like to join her at the event. Nita declined but suggested that her eighteen-year-old daughter, Tessa, might like to go in her place. Tessa had recently split up with her boyfriend and had lost her job at an aircraft factory. She was at a loose end and needed something to lift her spirits. Ginger told Tessa that they would be calling at her apartment in Cameo Lane, Berkeley, to pick up PKD and mentioned that he was a 'very famous author'. Tessa was clearly excited at the prospect of meeting him.

On arrival at the apartment, PKD was already outside waiting for them. He seemed in a bad mood and grumpily stated that he was going home. Ginger pleaded with him to come to the party and eventually he relented. At the party, Tessa was introduced to one of PKD's friends, Tim Powers, still a student at Cal State. As the party progressed, Tessa began to feel a little lost. Ginger got drunk and passed out on the sofa. Tessa got talking to PKD and ended up going home with him.

PKD would later describe Tessa as 'a little black-haired chick. . . exactly like I'm not supposed to get involved with'. Tessa's impression of PKD was of someone 'lost and helpless'. She said he was 'really paranoid. . . He thought I was a cop, that maybe I was underage and trying to get him busted for that, or else a narc who thought he was into drugs.'[132]

Noises in the night

Within a week, PKD had rented an apartment in Cameo Lane, Fullerton, determined to set himself up in a new life with his new love. Tessa states that this apartment was haunted. The two girls who lived there before had conducted an exorcism but this failed. PKD and Tessa heard unusual noises and one bedroom had, as Tessa puts it, a 'dense, swampy atmosphere'. Tessa describes how they would sometimes hear strange noises during the night and find that the next morning the furniture had been moved around. She has also said that the radio kept playing music even after it was turned off and unplugged. She said, 'It was playing songs like You're So Vain and You're No Good.' This may have been supernatural activity but PKD, who had not recovered from the November 1971 break-in, was convinced that his 'enemies' had not given up and that these nocturnal disturbances were evidence of break-ins taking place at the new apartment. Tessa said that they poked around in the vacant apartment next door and found mysterious electronic equipment.[133]

PKD later explained that, one day in 1973, he used adhesive tape to seal one of his hairs across the gap between the door and the door frame. In this way he would know if anybody had entered the apartment when he and Tessa were away. On their return, they found that the hair had indeed been broken, indicating that somebody had entered through the door. He subsequently discovered that 'a chick we knew, it turned out, had a key to the apartment, and had entered in our absence'.[134] Could this also be the explanation for the nocturnal furniture-movers?

Tessa gives yet another possible explanation for the nocturnal events that she describes taking place in Cameo Lane when she and PKD first moved in together. In her book *Philip K. Dick: Remembering Firebright*, Tessa explains how she had experienced a 'childhood form of epilepsy' that she grew out of by the time she was twenty.[135] Tessa was born in 1954, so in 1972 she would have been eighteen and therefore still affected by her epilepsy. We know from Tessa's account that on at least two occasions she experienced 'sleep paralysis' while in the apartment in Cameo Lane. PKD also experienced strange nocturnal sensations, in his case, of strangulation. Tessa states that he also saw 'shadows walking around' but there were no intruders to be found. It has been suggested that PKD may have experienced what is known as 'temporal lobe lability'. That Tessa also shared unusual incidents in Cameo Lane leads me to suspect that there may have been some form of electromagnetic field in or around the Cameo Lane property that was affecting them. Tessa later confirmed that all these events took place in the 'haunted' bedroom.

In early September 1972, PKD was asked to be a panel guest at the 30th World Science Fiction Convention, 'L.A.con1', which was being held in nearby Anaheim. Science fiction was now becoming mainstream, and the convention was attended by two thousand members, easily breaking the previous record set in 1971. Frederick Pohl and Robert Bloch were guests of honour and the Hugo Award for best novel went to Philip José Farmer for *To Your Scattered Bodies Go*. PKD was keen to mix with such a prestigious guest list, if only to dispel rumours that he was burned out.

During the convention, there was an incident between Tessa and David Gerrold, author of the famous *Star Trek* episode 'The Trouble with Tribbles'. According to Tessa, PKD was in the process of buying her a 'Tribble' mascot when Gerrold sneaked up behind her and grabbed her. Tessa was naturally startled and, she explained, 'almost as a reflex, I kicked him in the shin and pulled myself free.'[136] PKD gives a typically exaggerated version:

> 'The second day of the con, David tried to put his arm around Tessa's waist and she Kung-Fu'd him out of existence, something he deserved.'[137]

PKD was now keen to settle down with Tessa. It was at this time that PKD's marriage to Nancy was formally ending and on 14 October the couple flew to San Jose for the divorce hearing. PKD and Tessa were collected from the airport by Ray Nelson, who took them for a meal at Fisherman's Wharf. The next day they travelled on the ferry to Marin County where, at the County Hall, the divorce was finalized. Nancy was given custody of Isa and PKD was ordered to pay $100 a month to support his daughter. This meant PKD was free to marry again.

His first attempt to propose to Tessa did not go according to plan. In an article for the *OC Weekly*, Tim Powers explains how the three of them were sitting at a restaurant in Disneyland eating sandwiches and waiting for more friends to join them when PKD asked Tessa to marry him. Feeling embarrassed, Powers reached across and took a dill pickle from PKD's plate. Before Tessa could reply, PKD reacted with fury: 'Powers! What are you doing with my pickle?'[138] By the time the ensuing argument had subsided, their friends had arrived and the moment was lost. Despite the pickle theft, it is clear PKD was a very happy man at this time. He seemed to have recovered from the break-up with Linda Levy.

The undercover narc

Later that month, Linda dropped by to see PKD and Tessa and introduce them to her new boyfriend, 'George', a somewhat mysterious character with long hair and a very expensive sports car who claimed to be an undercover narcotics agent. To PKD, he was a typical 'freak'.[139] Someone very like him would feature in one of PKD's stories. PKD had already started on his award-winning novel *A Scanner Darkly* when this encounter took place. The novel would eventually be published in 1977. It is unclear if PKD had already created the character of the protagonist Robert Arctor/Agent Fred at this stage, but there are uncanny parallels between Linda's friend and PKD's fictional character, who leads a double life. PKD goes on to describe the rest of their evening with Linda and her boyfriend:

> 'He took us for a ride in his high-powered car, walked Linda
> into a liquor store handcuffed, drove wildly (he appeared very
> drunk but I doubt he really was), told us he would bust any
> of us any time he wanted.'[140]

In Tessa's version of events, Linda came round to the apartment one day
and secretly announced to PKD and Tessa that 'George' was an undercover
narcotics officer but she begged them not to tell anybody. When they
eventually met 'George' at Linda's apartment, PKD took with him a tin of
cheap snuff with the word 'cokesnuff' written in big letters on the top.
George took one look at the tin and disappeared into Linda's bedroom.

> 'Linda followed him and we could tell that they were having
> a tense conversation behind the closed door. Presently, Linda
> emerged and said, "George has asked me to inform you of
> his profession".'[141]

I took the opportunity to discuss this issue with Tessa in March 2013.
She confirmed that the wild car trip did take place. However, she recalls
it as being far less threatening and that 'George' seemed like a nice guy.
It is possible that PKD's suspicions regarding 'George' were simply a
reflection of his growing paranoia, as evidenced by a letter he wrote to,
of all organizations, the FBI, in October 1972 at around the time that
he met 'George'.

In this peculiar letter, PKD explained to the security services that he
knew of a secret neo-Nazi organization that was using selected science
fiction writers to advance its cause. PKD described how he had been
approached by a representative of the group, a person who identified himself
as 'Solarcon-6'. Solarcon-6 asked PKD to place coded messages in his future
novels that would be read by 'the right people here and there.'[142] PKD stated
that he refused to be involved but suspected that some of his fellow writers
had not been so honourable. This group was planning to bring about a
third world war by infecting the American population with a new, extremely
virulent form of syphilis, PKD said.[143] He went on to accuse a friend, fellow
science fiction writer Thomas M. Disch, of being one of the authors that
this sinister organization was using and claiming that Disch's novel *Camp
Concentration* contained coded messages.

In a later letter, PKD identified the 'Agent' of Solarcon to be a person
called Harold Kinchen. He accused Kinchen of being involved in a second
burglary at his home that took place in March 1972 and that Solarcon had
been interested in recruiting PKD for some time. Was Solarcon simply a
figment of PKD's fevered imagination or was there something more to this
curious episode? We will return to this mystery in Part Two.

Flow My Tears

Christmas 1972 was not a good time for PKD. He had been feeling unwell for most of the month and, as the holiday period approached, came down with double pneumonia. Tessa cared for him at home and helped him through a profound 'crisis' that we shall return to later. According to Sutin, PKD had worked himself to a standstill and was clearly exhausted. However, money was scarce, as usual, and the only way PKD could support the two of them was to write. In February 1973 he finally completed the much-revised manuscript for his novel *Flow My Tears, the Policeman Said.*

This novel is set in a future USA that has been torn-apart by a second civil war and is now ruled by a dictatorship, with the National Guard and the police keeping control. The central character is a genetically enhanced singer and TV host who narrowly survives an attack on his life by a former lover only to wake up in a hotel room without any means of identification. This puts him in a dangerous predicament as without proof of identity he could end up in a state labour camp. The novel would later be nominated for the Hugo and Nebula Awards and win PKD the John W. Campbell Memorial Award for Best Science Fiction Novel.

Also in early February 1973, PKD heard from his literary agent, Scott Meredith, that the BBC wished to conduct an interview with him the following month. The popular BBC TV arts series *Omnibus* was planning to devote a whole programme to review how 'the perception and acceptance of Science Fiction had constantly changed since its early beginnings in the time of Jules Verne'. This programme was to finish with a review of the vibrant science fiction culture found on the West Coast. As well as PKD, the programme makers planned to interview Ray Bradbury and Harlan Ellison. PKD was keen to be involved in this project and, on 10 March, a film crew, under the direction of Harley Cokeliss, spent a whole day with PKD shooting and re-shooting various scenes, including a short item to convey the reverse-time effect of the 'Hobart Phase' from PKD's novel *Counter-Clock World* (1967).[144]

The documentary makers filmed PKD sitting at his table eating break-fast cereal. The idea was to run the film backwards and seem to show PKD regurgitating the food onto his bowl[145] to illustrate PKD's idea that for him time could run backwards as well as forwards.

PKD believed that the recording of this interview was to be broadcast on the 9 December 1973 edition of the programme.[146] In actual fact it was broadcast a week later on 16 December under the title of *It's Fantastic, It's Futuristic, It's Fatalistic, It's Science Fiction.* Sadly, PKD's section was cut out of the programme at the last minute.[147] This is confirmed in Purser's *Daily Telegraph* article.[148] Curiously, Tessa has a different version in that she states the film was accidentally put through the X-ray machine at Los Angeles

Airport and on arrival back in London the whole reel was found to be fogged.[149] When I spoke to Tessa in March 2013, she was absolutely sure that this is what had happened. Is it possible that the BBC, in order to cover up their careless error, created a story that PKD's section was simply cut out of the final edit?

In January 1973, Tessa discovered she was pregnant. They were both delighted at this news. Tessa wanted a child and PKD felt that this was the perfect excuse to get married. It is possible that PKD had again written himself into a state of mental and physical exhaustion. From February to April 1973, he threw himself into the writing of a new novel, one that would fictionalize his experiences in 1971 when his home in Hacienda Way was the centre of a thriving drug scene. He wrote feverishly throughout the night, working in the spare bedroom so as not to disturb his partner. It is clear that by re-living those days of excess PKD put himself under great pressure. In a January 1978 entry in *Exegesis* he writes:

> 'Thinking back over my life I can see that I have survived many troubles – I look at the copies of the Ballantine SCANNER & I can see what I have done to transmute those terrible days into something worthwhile, lasting, good, and even important.'[150]

The resulting 82-page outline for *A Scanner Darkly* was accepted by Doubleday in April 1973. However, until the final manuscript was accepted, this was of no direct financial help. Luckily, that month PKD received a payment from his agent, which meant PKD and Tessa could now get married. He called a local minister and the wedding was held in the apartment.

Three months later, on 25 July 1973, Tessa gave birth to a 6lb 13oz (3.1kg) baby boy who they named Christopher Kenneth. PKD needed a financial lifeline. This came in September when United Artists bought the movie rights for PKD's 1968 novel *Do Androids Dream of Electric Sheep?* It would eventually form the basis for the classic sci-fi movie *Blade Runner*. PKD received an immediate annual option payment of $2,000, with the tantalizing possibility of a further $25,000 should a movie ever be made. That month, a French film crew recorded a rather surreal interview in which PKD and his good friend Norman Spinrad discussed politics while sitting in one of the spinning teacups in 'The Mad Hatter's Tea Party' fun ride at Disneyland.

Once more, a new baby led to a decline in PKD's mental state. In a letter sent to his Danish translator, Jannick Storm, in September 1973, PKD describes how after Christopher's birth he fell into such a deep depression that he considered suicide.[151] Such were the concerns regarding his mental health at this time that he was allocated a therapist at the Orange County

Mental Hospital (OCMH). In a later letter, dated 10 September 1973, PKD writes that his therapist at the OCMH gave him a 'straight, flat-out diagnosis of manic depressive' and gave him a course of lithium carbonate.[152]

Momentous days

The year 1974 was marked by a series of events that would change PKD's life forever. Such was the power of these experiences that PKD spent the rest of his life trying to understand them. He would later call them '2-3-74' or simply his 'Theophany'.

According to Tessa, PKD had been becoming increasingly agitated throughout the month of February 1974. He was visiting his psychiatrist once a week and was being prescribed medication to calm him down. Neither of these measures worked and as the month progressed he felt that some form of 'hit', similar to the one that took place in November 1971, was about to take place. The fact that he was responsible for a young wife and an infant played on his mind a great deal. Complicating PKD's psychological state was the fact that he was suffering permanent toothache. In her book *Philip K. Dick: Remembering Firebright* (2013), Tessa believes the cause was impacted wisdom teeth.

The pain was severe enough for PKD to overcome his fear of dentists and agree to take a taxi over to their local dental surgeon. When PKD came out of the surgery after the extraction, his mouth was numb from the sodium pentothal anaesthetic he had been given and the gauze dressings packed into the wound. He couldn't speak, and so on the way back he communicated with Tessa using a pencil and pad. Tessa asked the dentist to arrange for powerful painkillers to be made available to pick up from a nearby pharmacy. Tessa and PKD travelled back to the apartment in a taxi. While the taxi waited, Tessa tucked PKD up in bed, made sure he was as comfortable as possible and then took the taxi to the pharmacy to pick up the much-needed medication.

When she got back, PKD was howling with pain and bleeding profusely. The next day, their family doctor was called and confirmed that the surgery had been very badly performed. The doctor prescribed a strong painkiller, Percodan, containing aspirin and an opium derivative, oxycodone. The doctor also prescribed heat pads to help drain the haematoma (accumulation of blood) building up inside PKD's cheek. By this stage PKD had taken a cocktail of painkillers. As well as the Percodan, he had swallowed another opium-derivative, Empirin-Codeine. Added to this would be any residual sodium pentothal circulating in his bloodstream after the extraction. In other words, he would have been strongly 'drugged up'.

Tessa said that three days after PKD's dental surgery, she was sitting downstairs waiting for someone from the local pharmacy to make the regular delivery of PKD's high blood pressure medication when she suddenly heard PKD get out of bed. Tessa states that she felt that PKD had been awoken from his sleep by a premonition that something important was about to be delivered to his doorstep. Before Tessa could react, PKD had made his way to the front door just as the delivery girl knocked.

The delivery girl and the pendant

Tessa joined him at the door to see a young woman with long brown hair. Tessa noticed that PKD was staring intensely at a pendant resting in the plunging neckline of the young woman's blouse. He asked the delivery girl about the pendant and she explained that it was a fish symbol similar to the one used by the early Christians. According to his *Exegesis*, the pendant reflected a gleam of light that stunned him. He stopped and covered his eyes with his free hand, explaining to Tessa that he had been blinded by a flash of pink light.

He immediately returned to bed and, on awaking later, told Tessa that he had experienced something he termed an *anamnesis* – a recollection of memories that have been buried deep within the mind. It was first used as a concept by the Ancient Greek philosopher Plato, who suggested we are all reincarnated beings who are forced to forget our past incarnations. PKD believed that the pink light stimulated these lost memories and from that point on he was to slowly uncover who he really was and, by association, realize the true nature of reality. He went on to tell Tessa he believed the beam had opened up his third eye, allowing him to 'see' truths deep within himself.

PKD seemed to change from that moment on. He was to spend a great deal of his time in bed in a state of semi-consciousness when he believed he was accessing lost memories. The first discovery was that he had been abducted while he was in Vancouver. In one long hallucination, he saw himself being driven round the streets of Vancouver in a huge black limousine. He could see two large men in black suits interrogating him, although he could not recall the actual questions. On becoming fully conscious, he was convinced that this was a supressed memory of what really happened before his suicide attempt.

The Xerox missive

According to Tessa, in late February, a few days after his 'pink light' experience, PKD received a mysterious letter from Estonia.[153] He became very disturbed by this correspondence and, on discussing the mystery with Tessa, suddenly found words coming out of his mouth that seemed to have a source other than his own mind. The words were quite precise. 'Today is Monday,

1974 – Flow My Tears, the Policeman Said

'To live is to be haunted.'
– Philip K. Dick, *Flow My Tears, the Policeman Said*

PKD completed the manuscript in August 1970. It was bought by Doubleday in October of that year but not without revisions. Indeed another two full revisions were done before a final manuscript was delivered to SMLA on February 7, 1973. The hardcover edition was published by Doubleday in February 1974.

On the morning of 12 October, television star Jason Taverner wakes up to find that the world has forgotten him. Indeed it is as if he had never existed. With the help of a young woman called Kathy Nelson he is able to acquire the fake ID cards needed to exist in what is a police state. Taverner comes to the attention of a policeman General Felix Buckman and subsequently discovers that Buckman's sister Alys had taken an hallucinogen called KR-3. This was so powerful that Alys was able to create a world in which the TV star Jason Taverner did not exist, which is the problem to be solved.

Flow My Tears was awarded the 1975 John W. Campbell Memorial Award for best novel. In that same year it was also nominated for the Hugo Award.

on Wednesday, another letter will come. It is highly dangerous.' In Tessa's version of events, she states that PKD believed the letter would kill him.[154]

On the Wednesday, PKD became extremely agitated and sent Tessa to fetch the mail. There were seven items. Six were circulars, bills, or letters from friends. But the seventh was different. PKD knew that this was the letter that his subliminal mind had predicted two days before. The return address was a New York hotel but the postmark was said to be 'Austrian'. It is unclear what is meant by 'Austrian' postmark. One interesting possibility is that the postmark actually said 'Vienna', which is not only the capital of Austria but also a district located close to the CIA headquarters in Virginia.

He asked Tessa to open it and make sure he could not see the contents. Tessa opened the envelope and found a single sheet of paper with two photocopied [Xeroxed] images on it. Both were book reviews taken from the radical New York newspaper the *Daily World*. Tessa recalls that the book title had the word 'carousel' in it. The reviews bore no relationship to PKD in any way. They were written in praise of a Soviet writer based in the United States. Nervously, Tessa told PKD that two words had been carefully underlined in red, these were 'decline' and 'death'. On the back of the sheet was the name and address of the writer.

PKD asked Tessa to place the letter in a fresh envelope as he was planning to 'send it' to the FBI. In a letter dated 19 April 1974, sent to his FBI contact, William A. Sullivan, PKD claimed that later that night, presumably in a hypnagogic (or hypnapompic) dream-like semi-sleep state, he 'saw' the following: 'Antonetti', 'Olivetti', 'Dodd Mead Reinhart' and 'Holt'. PKD, then saw the words 'Olive' from 'Olivetti' and the word 'Holt' meld together to make the name 'Olive Holt', the name of his babysitter when he was three or four years old.

Later, PKD phoned the FBI to discuss the letter he had received from Estonia, a country that was, at that time, part of the Soviet Union and so firmly behind the Iron Curtain. He felt that the letter was some form of trap. He followed the call to the FBI with a letter, sent on the same day. But it was the letter that arrived the following Wednesday, containing Xeroxed book reviews, that had really disturbed him. In *Exegesis,* he calls this the 'Xerox Missive' but in *Radio Free Albemuth* (1985) it is the 'Shoe Ad'.

There is some doubt as to whether PKD really did send any letters to the FBI as there is no evidence of them in the FBI files. Tessa states that PKD used to place the letters in the rubbish bin, working on the assumption that if the 'Feds' were going through his trash for incriminating evidence that was a sure-fire way of making sure that his correspondence arrived on the right desk.[155] So it is quite possible that nobody other than PKD ever actually read these letters. However, PKD was to mention this incident again in *Exegesis*.

On 16 March, while in yet another one of his semi-sleep states, PKD perceived a series of geometric shapes and flashing lights of various colours. He was sure that he was, in some way, sharing these perceptions with another entity that was manifest in his mind. This feeling was reinforced on 18 March when he sensed that something other than himself was using his senses to understand the external world and that whatever it was did not believe what it was perceiving. By 20 March, the entity had gained full control and understanding and conveyed to PKD that the reality he took for granted was, in fact 'cardboard, a fake'. In a letter to his pen-friend Claudia Bush, from March 1975, PKD describes how this entity expanded his perceptions to know the world in its true sense, an illusion:

> 'Through its power I saw suddenly the universe as it was; through its power of perception I saw what really existed, and through its power of no thought decision, I acted to free myself. It took on in battle, as a champion of all human spirits in thrall, every evil, every iron imprisoning thing.'[156]

Accompanying this new awareness was a series of profound visions. In another letter, reproduced in his *Exegesis*, PKD describes how one night his mind was flooded with thousands of images that flashed one after another in front of him. He likened these to the non-objective paintings of Paul Klee and Wassily Kandinsky. He claimed that these visions went on for eight hours. We know from Tessa's account that at this time PKD was spending a great deal of time in bed dozing, so it is entirely possible PKD may have spent hours in this semi-sleep state. He likened the images to the 'flash cut' technique used in movies. He was completely at a loss to understand what these images were trying to tell him.

There is one intriguing letter, sent to his FBI contact Sullivan, and dated 14 April 1974. PKD starts off by explaining that he is still curious about the Estonia letter and states that he has been doing his own investigations. On checking a map, he notes that the capital of Estonia is Tallin and the nearest major Soviet city was Leningrad (which has now reverted to its old name of St Petersburg). From a 'paperback best-seller' that he bought in Grant's department store called *Psychic Discoveries Behind the Iron Curtain* and written by Sheila Ostrander and Lynn Shroeder, PKD found the names of two Soviet scientists working at the Physiology of Labour Laboratory at the University of Leningrad. They were Madame Lutsia Pavlova and her colleague Dr Genady Sergeyev, of the A.A. Uktomskii Laboratory. He explained to Sullivan that, under the legitimate guise of an American science fiction writer, he had written to them to ask about their work, specifically the 'long-distance transmission of "telepathic" communication'. He then quickly makes his own position clear in regard to this research when he states to Sullivan that he:

> '. . .personally consider[s] absurd and a crank preoccupation and without merit (our field here in the U.S. has debated ESP and so-called "psi" or parapsychological powers for years, and I am with the party which feels it to be a hoax on par with flying saucers and little green men).'[157]

This is a very strange comment from a person who, from other sources, seems to have recently experienced a series of profound paranormal experiences. According to Tessa, PKD was very interested in UFOs and had been very taken by Charles Tart's theory that flying saucers were actually life forms that lived in the upper atmosphere. Of course, it may simply be that PKD felt it better to come across as a strong sceptic as he was dealing with the FBI and not a group of his sci-fi fans.

Hidden presence

PKD became increasingly preoccupied by the being that 'shared his consciousness'. He began to sense a presence in the apartment and claimed that, on occasion, he would see it in the extreme periphery of his vision but, on focusing on it, the being would blend into the background. PKD called this entity 'Zebra' in recognition of its skills at camouflage. He perceived that Zebra had a third eye in the centre of its forehead, which it kept closed most of the time.

The true nature of the Zebra entity continued to preoccupy him. In November 1976, in a letter to Mark Hurst, PKD described a concept that he called 'The Zebra Principle'. In this, he suggests that some alien life-forms may be able to camouflage themselves against the background environment. PKD had long been intrigued by the suggestion by Roger Caillois, in his 1964 book *The Mask of Medusa*, that there may be creatures living among us who are able to disguise themselves so as to avoid detection. In his letter, PKD speculated on whether this is how higher, or even 'divine', intelligences can remain unseen. One cannot help but wonder if it was Callois' book that stimulated, albeit subliminally, PKD's encounter with Zebra.

Zebra's identity would finally be revealed to PKD by the next manifestation of his Theophany. It was an entity that Tessa and PKD called 'Firebright', and which first appeared on 22 March. In her book, Tessa describes Firebright as a sphere of blue light about the size of a baseball. PKD told her that it appeared as he was lying in bed in his usual hypnagogic state. He saw the blue ball of light dance around the room and then enter his head. She states that 'Firebright' was more a facilitator of communication between PKD and other entities called 'Teachers' than a sentient being in its own right.[158]

One of these 'Teachers' became more dominant than the others. Initially, PKD simply called it 'A.I.' for artificial intelligence. This was a mechanical female voice that sometimes seemed self-aware and sometimes not. PKD was eager to discover more about the source of the mechanical A.I. 'Voice' and simply asked her who she was. She replied that she was called 'Sadassa Ulna'. He asked where she was and she replied that she 'did not know'. PKD told Tessa that she then asked him to wait a second. It seems that she looked around and found an envelope on a pile of papers. She read out the address to PKD: 'F. Walloon, Portuguese States of America'. This was an intriguing response and it suggested to PKD that 'Sadassa' was living in an alternative universe in which Portugal had kept hold of its original colonies in the Americas (Newfoundland, Labrador and Brazil). This has interesting parallels with PKD's book *The Man in the High Castle* (1962), which features an alternative United States ruled by Japan and Germany.

In his discussion about this incident with Gregg Rickman in *Philip K. Dick: The Last Testament* (1985), PKD acknowledges that this could be a message from an alternative universe. He gives more details about the event and states that the 'Voice' actually said, 'Fan Walloon'. PKD considered this to be of significance. PKD wrote this down as he heard it. He later realized that the word he heard as 'fan' was actually spelt 'van', exactly the way a Belgian Walloon would pronounce the Dutch word 'van'. PKD insisted that he had never heard of the word Walloon before and had to look it up. For him this was clear evidence that the 'Voice' was not simply part of his own subconscious.[159]

The A.I. 'Voice' also made some very curious but incomprehensible statements to PKD. For example, she once announced to him that 'you have to put your slippers on to walk toward the dawn'. Although very poetic this made little sense to him. Later PKD was to use this as a song lyric in his book *Radio Free Albemuth* (1985).

Communications from VALIS

As with Zebra, PKD never really came to any firm conclusions as to what A.I. actually was. But this ceased to concern him because he was to realize that A.I. was just one aspect of a larger system that he was to call 'VALIS', an acronym for Vast Active Living Intelligence System. As we shall discover, a whole series of 'fictional' novels were written with VALIS as the central concept. For PKD, VALIS was not a fiction but a reality. He believed that VALIS was a kind of 'satellite' beaming messages down to Earth. These messages could be received by any brain that was open to such communication.

However, at the same time that PKD was looking to the skies for an explanation, another development took place that led PKD to believe that all reality, including the existence of the VALIS satellite itself, was part of a much more complex universe in which multiple levels of time all existed simultaneously, stacked up one on top of another like the layers of an onion. What PKD took to be late 20th century Los Angeles was actually a fabrication similar to the world of Ragle Gumm in his 1959 novel *Time Out of Joint*. It was not only AD 1974 but also AD 70. The Roman Empire had not really ended.

PKD came to this conclusion when he started to sense the presence of a person he came to know as 'Thomas'. Unlike 'Firebright' and the A.I. 'Voice', 'Thomas' was a human being who was (and is) living under Roman rule. PKD said he sensed that Thomas was a Christian who had been tortured for his beliefs. He saw 'Thomas' as a version of himself that had existed centuries earlier in linear time but, in PKD's new understanding of time, also shared the same present moment with him.

As we shall discuss later, PKD was of the opinion that this proved his belief that time has another form that our present science is unaware of, one that he would later describe as 'orthogonal'. The term literally means 'right-angled' but by extension has come to refer to something that acts separately or independently from other factors. This idea that we are all trapped in our own illusory version of reality was central to PKD's later thinking. PKD argued that there are two levels of 'reality' and both exist in different concepts of time.

Linear time is the one we all seem to exist within. It presents to our senses a sensation of movement or flow turning the future into the present and then into the past. Its flow is always in one direction and that is towards the future. However, he also proposed another time that exists at a right-angle to linear time. This presents, to those attuned to it, a permanent present moment that contains all our pasts and all our futures. This he termed 'orthogonal time'. From the viewpoint of an entity existing in orthogonal time, our universe of linear time presents a totally different perspective.

PKD also postulated in his *Exegesis* that 'Thomas' was his good friend Bishop James Pike, who was communicating with him from beyond the grave. PKD reflected upon the fact that Pike was a Biblical scholar and spoke fluent ancient Greek and Latin. He also felt that this entity was, in some way, trying to teach him to be a better, more effective human being. PKD found he stopped drinking wine and developed a taste for beer.

The entity Thomas/James told PKD that he had become far too slovenly in his appearance. Under this new influence, PKD began smartening up and trimming his beard and nasal hair. The new freshly scrubbed PKD then sorted out the chaos that was his tax affairs and even, for a time, dispensed with the services of his literary agent.

All this activity came about at a cost. PKD's blood pressure, which had always been high, was reaching a critical level. In early April, PKD was forced to spend five days in hospital undergoing tests. Tessa recalls that Dr Morrison, the family physician, suggested that PKD may have suffered a series of small strokes. On his return home, PKD's mood swings became quite extreme. Tessa states that he would lie in bed for days on end and was spending more and more time in his semi-sleep state. PKD found that while in these hypnagogic states he would experience more of his 'visions'. One can only imagine the strain this must have placed on Tessa. She was a young mother who suddenly seemed to be nursing two babies.

It was while in this peculiar state of exhaustion that PKD experienced probably the most regularly cited incidents of his whole 2-3-74 'Theophany', the seemingly miraculous diagnosis of Christopher's life-threatening hernia.

The Diagnosis

PKD himself was happy to repeat this story often and regularly. For example in his interview with D. Scott Apel in July 1977, he describes the circumstances as he recalled them:

'My little year-and-a-half year old son had a serious birth defect which the doctors failed to notice. And this . . .*mind*. . . which took me over diagnosed it and told my wife to take him to the doctor immediately and to tell the doctor what it was and to request immediate surgery. She did, and she came back and said "they are scheduling him for immediate surgery. He does have that birth defect". . . which could have proved fatal at any time.'[160]

Tessa tells the story from her point of view and, as the only other witness to these events, her version is of great importance. She describes how she had taken Christopher to see their family doctor in July because she had observed 'strange symptoms'[161] when changing his nappy. The doctor told her there was nothing to worry about. A few weeks later, in August 1974, PKD was taking one of his 'frequent naps' while she cooked breakfast. She heard noise from the bedroom:

'Phil got out of bed and walked down the hall, calling to me to get the doctor. At first I thought that Phil needed medical help, but then he told me that our baby had an inguinal hernia and was in danger of dying if it strangulated. He looked as if he was in an hypnotic trance.'[162]

PKD explained to her that he had 'heard our son telling him about the hernia'. A few days later, Tessa took Christopher back to Dr Morrison, who then referred him to a specialist. The specialist subsequently informed PKD and Tessa that, had they allowed their son to cry, the stress could have caused the hernia to strangulate and, in doing so, cut off the blood supply. This could, indeed, have killed him.

Compare this with PKD's version that appears in *Exegesis*:

'I am thinking back. Sitting with my eyes shut I am listening to "Strawberry Fields." I get up. I open my eyes because the lyrics speak of "going through life with eyes closed." I look toward the window. Light blinds me; my head suddenly aches. My eyes close and I see that strange strawberry ice cream pink. At the same instant knowledge is transferred to me. I go into the bedroom where Tessa is changing Chrissy and I recite what has been conveyed to me: that he has an undetected birth defect and must be taken to the doctor at once and scheduled for surgery. This turns out to be true.'[163]

Now there are differences between these two versions. Tessa describes PKD as in bed taking a nap, whereas PKD claims he was sitting down listening to the Beatles on his hi fi. Surely Tessa would have heard this? Indeed, in his 22 April 1981 interview with Gregg Rickman, PKD actually states that Tessa 'saw me sitting there listening to the Beatles'.[164]

In PKD's version, as told to Apel and Briggs, Tessa immediately takes Christopher to the doctor who, in turn, schedules Christopher for 'immediate surgery'. In Tessa's account there is no immediate rush to the doctor, nor does the doctor do anything other than refer Christopher to a specialist. It is clear from the above that something happened that day, but the circumstances are very confused, which suggests a degree of elaboration on the part of PKD.

You also get the idea that PKD had given a diagnosis that was totally beyond his own knowledge and experience. This is evidence of how much this story has changed over the years. For example, in his article *Philip K. Dick: The Other Side*, Paul Rydeen describes the same incident this way:

> 'While listening to the Beatles' "Strawberry Fields Forever" one day, Phil heard the lyrics change into a prophetic warning: "Your son has an undiagnosed right inguinal hernia. The hydrocele has burst, and it has descended into the scrotal sac. He requires immediate attention, or will soon die." Phil rushed him to the hospital and found every word to be true. The doctor scheduled the operation for the same day.'[165]

Here we have PKD being given a precise description of Christopher's problem, rushing his son to the hospital and the operation being scheduled 'for the same day'. No mention of Tessa, the family doctor, the specialist or any delay. This is, for me, evidence of 'Chinese Whispers' and all it does is obscure the truth and give the reader concerns over the validity of other elements of 2-3-74.

I have checked all PKD's letters from August 1974 onwards and no mention is made of this incident. We find the first reference to Christopher in a letter to Joanna Russ dated 23 September 1974 but only stating that he has a 'lovely wife and a lovely year-old baby.'[166] Indeed, in a letter to friend and fellow science fiction writer, Ursula Le Guin, dated 23 September 1974, he describes in detail 'the spirit which filled me starting in March', adding later that this spirit 'loved our baby and our cat'.[167] No mention is made of how this entity saved Christopher's life just a few weeks before, an event that must have been equally stressful and redemptive proof of the reality of this spirit being. Yet PKD is more than keen to re-tell the necklace incident from February of that year. Curiously, even in a letter to his mother dated 25 September 1974, he fails to describe the incident that saved her grandson's life. He does, however, describe the death of his cat, Pinky.

The most telling letter is one dated 18 October 1974 to his friend and fellow science fiction writer, Thomas M. Disch, in which PKD mentions, very much in passing, that 'we just learned that our baby is to have minor surgery next week – a birth defect previously undisclosed'.[168] It is this 'minor surgery' that brought about the postponement of PKD's planned *Rolling Stone* interview with Paul Williams. This is then followed by a very humorous letter, one clearly not written by a man who is hiding the fact that his only son may die. This may help explain PKD's error in ageing his son in the interview with D. Scott Apel and Kevin Briggs.[169] In this interview, he states that Christopher was 18 months old. As the 'pink beam' event can be dated by Tessa's account as taking place in July 1974, Christopher would have been twelve months old, having celebrated his first birthday on 25 July. Surely this is something PKD could not have failed to associate with the 'diagnosis'? However, it seems that he may have confused his dates in that he knew that Christopher's 'minor' surgery took place in mid-October 1974. By that time Christopher would have been fifteen months old, nearly the 'year-and-a-half year old' as described by him in the interview.

This makes more logical sense. Tessa informed me that for standard medical reasons the operation could not be performed until Christopher was around eighteen months old. The operation was then carried out by the specialist and their family physician, Dr Morrison. Tessa added that a similar problem had been found in her two brothers, which suggests an inherited condition.

We know that, in August, PKD himself had been in hospital for surgery to his right shoulder. We also know from the Henry Ludmer letter of 8 October 1974 that Christopher was okay and out of hospital.[170] Furthermore, in a letter to his daughter Laura, dated 29 October 1974, PKD tells her about Christopher's surgery and that he is okay. He adds that it was an 'abdominal birth defect which Dr Quack, as we call him, never noticed; I finally noticed it myself'. So here we have yet another version of the same story with PKD being the hero who finally identifies the problem.[171] Indeed, in this version his son's illness was life-threatening with Christopher being, as PKD terms it, 'in the horsepiddle for three days'.

> 'We had two priests praying for Christopher: our regular vicar (Episcopal) and the Catholic priest at the hospital whom I like a lot.'[172]

From then on, with the exception of a similar reference to that described above to Laura in a letter to his mother, Christopher's close shave with death is not mentioned again in the letters (at least not up to February 1975).

It is also regularly stated that PKD showed technical knowledge of the human body that he must have gained from 'other' sources. With regard to this diagnosis, this is not quite true. As previously stated, in the early 1950s, PKD developed a hernia after playing tennis. Kleo states that PKD was so concerned that this could affect his ability to have children that he spent a great deal of time reading up all he could about the inguinal region of the body.[173] Could PKD's access to this information twenty years later be related to a form of cryptomnesia?

There is evidence from other sources that PKD had not forgotten about his own hernia issue. For example, soon after marrying Anne he admitted that he had a hernia problem. It seems that he was too scared to go to hospital to have this treated.[174] One can only conclude that, as this is not mentioned again, PKD simply learned to live with it. As such, it is reasonable to suspect that when his son Christopher was born the question of an inherited hernia problem would have been on his mind.

Once Christopher's operation was performed, journalist Paul Williams could go ahead with his interview for the rock magazine *Rolling Stone*.

The *Rolling Stone* interview

After meeting Paul Williams for the first time at the 1968 World Science Fiction Convention in Berkeley, the two began regularly exchanging letters. They met again in San Rafael in 1970 when PKD told Williams that he felt he was running low on energy and was suffering a creative slump. Williams was keen to help PKD in any way possible and, as a well-respected writer for *Rolling Stone*, he was relatively free to choose his topics. He decided the time was right for the publication to feature an article on this great science fiction writer.

Williams flew into Orange County shortly before Halloween, 31 October 1974,[175] and made his way by taxi to PKD's home in Cameo Lane. The interview that finally appeared in the November 1975 edition of *Rolling Stone* was a fascinating snapshot of PKD's life at that time. It has some great photos of PKD, Tessa and Christopher and also gives another slightly different 'take' on the November 1971 break-in. Here PKD presents four different theories as to who may have been responsible for the burglary, all of which are contradictory. He does, however, acknowledge that it could have been an inside job planned by his 'friends' or, indeed, that PKD himself was responsible for it but had somehow forgotten.

What I find curious about this interview is that not once does PKD mention the events of 2-3-74, which is really quite odd. This reflects the fact that the events also fail to feature in his letters until much later in the year.

Soon after Williams left, PKD was struck down by a bout of 'flu'. This continued over Christmas and into the early part of 1975. However, according to his letters, he emerged from his sickbed and had a reasonably lively holiday period. As well as a visit by a group of Hollywood friends, including the actress Barbara Hershey, PKD was fit enough to be interviewed at home by Tony Hiss of the *New Yorker* magazine on 29 December 1974. Hiss and his associate, Henry Korman, stayed for six hours and discussed, among other things, the psychological theories of Robert Ornstein and the mystical implications of PKD's 2-3-74 experiences.

However, in a letter to Claudia Bush on 3 January, PKD says what a depressing, lonely New Year's Eve he had with Tessa, doing the laundry. He describes how, at midnight, he 'popped one of Christopher's balloons with a cigarette.'[176]

Chapter Nine

The High Earner (1975–80)

In early 1975, PKD's life took a distinct turn for the better, albeit for a short period of time. He could now afford to buy a new version of the *Encyclopaedia Britannica* to replace the one taken by Nancy when she left him. Tessa bought a brand new guitar and a 'fee-stabled' horse. In March 1975, the family moved from Cameo Lane to a larger, three-bedroom house at Santa Ysabel Avenue, Fullerton. It had a front garden and a yard at the back where Christopher could play. PKD also bought a sporty convertible, a red Fiat Spyder, the first luxury he'd given himself for years.

PKD began writing a short story entitled *The Eye of the Sybil*. It was PKD's first attempt to describe his 2-3-74 experiences in a fictionalized way. This story was originally intended to be turned into a comic book format, illustrated by PKD's friend Art Spiegelman, editor of the illustrated magazine *Arcade*. It proved impossible to present the story pictorially in this way, however, so PKD sent the manuscript to the Scott Meredith Agency on 15 May 1975, but they failed to find a buyer.

This setback was softened by the news, also in May, that his novel *Flow My Tears, the Policeman Said*, had won the prestigious John W. Campbell Award for science fiction. The award had been established only two years before, by science fiction writers Harry Harrison and Brian Aldiss, and is named in honour of a man who, as a sci-fi writer and editor of *Analog Science Fiction and Fact* magazine, is considered one of the pioneers of early science fiction. The John W. Campbell Award is judged by a small panel of science fiction experts and based on the best novels in the genre published the previous year. It is presented each June at the Campbell Conference, hosted by The Center for the Study of Science Fiction, at the University of Kansas. The previous year the award was won jointly by Arthur C. Clark and Robert Merle but PKD was judged the clear winner among the 1975 entries. His novel *A Scanner Darkly* (1977) would be one of the runners-up in the 1978 award.

PKD's mood swings, possessiveness and jealousy began to put a great strain on his marriage. Tessa was still a young woman who wanted more out of life than to be mother and homemaker. She enrolled in the local community college where she started courses in German and biology. PKD accused her of using this as an excuse to see other men when, in fact, it was he who used Tessa's absences to start a relationship with another woman.

This extreme jealousy was a major factor that undermined all PKD's relationships and his marriage to Tessa, his fifth and – as it turned out –

last, was to be no exception. In July 1975, Tessa and Christopher visited her family for a week. This was the first time that PKD and Tessa had really been apart yet PKD was reminded of how Nancy had left with Isa and saw this brief separation as a form of desertion. PKD would later describe Tessa's absences as 'fledgling adventures'.

PKD began to flirt more and more with women he met. Quite naturally, Tessa found this difficult to deal with. Just how overt this had become was described by PKD's friend, Tim Powers, in his introduction to the *Selected Letters Volume Four*. The following incident is described in the introduction.

PKD and Tim had not been in touch since early 1973 when Tim started dating Linda Levy. PKD had found this difficult to deal with at the time and continually made negative comments regarding Tim's new girlfriend. Tim was put out by this and they both stopped contacting each other. The friendship fell by the wayside. However, PKD and Tessa decided to have a party at their Santa Ysabel Avenue house on 3 August 1975. As well as a number of college students and academics, they decided to invite the only non-family member who had attended their wedding in April 1973, a young woman called Ila Howard. Ila didn't wish to come on her own and so asked if she could bring Tim Powers along as her guest. PKD agreed and, as soon as Tim arrived at the party, made it clear he wanted them to become friends again. Their resurrected friendship endured for the rest of PKD's life and Tim was immortalized as one of the central characters in PKD's novel *VALIS*.

Doris – a woman with a calling

PKD's behaviour was causing Tessa a great deal of worry and stress. In particular, he had made a new friend called Doris Sauter who was taking up more and more of PKD's time. PKD had first met Doris in the spring or early summer of 1972 when she was dating his friend and fellow science fiction writer Norman Spinrad. She was living in Tustin, a suburban city in Orange County, and Norman was in Laurel Canyon, a neighbourhood in the Hollywood Hills of Los Angeles. Doris and Norman would drive down to Fullerton to meet up with PKD and Tessa and go for a meal at a local Chinese restaurant nearby. When Doris and Norman split up, PKD continued his friendship with her and she became part of a small group, including Tessa and Tim Powers, who would spend hours discussing politics, religion and many other subjects.

In 1974, sitting in her tiny apartment, Doris had her own epiphany – a religious conversion that would eventually lead her to the priesthood. She initially toyed with Catholicism before settling on Episcopalianism. PKD was delighted about this and felt that here was somebody with whom he could discuss the religious implications of his 2-3-74 experience. When

PKD felt neglected in a relationship, he invariably sought support elsewhere, and his marriage to Tessa was no exception. Doris was a good listener and, with her own keen interest in theology, was more than happy to engage PKD in long discussions.

Tessa, meanwhile, had a young child to cope with as well as the everyday realities of running the household. Clearly, the marriage was in trouble and external help was needed and so they began attending marriage counselling. Adding to these complexities was PKD's worsening psychological state, including a return of his old phobias. PKD had already been diagnosed as 'manic depressive'. This condition may account for one particular event that clearly worried his young wife:

> 'One time he tried to take a letter to the mailbox on the corner, but as soon as he left our front yard he felt dizzy and actually fell down. He got up and ran back into the house.'[177]

The break-up

Things came to a head when PKD announced that he was planning to move out and look after his new friend, Doris. As we shall discover, PKD had already asked Doris to marry him even though he was still with Tessa. One February afternoon, Tessa decided she had had enough and took Christopher with her to stay the night at her father's house. The next day, she returned with her brother and his wife to pick up some clothes for her and toys for Christopher. In *Remembering Firebright*, she insists that she had told PKD that she would be away for two days and then would be back.[178] She describes how, as she walked round the house collecting things for her trip, PKD and his friend Tim Powers sat watching her in silence.

The next day, Tessa was horrified to discover that PKD had attempted suicide after she left and was now in the psychiatric ward at the county hospital. When she visited him she found him unconscious. On her return to the family home she found a note from a 'woman' stating that PKD needed some fresh clothes and the cats needed feeding. The next day PKD had regained consciousness but was too upset to speak to her. According to Tessa, on the third day PKD was released, being picked up by the mystery woman in 'his little red Fiat Spyder, which was the one shabby luxury that we had been able to afford'.[179] From this wording, it is clear that Tessa was feeling bitter at this turn of events.

The suicide attempt was a comedy of errors from start to finish. PKD took forty-nine digitalis tablets, and assorted Librium and Apresoline.[180] He then slashed his left wrist, went to his garage and sat in the Fiat with the engine running. This is described in detail in Chapter Four of *VALIS*:

Philip K. Dick showing every sign of enjoying a happy childhood, large portions of which seem to have been spent under a cowboy hat

In this photograph taken by his fifth wife Tessa Dick, PKD is with their son Christopher. PKD claimed a spiritual entity helped him to diagnose 'a life-threatening birth defect that no one had been aware of' in Christopher

PKD with wife Tessa Dick, who collaborated with him on *A Scanner Darkly*. He once wrote, 'Tessa and I started out with conflicting realities… but now we are shaping a joint one between us.'

PKD in the Cameo Lane apartment (in Fullerton, California) he shared with Pinky the cat and his wife Tessa. Pinky once cornered a mouse. To save the mouse, they shut Pinky in the bedroom. PKD tried to chase the mouse outside, but it ran straight under the bedroom door. When that was opened, Pinky was standing there looking delighted, mouse tail in mouth. It led PKD to conclude that only God decides who lives and dies

Life and soul of the party: PKD with friends in his apartment in San Rafael, California around 1971. On 17 November 1971, he came home to find his stereo had vanished and his safe had been blown, or so he alleged

PKD wears a delegates badge at Worldcon 72, the World Science Fiction Convention held in LA in 1972, as he lines up for a photograph with belly dancer Wanda Kendall, star turn of Wanda's Wigglers

Writer William S. Burroughs as photographed by poet Allen Ginsburg. PKD gave much thought to Burroughs' 'information virus theory', the idea that we have been invaded by an alien virus, deciding in the end that if such a virus exists then it would most likely be benign

Leader of the renegade Nexus-6 replicants Roy Batty (actor Rutger Hauer) from the film *Blade Runner*. Based on *Do Androids Dream of Electric Sheep?*, it was the first Philip K. Dick story to be adapted by Hollywood

THE RELIGIOUS EXPERIENCE
OF PHILIP K. DICK

PHILIP K. DICK WAS A WRITER OF SCIENCE FICTION. IN 1982 HE DIED SUDDENLY OF A STROKE. HIS BOOKS OFTEN DEALT WITH THE ILLUSORY QUALITY OF REALITY AS WE KNOW IT. IN MARCH, 1974 DICK SAW WHAT HE LATER DESCRIBED AS "A VISION OF THE APOCALYPSE," AND SPENT THE REST OF HIS LIFE TRYING TO UNDERSTAND WHAT HE HAD EXPERIENCED. WAS IT THE ONSET OF ACUTE SCHIZOPHRENIA, OR WAS IT A GENIUNE MYSTIC REVELATION, AND THEN AGAIN, IS THERE ANY DIFFERENCE ??

FULLERTON, CALIFORNIA, MARCH, 1974:
"I HAD A WISDOM TOOTH EXTRACTED. THEY GAVE ME A TREMENDOUS AMOUNT OF SODIUM PENTOTHAL. I CAME HOME AND WAS IN GREAT PAIN. HE HADN'T GIVEN ME ANY PAIN MEDICATION AND MY WIFE CALLED THE PHARMACY."

"I WAS IN SUCH PAIN THAT I WENT OUT TO MEET THE GIRL WHEN SHE CAME. SHE WAS WEARING A GOLDEN FISH IN PROFILE ON A NECKLACE. THE SUN STRUCK IT AND IT SHONE, AND I WAS DAZED BY IT."

Counter-culture cartoonist Robert Crumb claimed never to have read any of PKD's novels, but that didn't stop him from including the writer in his series of comic strips based on strange events in offbeat lives. PKD appeared in issue 17 of Robert Crumb's *Weirdo* comic – this is the opening page of eight

Russian TV reporter Vladimir Lenski interviews the Philip K. Dick android in Chicago in
2005. Kitted out in clothes donated by the Dick family and with skin made of 'Frubber',
the robot made use of its advanced software to respond to questions, drawing on a vast
database of words from PKD's novels and interviews. (Journalists' most commonly asked
question? 'Do androids dream of electric sheep?') Later that year, the android's head was left
on a plane and never seen again

Philip K. Dick saw empathy as humanity's best hope. As he put it, 'The true measure of a man is not his intelligence or how high he rises in this freak establishment. No, the true measure of a man is this: how quickly can he respond to the needs of others and how much of himself can he give?'

'In 1976, totally crazy with grief, Horselover Fat would slit
his wrist (the Vancouver suicide attempt having failed), take
forty-nine tablets of high-grade digitalis, and sit in a closed
garage with his car motor running-and fail there, too. Well,
the body has powers unknown to the mind.'[181]

The Fiat stalled, he vomited up the tablets and the bleeding stopped.
According to Sutin, it was PKD who decided he didn't want to die so he
phoned his therapist who called an ambulance at his behest.[182] Tessa tells
a different story. She writes that after an unsuccessful attempt to slash his
wrists with a razorblade he was in a great deal of pain. He decided to ring
his pharmacy to get his prescription refilled. The pharmacist could tell that
PKD was in distress so decided to call the emergency services, which then
dispatched a team of paramedics.[183]

Sutin says that PKD was in hospital for fourteen days, initially in a
cardiac intensive care section and then in the psychiatric ward of Orange
County Medical Center.[184] This contradicts Tessa's account in which she
specifically states that PKD was released after only four days.[185] We know
from her account that Tessa visited PKD the next day in hospital but he
was unconscious. She returned to the house on the second day to find the
note telling her to feed the cats and to bring PKD some clothes.[186] Although
she never mentions the name of the person who left the note in her book
Remembering Firebright, she has confirmed to me personally that it was not,
as I had assumed, Doris, but a student from one of Professor Willis
McNelly's classes by the name of Sue. According to Sutin, Doris also visited
PKD in hospital and, from his account, we understand that PKD was keen
for Doris to move in with him.

I was surprised to discover from Tessa that the woman that PKD was
planning to move in with was not Doris, but another woman called Kathy.
It seems that PKD had met Kathy at Christopher's 'Baby Shower' and
another of PKD's 'friendships' ensued. Clearly Doris was not aware of this
arrangement.

According to Tessa, it was Sue who was given PKD's credit card and his
car for safekeeping. It seems that Tessa does not recall PKD's stay in the
psychiatric ward. *VALIS* specifically says that Horselover Fat is 'locked up
in the Orange County mental hospital' and that Fat is very upset that his
wife Beth, clearly based upon Tessa, does not bother to visit him in hospital
after his suicide attempt.[187]

Anne Dick recalls phoning PKD in the psychiatric ward on the Friday.
PKD informed her that the specialists had decided to keep him in for an
indefinite period. PKD told Anne that Tessa had been too busy to visit
him, adding, 'I hope she rots in hell for twelve eons'. Intriguingly, Anne

states that Tessa eventually turned up *after* PKD had been transferred to the psychiatric ward.[188]

What can we make of this? Was Tessa unaware that PKD was incarcerated for at least a week, maybe longer, in a secure mental unit? Or could it be that Sutin used the fictionalized VALIS account rather than the version given by the person who was actually a witness to the events?

It is clear that both Doris and Tessa visited PKD during the shorter stay at the cardiac section. Of possible significance is that Doris, in her introduction to *What If Our World Is Their Heaven* (2009), does not mention the suicide attempt, simply stating:

> 'Phil's relationship with Tessa was disintegrating rapidly – it was clear that his marriage was at an end. Phil soon proposed to me, but I turned him down.'[189]

As we have already discovered, it was the student Sue who drove PKD home to Tessa in the Fiat Spyder. According to Anne, Tessa had, by this stage, returned to the house with Christopher. If it had always been Tessa's intention to just have a short break from PKD this is not surprising. Indeed, Tessa was at home when Sue dropped him off. Tessa informed me that she was not at all happy about this; particularly as Sue's aggressive driving style had badly damaged the Spyder's synchromesh.

Although Tessa was pleased to have PKD home, the damage had been done. At the time she was fully occupied as a housewife and mother and was finding it difficult to cope. She had heard PKD's descriptions of his experiences many times and had ceased to be as interested as PKD would have liked. She had difficulty in accepting that PKD's experiences were anything other than hallucinations or a reflection of his confused mental state. For her, they were not real. In a 2002 interview with Chris Ziegler for *OC Weekly*, Tessa said she didn't mind the first few times PKD reported seeing visions. 'At first it was exciting. But after a while, it was like, "I don't want to hear about your visions!"'[190]

For PKD, however, they were the most real thing that had ever happened to him. The strain was simply too much. PKD was looking for somebody more sympathetic to his 'conversion experience' and Doris, having experienced one of her own, albeit far more traditional in both its circumstances and its outcome, was ready and waiting. PKD had another excuse for moving in with Doris. In May 1975, Doris was diagnosed with a form of blood cancer, non-Hodgkin lymphoma, then known as histiocytic lymphoma. She underwent a series of chemotherapy sessions and PKD was keen to help her cope with the unpleasant side effects, which included seizures and nausea. His suicide attempt and subsequent hospitalization allowed him to put pressure on Doris to move in with him.

Doris finished one particularly intensive session of chemotherapy and radiation treatment that had not gone well and, according to Tessa, she had been given less than six months to live. Doris had, in the past, experienced three severe seizures as a result of her treatment.[191] This was PKD's excuse. He knew that Doris would struggle to cope on her own, having regularly visited her tiny one-room apartment in Santa Ana.[192]

PKD also argued that he was in need of care too, because of his tachycardia. Doris eventually gave in and, in May 1976, PKD moved out of the Santa Ysabel Avenue house and rented a two-bedroom apartment in East Civic Center Drive, Santa Ana. Doris soon moved in with him. Tim Powers lived nearby. This new apartment had two bedrooms and two bathrooms. It was located on the top floor of the apartment block with a balcony overlooking Civic Center Drive. As Doris described it 'on a clear night you could see the Disneyland fireworks.'[193] As we shall discover later, PKD believed that he had 'precognized' (or retro-cognized) living in this place in a dream from years before.

After a few weeks of living alone, Tessa had to give up the Santa Ysabel Avenue house as she could not afford the rent on her own. She packed up her belongings and with Christopher drove the Fiat Spyder up to Napa to stay with relatives for the rest of the summer.[194] The marriage was effectively over.

Initially, the relationship with Doris went well, with PKD playing the role of doting carer. Echoes of this period can be found in PKD's description of the relationship between the dying Rybys Romney and her neighbour Herb Asher in his 1981 novel *The Divine Invasion*.[195]

May 1976 proved to be a life-changing month for PKD's writing career, too. Bantam had acquired three of PKD's novels, *Palmer Eldritch*, *UBIK* and *A Maze of Death*, all down to a keen young editor called Mark Hurst. PKD received $20,000 for these three books, plus an advance of $12,000 for his planned book *Valisystem A*.

This should have been a happy period for PKD yet, again, his obsessive possessiveness came to the fore and he became very jealous of all Doris's male and female friends. His old phobias returned, including his inability to eat in public. PKD had always found the idea of 'cohabitation' difficult. He had asked Doris to marry him on various occasions but Doris did not wish to be tied down at that stage in her life. She had been told that she had only a short time to live and so wanted to use that time to fulfil whatever ambitions were left to her. Such was PKD's anxiety on the subject that, in August, he cancelled a planned visit by his eleven-year-old daughter Isa because he was worried what his daughter would make of her father's new domestic arrangements.

At that time there was a great deal of disruption in his life. The apartment that he was living in was about to be converted to a condominium, which meant it would be put up for sale and no longer available for rent. He would later take up the option to buy it. Caring for Doris Sauter was also draining him of energy. Clearly, his search for an understanding of the events of 2-3-74 was also frustrating him. 'Every now and then I imagine that I've figured out some small clue in my epistemological search. But every clue I figure out, ten more unexplained things pop up.'[196]

Things came to a head later that month. Doris decided to return to college in the autumn. Her cancer was in remission and she was keen to follow up her ambition to become an Episcopalian priest. At first, PKD offered to pay $2,000 towards her costs but then changed his mind so Doris had to find an alternative source of finance. This change of heart on PKD's part, together with his mood swings, were proving too much for her. She didn't wish to end the relationship but felt that maybe they needed their own space. When an apartment next door became available, Doris took the opportunity to move out as she would still be close by if PKD needed her. She continued to pop round to cook dinner for him and watch movies. This situation continued even after she was forced to move out when the apartments were converted into condominiums and put up for sale.

Eventually, Doris followed her calling and began to study for the Episcopal priesthood. She was keen to be ordained but it was clear to her that this would not be in Los Angeles. She decided to move to Yuba City, in the north of the state, which had a more liberal attitude to women priests. PKD saw this as yet another abandonment and refused to visit her in her new home.

By now, Tessa and Christopher had moved back to Orange County. Tessa states that he wanted her and Christopher to move back with him but this was not possible as a clause in the new apartment's lease did not allow children to live there.[197] Although Tessa now began divorce proceedings, she says their friendship remained strong and she continued to assist him with his writing. The divorce was finalized in February 1977.

PKD would later claim that the reason all his relationships ultimately ended in failure was that 'I am so autocratic when I'm writing. . . completely bellicose and defensive in terms of guarding my privacy. . . It's very hard to live with me when I'm writing.'[198] Yet despite the often turbulent break-ups, he said, 'I still have a good relationship with my ex-wives' and especially Tessa, with whom he remained 'very, very good friends'.

Doris eventually graduated from Chapman College in 1981 and started the process of ordination into the priesthood. She took up a pastoral position in Yuba City. PKD, as usual, was not alone for long.

1977 – A Scanner Darkly

'Everything in life is just for a while.'

– Philip K. Dick, *A Scanner Darkly*

This novel had a long gestation period. The original idea was developed by PKD in 1972 but it was only in 1973 that the story gained a structure. He wrote an outline of 82 pages which was submitted to Doubleday. Doubleday were interested and accepted it in principle in April 1973. After a series of revisions the novel was eventually published in January 1977 in hardcover.

The novel is based in Orange County in California. It focuses on a group of drug users and the complex and sometimes amusing world they inhabit. One of the group, Bob Arctor, is, in fact, an undercover narcotics agent called special agent "Fred" who is employed by the local authorities to report back on the activities of the group. A new narcotic called "Substance D" is on the streets and in his role of Bob Arctor Fred ends up taking large amounts. This further splits his brain into two elements and Fred and Bob become separate personalities.

This book deals with the illusory nature of reality from the viewpoint of a character existing in two separate states of consciousness. What is real and what is illusion becomes a fascinating meditation on sanity and insanity. Many of the events described in the book were actually witnessed by PKD in his time sharing his property in Santa Venetia with a series of ever-changing groups of teenage drug-users.

In 1978 *A Scanner Darkly* won the British Science Fiction Association "Best Novel" award followed, in 1979, by the Graouilly d'Or at the Metz Festival in France.

Joan the social worker

Joan Simpson was a thirty-two-year-old psychiatric social worker based at Sonoma State Hospital, about forty-five miles to the north of San Francisco. She had become a collector of PKD's early works and had struck up a close friendship with her book dealer, Ray Torrence. In March 1977, and unknown to her, Torrence wrote to PKD describing how she was very keen to meet her writer-idol. In February 1977, PKD said he had experienced a series of hypnagogic premonitions in which he felt the presence of a woman next to him. These sensations became so strong that he was convinced that a new love interest was soon to appear in his life. The letter from Torrence was therefore of no surprise to him and PKD immediately invited her to stay with him in Fullerton. Joan was delighted to accept and, in April 1977, embarked on the twelve-hour drive down to Orange County.

During her three-week stay, PKD described his 2-3-74 experiences in detail. This clearly did not worry Joan. What did disturb her, however, were the conditions that PKD was living in. She described to Sutin how there were cat flea eggs all over the two glass-topped coffee tables, bottles of pills stacked up everywhere and pages of his *Exegesis* lying all around the apartment. Much to her surprise, PKD agreed to return with her to Sonoma. Although he decided to keep up the rent on the Santa Ana apartment, it was clear that PKD was more than happy to return to his Bay Area roots.

In May, the couple began renting a house in Chase Street, Sonoma. PKD was with his old friends again. Ray Torrence, the engineer of PKD's new relationship, was delighted to have him back, as was another friend, Paul Williams, the author of the famous *Rolling Stone* interview. But PKD was still fighting his demons. As was clear from his initial conversations with Joan, the events of 2-3-74 were still playing on his mind. He was still writing his *Exegesis* but he felt he needed to describe his experiences in the best way he knew how, in a novel. He had been working on a manuscript he had called *Valisystem A* but this was not going at all well. However, things were about to change.

A few weeks after his move, he was delighted to receive a letter from two young college graduates who were requesting an interview with him for a planned book on science fiction writers. D. Scott Apel and Kevin Briggs had embarked on a project they called *Approaching Science Fiction Writers*. As the title suggests, the book would not only incorporate in-depth interviews with writers but also describe how they approached their heroes for the interviews. They had already recorded two-hour interviews with Norman Spinrad, Roger Zelazny, Robert Anton Wilson and Fritz Leiber. Their next quarry was Philip K. Dick. So they were understandably pleased to discover that PKD had recently moved from Los Angeles to Sonoma, around ninety miles north of where they lived.

They sent a letter off to PKD as much in hope as expectation and so were delighted when he telephoned Apel to arrange a meeting. However, a day or two later, Apel received a second call, this time from Joan. PKD's depression had returned and he was not in the right frame of mind to do a series of interviews. However, Joan told Apel that, in her opinion, the interviews could be exactly what PKD needed to break out of this cycle. She promised that she would speak to him and see what she could do.

Clearly, her approach worked and on 20 June 1977 Apel and Briggs arrived at PKD and Joan's Chase Street house. They were greeted at the door by Joan. Apel describes her as 'slim, dark-haired and very cute, with an engaging voice and manner'.[199] In a much-quoted description of PKD he writes:

> 'He was not what I expected. Photos do not do him justice. He was large, physically imposing and hairy. He was wearing slacks and an open shirt, as if his hairy barrel chest and barrel belly couldn't stand being confined.'[200]

The interview went extremely well and, as we shall discover later, PKD made some fascinating off-tape comments that suggest yet another interpretation regarding the 2-3-74 events.

Thirty-four years later, journalist Jamelle Morgan interviewed Scott Apel and discussed with him in some detail his thoughts and impressions of PKD in the summer of 1977. Morgan was keen to understand if Apel was of the opinion that PKD was insane at that time. Apel was quite sure that PKD was completely sane.

> 'And I can make a claim like that if only because I have a degree in psychology and I've worked in mental asylums. They train you to tell the difference between people who are sane, people who are insane and people who are acting insane. Phil was in no way crazy. There may be some biological explanation for some of his experiences; you know a brain embolism or over-medication. I am not a medical doctor. But I do know the man was absolutely sincere in his belief that he had an experience that was in some way outside the realm of normality.'[201]

In both the Morgan interview and in the introduction to *Philip K. Dick: The Dream Connection* (1987), Apel suggests that, in some respects, he and his associate Kevin were the models for 'David' and 'Kevin' in *VALIS*. The names are a strong clue. In a subsequent phone call, PKD confirmed to Apel that the characters were indeed based on him and Kevin. However, Tim Powers and Kevin Jetter have claimed the characters were based on them.[202] An analysis of the characters of Powers and Jetter do tend to bear this out. Powers is a Catholic, as is 'David', and Jetter was and, as far as I am aware, still is, a grounded rationalist in a similar vein to 'Kevin'.

The Metz Festival

In September 1977, Joan accompanied PKD to France. He had been invited to give a talk at the Second International Science Fiction Festival, in Metz. PKD was one of the guests of honour at the event, the other two being his good friend Roger Zelazny and his erstwhile adversary Harlan Ellison.

However, it was PKD who was to give the keynote address. This was clear evidence of how his work was taken very seriously in France. To commemorate PKD's appearance at the festival, organizers had even commissioned a limited edition booklet of his short story *Explorers We*, written in 1958 and published the following year in *Fantasy and Science Fiction Magazine*.

PKD had hand-written his speech in advance and these notes were supplied to the organizers for translation into French. The plan was that PKD would read out a paragraph in English and the translator would repeat it in French.

His original speech was entitled *'If You Find This World Bad, You Should See Some of the Others'*. In this, PKD presented some fascinating ideas regarding the implications of his 2-3-74 experiences. The transcript of the speech is alive with speculation and intellectual gymnastics and is the perfect introduction to PKD's thinking in 1977.[203]

Sadly, this is not how the speech came across on the day. Just as PKD was about to start, he was informed that he had to shorten his presentation by twenty minutes. PKD quickly went through the manuscript and took out a series of sections. His translator was obliged to do the same for his document but, unfortunately, removed different sections. What resulted was utter confusion. Fortunately, those of us who were not there that day can simply read PKD's staggering prose.

In his introduction to Gregg Rickman's *Philip K. Dick: In His Own Words* (1984), Zelazny describes the outcome of the speech from his point of view. Zelazny had to attend a book signing event at a local bookshop so his feedback on what took place was second hand. The first idea he had that something had gone wrong was when French attendees to PKD's talk began turning up at the bookshop. One asked Zelazny if it was true that PKD planned to set up his own religion and another claimed that after the talk PKD had given him the power to forgive sins and kill fleas.

Joan came down with a stomach bug and spent most of the time confined to her hotel bed. After the break-up, PKD was to tell friends that she had experienced a mental breakdown.

On their return to California, Joan hoped PKD would join her in Sonoma. However, PKD was now far too settled in Orange County to move to Northern California. As Joan was not willing to live in the Los Angeles area, the relationship came to an end. PKD was back being single. This was a position he had been in before but now there was one huge difference: he had money, lots of it. According to Lawrence Sutin, in 1977, PKD's earnings grossed roughly $55,000 and in 1978 this had increased to $90,000. As well as increasing the amount of money he was paying in maintenance to his ex-wives and children, he was able to buy a brand new Mercury Capri for cash and to donate sums of money to his favourite charities.[204]

In August 1978, his mother, Dorothy, died. PKD's reaction was shock and grief at first but this soon changed to relief as he felt that yet another burden had disappeared. He was free, single and relatively well off. His world suddenly looked good. PKD entered the final stage of his life with a golden opportunity to write the books he really wanted to write: stories that would describe, in various ways, what happened to him in 1974.

Chapter Ten

The Final Years (1979–82)

PKD had lost his mother but his father was still very much alive. They had been estranged for many years but they were to have a rapprochement thanks to PKD's first daughter, Laura.

In the late 1970s, Laura had been studying at Stanford University, in the San Francisco Bay area. Quite by chance, she discovered that her grandfather Ted Dick was living very close to her on the edge of campus. Clearly a determined young woman, she simply climbed over the fence and introduced herself to her long-lost relative. One can imagine the surprise on the faces of the elderly Ted and his third wife Gertrude. They struck up a strong relationship and Laura spent many hours doing her studies on the couple's living room floor. Anne Dick describes how she informed PKD of this discovery:

> 'The next time I talked to Phil on the phone I told him, "Your father is okay, Phil." Phil called his father, and a telephone dialogue began between the two of them that continued until Phil's death. Phil sent his father autographed copies of some of his novels and copies of magazine interviews. His father was immensely proud of them.'[205]

In late May, PKD wrote to Laura describing how he was totally exhausted. He added that in some way he also felt 'damaged'.

> 'I sense myself taking the line of least resistance, in every situation. I am conserving my psychological energy. But only an organism preparing to die does that. Am I withdrawing from life itself? Maybe that is it. I don't know.'[206]

On 25 February 1980, Laura celebrated her twentieth birthday. PKD, who was suffering a sprained back, sent her a letter in place of a card.[207]

Laura was now engaged and was keen for her father to attend the wedding at Point Reyes Station in August 1980. For a time, it looked as if he would do so. According to Anne, he had even asked Laura to supply him with a list of his obligations on the day. Unfortunately, as the wedding got closer PKD had an attack of tachycardia and he told Anne that any excitement could kill him. However, the version of events he told Tim Powers and Doris Sauter was that Anne didn't want him to attend. It was clear that even after many years, the situation between Anne and PKD was still fraught. It can only be imagined how sad Laura must have felt not to have her father there to give her away at her wedding.

PKD seemed to be sinking into himself. Success had not made him happy. He continued writing his *Exegesis* and continued to think deeply about the events of 2-3-74. But he began to believe that such powerful experiences were now fading memories. However, VALIS was about to reappear in his life.

The Second Theophany

On 12 January 1981, PKD wrote a fascinating letter to Patricia Warrick describing in great detail what he terms his 'Second Theophany', which took place on 17 November 1980. PKD describes how at 11 am on that day he was standing in his kitchen with his friend Ray Torrence. PKD suddenly found himself in a powerful hypnagogic state:

> 'I saw an infinite void, but it was not the abyss; it was the vault of heaven, with blue sky and wisps of white cloud (I am quoting the notes I made that night). He was not some foreign God but the God of my fathers. I saw nothing, but I experienced his presence, his personality. And I was aware of him addressing me.'[208]

This being then explained to PKD that he was infinity:

> 'Where I am, infinity is; where infinity is, there I am. I am everywhere and all roads, all lives, lead to me. Everyone will find me in the end. I revealed myself to you (in March 1974) and you saw that I am the infinite void.'[209]

PKD was convinced that this was, indeed, God, and that God had manifested in his life as VALIS. After this encounter, PKD believed this entity to be a personality of pure love and to be totally transcendent. For him, this later Theophany was a direct encounter with the true God, whereas his March 1974 experience was more of an encounter with God's will in the world. In this way PKD believed that this VALIS was more akin to his own concept of Ubik. Indeed, I cannot help but be reminded of how Ubik described itself in 1969.

> 'I am Ubik. Before the universe was, I am. I made the suns. I made the worlds. I created the lives and places they inhabit; I move them here, I put them there. They go as I say, they do as I tell them. I am the word and my name I have never spoken, the name which no one knows. I am called Ubik, but that is not my name. I am. I shall always be.'

1981 – The Divine Invasion

'Sometimes I think this planet is under a spell,' Elias said. 'We are asleep or in a trance, and something causes us to see what it wants us to see and remember and think what it wants us to remember and think. Which means we're whatever it wants us to be. Which in turn means that we have no genuine existence. We're at the mercy of some kind of whim.'

– Philip K. Dick, *The Divine Invasion*

This novel was very much influenced by Phil's writing of his *Exegesis*. He was looking for a follow-up novel to *VALIS*. Indeed, he initially called the book *Valis Regained*. The novel was eventually written in two weeks in March 1980. He used as the beginning his short story 'Chains of Air, Web of Ether'. It was eventually published by Simon & Schuster in June 1991.

The story begins with a young boy called Emmanuel starting school on Earth. He knows that his mother Rybys Romney is dead and that his stepfather, Herb Asher is in cryonic suspension, clinically dead.

What he doesn't know is that Herb's mind is alive with lucid dreams in which he is re-experiencing the last six years of his existence, including the time when he lived as a recluse on the distant star system CY30-CY30B, where a local god, Yah, appeared to him in a vision and told him to go and visit his neighbour who was terminally ill. That neighbour was Rybys Romney.

At school Emmanuel is approached by a strange, intense, little girl called Zina. Zina tells him that he needs to awaken to realise his true identity.

Again PKD weaves into a novel the idea that there are two gods (Bitheism): one that is immanent in the world and one that is in a state of forgetting its true role. This idea features in earlier novels such as *The Cosmic Puppets*, but in *The Divine Invasion* we have a full explanation of anamnesis, the recovery of lost memories and a realization of origins.

The idea that the mind feeds on past-life memories as a form of passing the time while in cryonic suspension appears again in this novel. This is again a version of the 'half-life' presented in PKD's earlier novel, *UBIK*.

The idea of a young girl being a manifestation of 'Wisdom' (Sophia) recurs from Phil's earlier work, *VALIS*. Here we have Zina taking the role. To this PKD adds the Kabbalistic concept of the 'Shekinah'.

Rumbling back to life

PKD was fired up again. VALIS was back in his life and he needed to know why. Possibly stimulated by this event, in April 1981 he began writing *The Transmigration of Timothy Archer*, sending off the manuscript on 13 May. The story, which PKD says 'is in no way science fiction', begins on 8 December 1980 with the killing of singer/songwriter and musician John Lennon, co-founder of the Beatles, and then goes into flashbacks. Lennon was shot dead outside his apartment building in Manhattan, New York.

His killer, security guard Mark Chapman, claimed he was incensed by Lennon saying The Beatles were 'more popular than Jesus'. Lennon was a big fan of PKD's work and during the time leading up to the shooting had been talking about making a movie of his novel *The Three Stigmata of Palmer Eldritch* (1965).

The Transmigration of Timothy Archer was the last novel that PKD was to finish and, in many ways, it pulled together many of the issues that had been playing on his mind for years. He always claimed this new work might be thematically linked to *VALIS*, *The Owl in Daylight* and *The Divine Invasion*, but it was never meant to be part of the 'trilogy'. Narrated by Bishop Archer's daughter, Angel, it is one of his most complex novels and, some say, a riposte to those who said he couldn't write strong women characters.

In one section, clearly based on PKD's experiences, a dead character seems to take over the mind of a living one and, in so doing, reflects what PKD thought really took place in his life in March 1974. In the novel, Bishop Timothy Archer dies in the Israeli desert and his personality seems to 'transmigrate' into the mind of a schizophrenic called Bill Lundborg. In reality, or at least this one anyway, PKD's friend Bishop James Pike dies in the Israeli desert and, for a short time, seemed to have 'transmigrated' into the mind of PKD, an author living in Fullerton.

Except for a short period in 1974, PKD had remained with the Scott Meredith Agency for his whole writing career. A new and very keen member of the Meredith staff, Russell Galen, had been assigned PKD as his client. Galen was a huge science fiction fan and was keen to boost PKD's career.

Birth of Blade Runner

One of the major projects Galen took over was the movie rights to *Do Androids Dream of Electric Sheep?* (1968). The business of transferring androids to the silver screen had been a long, drawn-out process. Director Martin Scorsese had shown interest in it initially, soon after it was published in 1968, but it was producer Herb Jaffe who first took out the option of filming it. His son Robert produced a screenplay but PKD was less than impressed. When Robert Jaffe flew down to Santa Ana to talk about the project, PKD said, '. . .the first thing I said to him when he got off the plane was, "Shall I beat you up here at the airport, or shall I beat you up back at my apartment?".'[210]

In early 1981, Galen's hard work came to fruition. English producer Michael Deeley decided that the book would make a perfect movie and quickly got Ridley Scott on board as director. The Ladd Company signed up for the distribution.

PKD was initially delighted at this news but then he began to worry about what Hollywood would do to his novel. Things did not start well. PKD discussed the plot with the screenwriter Hampton Fancher, but when he read the finished product, in December 1980, he was horrified. Fortunately for PKD, Deeley and Scott felt the same way about Fancher's script and, in early 1981, David Peoples was called in to do a major re-write. PKD was much happier with the new story-line.

PKD was also pressured into writing a 'novelization' of the screenplay but he refused. In the last interview he gave before his death, PKD said he thought that holding out against doing a novelization might have saved the movie as it meant that the original novel had to be reissued. He said, 'I think that one of the spin-offs was they went back to the original novel. . . So it is possible it got fed back into the screenplay by a process of positive feedback.'[211] Despite being invited to visit the studio to see the filming, he resisted the offer, worried that he might be so incensed by the way they were interpreting his novel that he would go berserk.

> 'They'd have to run in and throw a blanket over me and call the security guards to bring in the Thorazine. And I'd be screaming, "You've destroyed my book!" They'd have to ship me back to Orange County in a crate full of air holes. And I'd still be screaming.'[212]

Anxiety over *Blade Runner* started to take its toll. PKD began drinking heavily and taking aspirins until, in May 1981, he suffered gastrointestinal bleeding. He said, 'Hollywood's going to kill me by remote control!'

On 29 July 1981, PKD watched a short clip of *Blade Runner* on KNBC-TV News. He was amazed how the film managed to reflect his own internal images of his characters and their environment. He was to tell Gregg Rickman that the special effects by Douglas Trumbull 'terrified me,' adding 'it was as if my brain was projecting its worldview into my TV screen'. [213]

PKD was sent an updated screenplay and realized that it had been 'rejuvenated'. As he said to John Boonstra, 'I got the novel out and looked through it. The two reinforce each other, so that someone who started with the novel would enjoy the movie and someone who started with the movie would enjoy the novel.'[214]

PKD was to have a much easier passage with the script adaptation of his story *Second Variety*, which was subsequently released in 1996 as *Screamers*. The screenplay was written by Dan O'Bannon, who also wrote the screenplay for *Alien*. 'They're very nice. I really like them. Every change that's made, they send me a copy to get my opinion. They treat me just like a human being.'[215]

VALIS

PKD's novel *VALIS* finally appeared in February 1981. In an interview with John Boonstra, on 22 April, PKD describes how he wanted the novel to be, as he termed it, picaresque. He states that he had been very influenced by J.P. Donleavy's novel *The Ginger Man* (1955) in this respect. He saw this writing style as a protest against the rigid structuring found in most novels. This style has a group of central characters who are 'picaroons', or rogues. The plot line is then a rumbustious adventure with no real structure or form. He was hoping that by using this format he would break out of the science fiction ghetto and reach a wider audience.

The opening of the book involves the suicide of a woman called Gloria Knudson who jumps off the Synanon building, the headquarters of a drug rehabilitation group in Santa Monica, California. This describes a real event. In early 1971, PKD had met a young woman called Gaylene Cunningham who committed suicide in the same circumstances. This is strong evidence of PKD's autobiographical intentions towards this book and is reinforced in a letter sent to Claudia Bush on 5 March 1979.

> 'I sent off my new novel in December called <u>VALIS</u>, which is not a novel and not sf, and yet is both. It's autobiographical and depicts. . . my experience of March 1974 which I am still trying to understand. . . All my book titles have been or will be restored to print. . . I think I will travel all over the world, except I can't figure out what to do with my two cats.'

The novel is narrated from the viewpoint of a science fiction writer called Phil Dick. Dick describes in detail the life of his seemingly schizophrenic friend, 'Horselover Fat'. The name 'Horselover Fat' is a clever linguistic pun on the name Philip (Phil-Hippos – 'horse lover' in Greek) Dick (dick, is German for 'fat'). This was clearly an attempt by PKD to inform his readership that the two characters are aspects of the same person. He confirms this to be the case in a letter sent to his literary agent Russ Galen dated 12 July 1980:

'Horselover Fat, is the psychotic self of the 'I' narrator. Fat has so to speak been struck off from the narrator and assumed a separate identity, due to the death of the girl (Gloria) . . . Fat is the narrator's psychosis, objectively given, which is to say, the narrator has split into two people and retains, throughout, an objective view-point vis-a-vis his own psychosis. The novel is the narrator's odyssey to exorcise his psychotic self, and this odyssey is at last successful. . .'[216]

However, by early 1981, PKD was strongly denying this link. In a letter published in a science fiction magazine and referring to comments made by his good friend Ursula Le Guin, he states:

'Although on page three I say "I am Horselover Fat, and I am writing in the third person to gain much-needed objectivity" it is clear from internal evidence in the novel that Phil Dick and Horselover Fat are two people. Ursula, you have fallen victim to a fictional device by which I establish at the beginning of *VALIS* that this is a picaresque novel.'[217]

This is a very curious denial in that PKD clearly created the character to be the voice of Philip K. Dick the experiencer of VALIS. This is also a very intriguing statement because we know that his earlier novel, *A Scanner Darkly* (1977), has, as its central premise, the idea that the two characters S.A. Fred and Arctor are the same person. Of course, in that case Fred is a narcotics officer working under cover and pretending to be the drug addict Arctor.

By September of that year, Horselover Fat was back in control. On the 23rd PKD sent a letter to Edmund Meskys, a publisher of a fanzine called *Niekas*. According to Gregg Rickman, he also sent a photocopy of the letter to around eighty-five people, including Rickman himself.[218] Rickman states that his copy was accompanied by a hand-written note in which PKD explains that his friend, Horselover Fat, has asked him (PKD) to write this letter to explain to as many people as possible that Fat has had a vision in which he 'actually saw the new savior'. In the letter PKD describes what happened next.

'I asked Fat if he was sure he wanted to talk about this, since he would only be proving the pathology of his condition. He replied, "No, Phil; they'll think it's you." Damn you, Fat, for putting me in this double-bind. Okay; your vision, if true, is overwhelmingly important; if spurious, well, what the hell. I will say about it that it has a curiously practical ring; it does not deal with another world but this world, and extreme is its message — extreme in the sense that if true, we are faced with a grave and urgent situation. So let 'er rip, Fat.'[219]

PKD goes on to explain that in the vision 'Fat' was informed that the new saviour is living in Sri Lanka and is called 'Tagore'. He is burned and crippled and must be carried everywhere. His burns are caused by mankind's destruction of the natural environment and his suffering will continue until mankind turns away from this destruction.

In a separate letter sent to his agent, Russell Galen, on 19 September 1981, PKD stated that VALIS had first informed him back in 1974 that a 'new savior' would soon be born. In 1979, the 'Voice' told PKD, 'The time you've waited for has come. The work is complete; the final world is here. He has been transplanted and is alive.'[220]

PKD was convinced that the being that had manifested in his 2-3-74 experiences was, in fact, Tagore. He had tried to identify this being many times and had called it many names, but here, in the last months of his life, he seemed to settle on the idea that this was all part of God's return to Earth.

However, it is also clear from *The Exegesis* that PKD believed Tagore to be a part of himself in the same way that Horselover Fat was a fictionalized version of his own psyche.

> 'The effect resulting is that one sense that Tagore, like Fat, is not imaginary, not a fantasy or hallucination but, like Fat, a way of talking about myself: a further hypostasis of me (like Thomas and Fat). Yet Tagore is Lord Krishna/Christ, i.e., divine, so I now possess or reveal a saintly hypostatic identity, one which speaks for the ecosphere and also takes on the sins against the ecosphere as stigmata: punishing himself for the sins of man. Interestingly, it is in my legs that I feel pain. And my response today regarding T-2 was to punish myself — I destroyed my stash and also destroyed my *Exegesis*, not quite as self-punishment but more as a sacrifice.'[221]

This certainly caused a fair degree of concern for those who received copies of this letter. They worried that PKD really was descending into mental illness. However, PKD continued to be the complex but amusing character he had always been. Sutin highlights this when he quotes from a self-parody that PKD wrote for the fanzine *Venom*. In this, PKD writes a 'review' of his novel *The Divine Invasion* (1981).

'It is glib enough, but apparently Dick is trying to work off the bad karma he allegedly acquired during his year or years with street people, criminals, violent agitators and just by and large scum of Northern California (this all took place, apparently, after the collapse of one of his many marriages). This reviewer suggests that a better way to make amends would be to take some much-deserved R&R: stop writing, Phil, watch TV, maybe smoke a joint – one more bite of the dog won't kill you – and generally take it easy until both the Bad Old Days and the *reaction* to the Bad Old Days subside in your fevered mind.'[222]

Multiple personalities

I find this review interesting. In *VALIS* he writes from the viewpoint of 'Phil Dick', a science fiction author who comments, usually negatively, on the behaviour of his friend Horselover Fat. The Tagore Letter similarly has 'Phil' informing the world that the communication was at the request of Horselover. The above review takes a similar, distanced approach in that PKD seemed keen to keep his more eccentric self at arm's length. It was as if in his real life he was splitting into two personalities as Arctor/Fred does in *A Scanner Darkly* (1977). In order to accommodate his own extreme beliefs, his more rational personality has split off and acts as a dispassionate observer of seemingly crazy behaviour.

This is the opinion of Tessa Dick. In her review of my own book *The Daemon, A Guide to Your Extraordinary Secret Self*, she writes:

'Let's move on to the chapter about Philip K. Dick. Chapter 10, "Summary: One Man's Experience", looks at Phil's extraordinary visions of March 1974. I won't spoil it for you. I simply need to say a couple things. First, Phil did not have migraines – he had bad teeth that gave him pain. Second, he was not epileptic – he had multiple personalities. Third, it focuses too much on *Minority Report* and too little on *UBIK*.'[223]

I shall return to the migraine argument later, but what I feel is of great relevance is that she is sure that PKD had 'multiple personalities'. Is this what was happening to him throughout 2-3-74 and finally reduced down to 'Phil' and 'Horselover Fat' in the early 1980s? If so, this would certainly explain why his seemingly bizarre behaviour in no way isolated him from his community. Indeed he continued to attract friends and, more importantly, lovers.

1981 – VALIS

'It is sometimes an appropriate response to reality to go insane.'
– Philip K. Dick, VALIS

In 1978 PKD was writing a considerable amount of material for his *Exegesis*. However in October of that year he started on a new novel based, in part, on his experiences of February and March 1974 and his subsequent speculation as to the cause and significance of these events. He completed the manuscript on November 29, 1978 and sent it to SMLA. The novel was published in paperback by Bantam in February 1981.

The narrator is a science fiction writer called Phil Dick. He describes the 'madness' of his close friend Horselover Fat. Fat has had a series of powerful experiences that lead him to believe that there is an alien satellite beaming messages to him from space. He convinces a group of friends that they need to search out evidence for this.

The group eventually find their way to the estate of a British rock musician called Eric Lampton. Here they are shown a movie that Lampton has financed. This suggests that others have had similar experiences. They realise that Lampton's two-year old daughter, Sophia, is the Gnostic incarnation of Holy Wisdom (Hagia Sophia). Sadly Sophia is accidentally killed. Fat refuses to give up on his search and heads off on a global journey to find the next incarnation of the 'Holy Wisdom'.

The name 'Horselover Fat' is a cryptic clue to the reader. The English 'Horselover' translates in Greek to 'Phillipos' and 'dick' is the German for 'fat'. Horselover Fat and Phil Dick are the same person. Indeed PKD has Fat experience all of the phenomena that he encountered in February/March 1974 so in effect what we have is an author (Philip K. Dick) having a fictional narrator (Phil Dick) describe the experiences of another fictional character (Horselover Fat) that mirrors the real-life experiences of the author. No wonder fellow Science-Fiction writer Ursula LeGuin described PKD as 'America's home grown Borges'.

PKD had earlier written a then unpublished novel *Radio Free Albemuth* which contained many similar biographical details regarding his experiences in February/March 1974 as appear in VALIS. From this, it may be concluded that Phil had sacrificed *Albemuth* to create *VALIS*. Indeed, many elements of Albemuth appear in the film sequence in the middle of *VALIS*. Phil was not to know that in 1985, over, three years after his death, that *Albemuth* would appear in the bookshops.

In early October, PKD began exchanging a series of letters with some-body called Susan. They had first conversed on the phone and he now began wooing her with poems. He was fairly plain speaking in his intentions. He invited her to the 'gala closed premier' of *Blade Runner* that was to take place in February 1982. Susan's husband was called Wendall and her daughter Stephanie. In his letter, dated 27 October 1981, it is clear that he had met Susan and her daughter together. It seems that Susan planned to leave California and that PKD would join her and Stephanie in whatever location they planned to go to. But PKD was not keen to move away and writes of loving another woman 'very deeply'. Another letter on 4 November 1981 suggested that he was becoming a pest. It is clear that they were lovers and that she had, at least, met his friend Tim Powers and Tim's wife Serena.

On 25 December 1981, PKD wrote to Sandra that he was now seeing a lady called 'Karen' who lived in the same building and that, 'I've known her for almost two years. She is bright and pretty and I fell in love with her long ago.' It seems odd that only a few days before he was in love with Sandra. He seemed to take great pleasure in telling one 'love of his life' how beautiful and bright another 'love of his life' is – 'love bombing' and then backing off rapidly. He had been doing this in his letters for years and was still using the same approach. At an ON-TV airing of a live Rolling Stones concert, he even 'confessed his total and undying love for her'.[224] It seems that he had phoned Sandra in New York on Christmas Day to be informed that she was back with her husband. In a letter dated 26 December 1981, PKD makes out to Sherie Rush that it was always his intention to get Sandra back with a guy called Greg. His letters did not make that clear at all. His statements of undying love suggest other motives.[225]

Tessa brought Christopher and her niece Jenny to visit PKD on Christmas Day. They said they had been followed by persons unknown all the way from Tessa's apartment in Orange County to PKD's place and Tessa had called the police about it. PKD phoned Tessa on the evening of 28 December. During their conversation she gave him an ultimatum about moving out of Santa Ana and back with her and his son. This had made PKD decide that he was going to sell the condominium and start looking for a house.[226] He had great hopes for the following year.

Premonitions of doom

PKD's comments and behaviour over the last few months of his life lend some support for his belief that time was 'orthogonal', by which he meant that information from the future could be projected into the past in the form of precognitions. There is strong evidence that PKD felt a degree of foreboding at this time. He seems to have sensed that his life was coming to an end and he needed to prepare himself by tying up a few loose ends. There were several curious examples of this.

In an *Exegesis* entry from September 1981, PKD makes the following comment:

> 'I have sensed for a while that I am dying. Yet I am not physically ill but I become more and more tired, and where I feel it is in my legs; I feel there is so much to do, to be told in my writing: novels about Christ and Krishna and God.'[227]

In late December 1981, PKD wrote a letter to someone called Sherie. In this he makes yet another odd statement that could be interpreted as being precognitive, particularly as the section is not in keeping with the generally upbeat tone of the rest of the letter.

> 'Am I trying to stave off death, like the knight in *The Seventh Seal*? I am playing a chess game with death and death will win but in the meantime I want – I don't know what.'[228]

The end approaches

At a meeting in January 1982, Tessa describes how PKD invited her and Christopher over to his condominium in Santa Ana for some coffee and doughnuts.[229] Soon after she arrived, PKD announced that he had something important to tell her. He recapped in great detail his visionary experiences of 1974 as if he wished to remind her of the details. He then stood up and paced round the room repeating over and over again, 'You will remember, and you will write about it.' He felt that he had only a short time to live and that this information should be written about in detail. Tessa agreed to this, thinking quietly to herself that PKD had at least another ten, possibly twenty, years left to write up his experiences himself.

This feeling of foreboding is also reflected in an interview with Gwen Lee recorded on 15 January 1982. Gwen had been introduced to PKD by his ex-girlfriend, Doris Sauter. Although PKD's relationship with Doris was over, PKD was more than happy to discuss with Gwen his state of mind at that time. Gwen drove up three times from her home in Carlsbad in North San Diego County, Southern California, spending the whole day discussing PKD's concerns with him. The full transcripts of these interviews can be found in *What If Our World Is Their Heaven – The Final Conversations of Philip K. Dick* (2009).[230]

In one intriguing section, PKD describes another version of his planned next novel, *The Owl in Daylight*. He explains what his intentions were:

1982 – The Transmigration of Timothy Archer

'Madness, like small fish, runs in hosts. . .'
– Philip K. Dick, *The Transmigration of Timothy Archer*

PKD started writing *The Transmigration of Timothy Archer* in April 1981 and finished it by 13 May. It was published in April 1982 by Timescape Books.

Unusually for PKD the narrator of this novel is female, an determined young woman called Angel Archer. She describes her relationship with her father-in-law, Timothy Archer, the Episcopal Bishop of California. Timothy is a controversial figure whose theological beliefs bring him into conflict with the elders of his church. He becomes intrigued by a set of recently discovered religious writings suggesting that the sayings of Jesus had been written down two centuries before his birth. Bishop Archer decides to visit Israel and gets lost in the Judean desert before being killed in a fall. After his death his personality seems to take over the mind of Bill, the schizophrenic/autistic son of his ex-lover, Marin.

This novel is a fictionalized account of actual events that took place in the late 1960s. PKD was introduced to Bishop James Pike in 1964 by Marin Hackett, the mother of his then wife Nancy. Indeed Marin is the character Kirsten Lundborg who similarly ends up having an affair with the bishop. There is also a series of suicides that mirrors actual events. Indeed in his 1965 novel *Dr. Bloodmoney*, submitted to SMLA in February 1963, PKD has a character called 'Bill' who claims to be the reincarnation of dead character, 'Jim'. Here we have a fictionalised account of the life of Bishop 'Jim' Pike which ends with another character, 'Bill', claiming that he has been taken over by the personality of the dead Bishop, Jim.

The Transmigration of Timothy Archer was nominated for Best Novel in the 1982 Nebula Awards.

'I wanted to write about a guy who pushes his brain to its limit, is aware he has reached his limit, but voluntarily decides to go on and pay the consequences.'[231]

On Wednesday 17 February 1982, Gregg Rickman called on PKD to conduct an interview that was to form the final third of his biography *Philip K. Dick: The Last Testament* (1985). This section of the book consists of a virtual monologue by PKD explaining in great detail his thoughts regarding his latest, and final, angle on his 'Theophany'. Rickman describes this.

'Much of the initial chapters of this section are not so much conversations as dictations, Phil rattling off what he later told me was "the party line" of the New Christ. I danced around verbally, a lightweight sparring with a heavyweight, trying to rouse the funny, skeptical Phil I knew.'[232]

The interview with PKD went on far later than Rickman had anticipated. It was clear that PKD had a great deal to impart that February evening. His last recorded comments concerned the meaning of the message that VALIS had given him.

'It is very important that that cipher not be read by anyone else. But who read it, I don't know. I have no idea who read it. I'd like to know. Whoever was supposed to receive it, I presume they received it. Because the month it came out I was just zapped with the coloured lights and so on. . . I would like to know who got that cipher. It was very important that cipher got out. It was a matter of life and death that cipher get out. But it did, and it got read and there was a response. There was an immediate response.'[233]

Although PKD seemed to be less convinced about all of this after the interview had finished, it is the interview that stands as his final recorded testament. Rickman left at about 10 pm.

The interview PKD gave that day was somewhat rambling and contradictory. He also made some curious grammatical errors that seem odd for somebody who clearly had an excellent understanding of the English language.

From this point onwards, it is clear PKD had a growing sense of dread. After Rickman had left that evening, PKD telephoned his therapist Barry Spatz and informed him of the problems he had experienced during his interview. He told Spatz that, as well as a general feeling of confusion, he had also noticed problems with his eyesight. Spatz was very concerned about these symptoms and advised his client that he should see a doctor as soon as possible.[234]

On the day of Rickman's interview, PKD received a phone call from Patricia Warrick, an academic at Wisconsin University. The two had met three times in person in 1979 and became good, if geographically distant, friends, phoning each other regularly for long discussions about PKD's work. Patricia had called PKD for a chat, but this time he was unusually quiet and announced that he was really not up to talking. He told her that he was not well but would call her back later. He never did. It is unclear if this phone call came before or after Rickman had been there.

Missed meeting

The next morning, PKD was observed by a neighbour going to buy a news-paper. This was the last time he was seen fully conscious. During the afternoon, PKD's friend Mary Wilson made a series of calls to PKD's house but received no answer. This really worried her.

That Thursday evening, PKD was due at an informal gathering held each week at the home of his friends Tim and Serena Powers. The group usually turned up after Tim got back from work at 9 pm. However, just before Tim arrived, Serena took a call from a very concerned Mary Wilson. She had continued to call PKD but had received no answer.[235] Tim was not too concerned; PKD never missed their Thursday night meetings. Clearly, if he failed to show then there may be cause for worry and Tim would give PKD, or his neighbours, a call.

The first guest arrived soon afterwards. As Tim stood in the doorway the phone rang again. Serena took the call and immediately made a gesture asking for silence. On the phone was Mary's mother, Elizabeth. PKD's front door had been left open and a group of neighbours went in to find him unconscious on the floor. Mary went on to explain that at first they thought that nobody was home, but then they spotted PKD's feet sticking out from behind a coffee table. Tim described what happened next in his introduction to *The Selected Letters of Philip K. Dick, Volume Four*.

> 'I got back into my jacket and left Serena to greet guests and clattered back down the stairs. As I was putting the key in the ignition of my motorcycle I heard the sirens of the para-medics howl past me down Main Street. When I got to Phil's place the paramedics and Mary Wilson were already there and the paramedic had lifted him from between the coffee table and the couch and carried him to his bed, and Mary and I answered a few hasty medical questions about him before they got him into a stretcher and carried him downstairs to the ambulance.'[236]

Tessa Dick describes how she turned up to visit PKD in the hospital's intensive care unit on the Friday morning. She reports that he had been partially paralysed by a stroke but was clearly conscious as he had been 'agitated and communicative' when brought in the night before. She had brought with her a small notebook so that PKD could communicate with her by writing notes. This was impossible because the medical staff had placed an intravenous needle into his right arm and strapped it down on to a board. PKD simply could not move his arm to write. A few minutes later, he was taken away for a CT [US CAT] scan. Tessa said, 'The next time I saw my husband, nobody was home behind those blank, staring eyes.' [237]

On Tuesday 2 March 1982, PKD's life support system was switched off, and so the world, with the flick of a switch, lost one of its most enigmatic, talented, complex and ultimately fascinating, writers.

According to Tessa, for some reason a person, or persons, unknown instructed the medical staff not to allow her access to PKD in his final few days. And she was not the only one. She states that both his priest and his psychiatrist, Barry Spatz, were told to stay away. Tessa was told that these instructions had not come from his eldest daughter Laura. Later, Tessa received a call from PKD's father, Ted, who was upset that the nurses had refused to tell him if his son was alive or dead. Tessa claims that she even had to hire an attorney to allow Christopher to see his father before they unplugged the ventilator and declared him dead.

After PKD's death, Tessa concluded that his precognitive abilities had allowed him to see what was to come. She refers to the January 1982 discussion over coffee and doughnuts mentioned earlier.

> 'I soon realized that he had foreseen his own death and had conveyed that to me in such a cryptic way that I didn't understand the full implications of what he had told me less than two months earlier.' [238]

Of even greater significance is the content of a letter written to Claudia Krenz on 25 February 1975. In the postscript PKD writes the following:

> 'I was up to 5 a.m. on this last night. I did something I never did before; I commanded the entity to show itself to me – the entity which has been guiding me internally since March. A sort of dream-like period passed, then, of hypnogogic images of underwater cities, very nice, and then a stark single horrifying scene, inert but not still; a man lay dead, on his face, in a living room between the coffee table and the couch.' [239]

I first came across this uncanny postscript while researching material for my book *The Daemon – a Guide to Your Extraordinary Secret Self*. [240] In that book I incorrectly stated that this letter had been unpublished at that time (2008). I am now aware that I was not the first person to make the link between this letter and the events of 18 February 1982. In his introduction to the fourth volume of PKD's selected letters, Tim Powers also notes the uncanny way in which PKD's hypnagogic dream-sequence mirrored the circumstances of his stroke. Tim describes the scene at the apartment that day:

1985 – Radio Free Albemuth

'There was a beauty in the trash of the alleys which I had never noticed before; my vision seemed sharpened, rather than impaired. As I walked along it seemed to me that the flattened beer cans and papers and weeds and junk mail had been arranged by the wind into patterns; these patterns, when I scrutinized them, lay distributed so as to comprise a visual language.'

– Philip K. Dick, *Radio Free Albemuth*

Radio Free Albemuth had a curious history. It was first conceived as a short story called 'A Man for No Countries'. This was in response to a 1974 request by his friend Philip Jose Farmer for PKD to contribute a story to a planned anthology. The story was never written but was adapted to become a novel entitled *Valisystem A*. It was completed in the summer of 1976 but it was not published until December 1985 when Arbor House realized a hardback edition. PKD took the basic premise of *Radio Free Albemuth* and used much of the autobiographical elements for inclusion in his novel *VALIS*.

The novel is set in California. Its central character is music industry employee Nicholas Brady. Brady has started to receive messages from an entity that calls itself Valis. Nicholas is not sure if the source is Russians conducting experiments in telepathy, God attempting communication or aliens from the star system Albemuth beaming information into his head from a satellite.

This novel has two narrators: a writer called Phil Dick and the central character Nicholas Brady. This idea of having a narrator identified with the author was to appear again in his later novel *VALIS*. It allows PKD to observe his own real-life behaviour in a dispassionate and detached way. It is clear that Brady is PKD. The novel describes, in some detail, the events that occurred in February and March 1974. In many ways this is similar to *VALIS*. However *Radio Free Albemuth* is as much a political novel as it is a science-fiction narrative.

'When I got to Phil's place the paramedics and Mary Wilson were already there and the paramedic had lifted him from between the coffee table and the couch and carried him to his bed. . ..'

Both the letter and Tim Power's description of the scene are identical. . . 'between a [the] coffee table and the couch.' Every time I read this it sends shivers up my spine. Tim, in his introduction, states:

'So, was this a genuine vision of Phil's own death, which was then seven years in the future? – I don't know – but remember – trust me – neither do you.'[241]

PART TWO

THE ESOTERIC EXPLANATION

Philip K. Dick was a complex individual who tended to give widely differing versions of events (and ideas) depending on who he was talking to. Unfortunately, this means that it is very difficult to isolate exactly what he really believed. This is particularly so in regard to PKD's so-called 'mystical' experiences. For example, in an interview with Gregg Rickman recorded in October 1981, PKD states quite categorically, 'No, I don't have any psychic ability. I don't even believe in psychic powers, that there are such things.'[242]

Another example of PKD's mercurial attitude to psychic phenomena can be found in his 1974 letter to his local FBI agent.

> '(These things I) personally consider absurd and a crank preoccupation and without merit (our field here in the U.S. has debated ESP and so-called 'psi' or parapsychological powers for years, and I am with the party which feels it to be a hoax on par with flying saucers and little green men).'[243]

However, according to Tessa, PKD was convinced that the apartment they shared in Cameo Lane, Berkeley, in 1972 was not only haunted but that the 'entity' was some form of 'psychic vampire'. This is hardly the conclusion one would expect from somebody who had no belief in such things.[244] We also know that PKD regularly discussed the existence of flying saucers and had once suggested that they were actually sentient life forms, similar to those he described in his novel *The World Jones Made* (1956).

That PKD admitted to inexplicable happenings in his own life is beyond dispute. For example, when he was living with Anne Dick in the early 1960s, he claimed that he saw the ghost of an old man walking round the house. What is strange is that PKD identified the spectre as probably the spirit of an 'elderly Italian gentleman'. He had said to Anne that it 'may have been the ghost of the man who used to live on the farm that was once here.'[245] Unfortunately, in her account of this incident, Anne does not say why PKD was so precise in this description. PKD also claimed that on still nights he occasionally heard the sound of a narrow-gauge railway locomotive making its way through Point Reyes Station. However, the locomotive had ceased to run along the tracks in 1920. Anne was convinced that what PKD was hearing was simply the wind but this was not how PKD perceived it. It is evident from these anecdotes that PKD was more willing to accept an otherworldly explanation than a prosaic one.

This may, in part, be due to the fact that he may have been influenced by his much-loved Aunt Marion who was a 'spiritualist medium'. She was known to regularly go into 'trance states'. Indeed, Tessa claims that Marion's death was brought about when her family mistook a massive stroke for one of these trance states. This confusion caused a crucial delay in getting her to hospital. By the time she got there it was too late.[246] PKD would have been well aware of Marion's 'skills'. So it is not at all surprising that, in the mid-1960s, PKD was keen to involve himself in Bishop James Pike's attempts to contact his dead son, Jim Junior, by using the services of various mediums. PKD has described how he took notes at the séance held at the home of famed psychic George Daisley in Santa Barbara. PKD refers to this visit in his letters[247] and also describes them in a positive way in his fictionalized account of the final years of Pike's life, *The Transmigration of Timothy Archer* (1982). Clearly, these are not the actions one would expect of somebody who thought such beliefs to be 'absurd'.

But for PKD the real mystery of his life was his apparent ability to see the future. He may have denied such experiences to those he believed would not accept them but in his private journals it is clear that for him these perceptions were very, very, real. In *Exegesis*, for example, PKD includes a section in which he postulates that he had spent most of his life 'precognizing' events from his future life and using them as plot devices. In other words, he experienced events in the future that seeded ideas for novels in the mind of his earlier self. This had obviously intrigued him for many years. For example, in late September 1974, PKD wrote one of his many letters to a pen-friend, the graduate student Claudia Bush. In this he makes the following observation:

> 'I just finished rereading *UBIK* for the first time since I wrote it (circa 1968) and I found that a number of my post-March dreams are absolutely for sure scenes from the book, down to the last detail. If I had a better memory I'd have realized it sooner. Well, all I can say is what I said; there is an airtight and super-close relationship between UBIK, phildick and my post-March experiences.'[248]

PKD was to suggest a very elaborate theory to explain these experiences. We shall return to this later on. For now I would like to review the evidence, from PKD's own writings, that he was, indeed, what he would term a 'pre-cog'.

Precognition

If PKD really could perceive events before they actually took place then this skill would have been manifest throughout his life. After reading all of his biographies, a large number of his personal letters and all of his recorded interviews, I have discovered many and varied examples of this ability. Of course, many of them are recorded by PKD himself so we have no way of confirming them independently. However, there are some examples that can be verified and these tend to lend credence to the others. I would now like to describe a selection of these incidents and allow you to come to your own conclusions.

1938: The Bookshop Dream

According to Emmanuel Carrere in his semi-fictionalized biography, *I Am Alive and You Are Dead*, when PKD and his mother were living in Washington in the late 1930s PKD had a curiously similar recurring dream involving the search for a mysterious piece of writing. In this case PKD found himself in a bookstore looking through a seemingly endless pile of *Astounding* magazines. He was searching for the magazine that would complete his collection. He knew that this rare edition would contain a story called *The Empire Never Ended*. This younger version of PKD also believed, like his older self, that this much sought-after story would reveal the secrets of the universe to him. Every time the dream ended he had managed to get further and further down the pile. As each recurring dream started PKD was closer to his goal than the previous one. PKD knew from his readings of H.P. Lovecraft that powerful knowledge can sometimes destroy the person finding it, driving them mad with terror. He was never to find the magazine, however, as the dreams suddenly stopped.[249]

The phrase 'the Empire Never Ended' was to have a profound effect on PKD during his 2-3-74 experiences. It became his mantra with regard to his belief that we were still under the yoke of ancient Rome and that the present world is simply an illusion disguising another world trapped in 70 AD. For example, it appears at least twenty times in his novel *VALIS* (1982) and it is quoted three times in his *Exegesis*. However, and to me this is of significance, as far as I can check, it does not appear in any of his other novels.

1956: *Invasion of The Body Snatchers*

Jack Finney's movie *The Invasion of the Body Snatchers* was released in 1956. PKD was initially convinced that somebody had stolen his story *The Father Thing* and made it into a movie. He later revised this opinion and concluded that maybe it was simply part of the Zeitgeist. However, there are some interesting similarities that suggest that PKD may have precognized the plot of the movie and written it into his short story.

1961: Anne's Abortion

When Anne became pregnant in the autumn of 1960, she decided that a termination was the only logical route to follow. Their previous baby, Laura, had been born in the February and Anne was not ready for another child. She also felt that the family finances were simply not healthy enough at that time. Although PKD objected strongly he had little choice but to go along with the termination. In his novel *The Man Whose Teeth Were All Exactly Alike* (1984) he describes in detail the pregnancy of a character called Sherry Dombrosio. She wants an abortion but her husband, Walt, is dead-set against this course of action. This action is all set against the background of Marin County in the early 1960s.

1962: *The Man in the High Castle*: Precognition of 'The Necklace'.

The original version of *The Man in the High Castle*, completed in November 1961 and published in 1962, contained a sequence that mirrored PKD's anamnesis incident of February 1974. One of the central characters of *High Castle* is a man called Nobusuke Tagomi. Tagomi lives in a San Francisco under Japanese occupation. Having lost the Second World War to the Axis powers, the USA has been partitioned. The West Coast is occupied by the Japanese while the eastern seaboard is under German control; the South is ruled by a Vichy-type regime with the strings pulled by Nazi collaborators, while the Midwest and Rocky Mountain regions are quasi-independent, buffer zones separating the two occupying powers. Tensions between Germany and Japan simmer beneath the surface, and the threat of nuclear conflict between them is ever present. Tagomi is the head of the Japanese trade mission. He is a gentle, reflective man who is greatly influenced by his Buddhist and Confucian beliefs. In one scene, Tagomi is sitting in a small city centre park contemplating a piece of silver triangular jewellery that he has recently purchased. He has just shot dead several German agents and he is having great difficulty in dealing with the moral implications of such actions. As he looks at the silver triangle, it reflects the flickering light of the midday sun into his eyes.

> And yet, in the sunlight, the silver triangle glittered. It reflected light. Fire, Mr. Tagomi thought. Not dank or dark object at all. Not heavy, weary, but pulsing with life. The high realm, aspect of yang: empyrean, ethereal (. . .) What is the space which this speaks of? Vertical ascent. To heaven. Of time? Into the light-world of the mutable. Yes, this thing has disgorged its spirit: light. And my attention is fixed; I can't look away. Spellbound by mesmerizing shimmering surface which I can no longer control. No longer free to dismiss.

This powerful 'blinding clear white light' engulfs Tagomi, eliciting images in him of the *Tibetan Book of the Dead*, the cycles of death and re-birth and the illusory nature of reality. It then stops suddenly and Tagomi sees a police officer standing in front of him. The policeman asks about 'the puzzle' that Tagomi had been playing with. Tagomi, frustrated that his reverie had been broken so abruptly, angrily responds that what he was looking at was no childish puzzle. He then walks out of the park to find a 'pedecab', a mode of transport introduced by the Japanese after the occupation. He then notices a huge construction blotting out the skyline. He asks a passer-by what it is and is informed that it is the 'Embarcadero Freeway'. From this information, we discover that Tagomi has entered an alternative history from the one he previously existed in. PKD chose this particular structure as a well-known symbol of post-war America built in the late 1950s, something that clearly did not exist in Tagomi's Japanese-ruled San Francisco. This realization of an underlying reality that contains a different history and present state is exactly what PKD 'discovered' after his own incident with reflected light in February 1974. For him the under-lying reality was the Roman Empire of 70 AD. For Tagomi, it was a world where the Axis powers had been defeated. The same experience described as a fiction in 1961 to be discovered as a 'reality' thirteen years later.

In February 1982, in one of the last few entries in his *Exegesis*, PKD made reference to this link.

> 'In 2-74 there was no pink light as such. But sunlight. Fish sign and light. Like Boehme. And Mr. Tagomi.'[250]

In 1961 PKD had Mr. Tagomi describe the experience thus:

> 'This hypnagogic condition. Attention-faculty diminished so that twilight state obtains; world seen merely in symbolic, archetypal aspect, totally confused with unconscious material. Typical of hypnosis-induced somnambulism.'

After his 'theophany' of 1974, PKD became convinced that information flowed in both directions, from the future into the past and from the past into the future. He was fascinated as to why so many of his later-life experiences had regularly turned up in his earlier fictions. It was as if he 'remembered' what had happened to him and unconsciously used these future experiences as plot devices in his novels and short stories. As we have already discovered, the source of the A.I. 'Voice', the mysterious Sadassa Ulna, claimed that she was living in the Portuguese States of America, an alternative America that was the result of a different time-line. PKD had used the idea of alternative Americas co-existing within the same time-space in his 1962 novel *The Man in the High Castle*. Was this a form of precognition on PKD's part?

Of course, one could apply a far simpler interpretation and suggest that

PKD was aware (subliminally or otherwise) of his own earlier plot-line and subconsciously embroidered this into his 1974 experiences.

1964: What Dead Men Say – Voice on the radio precognition in 'What Men Say'

In 1974, PKD heard the radio speaking to him even though it was not plugged in. Tessa described her version of this to me in a personal SKYPE call in March 2013. She confirmed that the radio had been turned off. But for me it is not simply how odd it is that an unplugged radio can pick up a signal but more that PKD may have precognized this event eleven years earlier.

A virtually identical experience is described in PKD's short story *What Dead Men Say*, which was written in early 1963 and published in the *Worlds of Tomorrow* magazine in June 1964. The central character, Johnny Barefoot, hears the voice of his dead boss Louis Sarapis beamed to him from outer space. Here we have elements of both *UBIK* ('half-life') and the *VALIS* trilogy. However, what is of greater significance is that we have a theme of messages from a disincarnate being manifesting in the mind of a person on Earth. This is what PKD claimed happened to him on 2-3-74. Indeed we also have this trope of messages from space in *Dr Bloodmoney*. What is happening here? Is PKD simply confusing his own fictions with actuality or did his mid-1970s experiences create ideas and images in his mind through a form of retro-precognition?

There is a second curious precognition in *What the Dead Men Say*. One of the negative characters is called 'Kathy' and she is an amphetamine addict. We know that Kathy was to play a central role in PKD's life in the early 1970s. It is accepted that Kathy is a fairly common name but it is intriguing that both the real and the fictional Kathy were involved in the drugs scene. Indeed, as we shall soon discover, Kathy will feature again and again in PKD's precognitions.

1964: Palmer Eldritch: Retro-Precognition

PKD's 'vision' of the face in the sky on Good Friday 1962 (or 1961) was of profound significance for him. Not only did it create in his mind the ideas that were to bring about his novel *The Three Stigmata of Palmer Eldritch* but it also reinforced his belief that there are powers in the universe that are far stronger than humanity and that this reality is simply an illusion overlaying a deeper, more profound state of existence. He was later to write extensively about the nature of time and the way that consciousness can access information from a timeless state in which everything exists in an eternal 'now'. He was sure that the themes from his early works had been seeded from his later experiences. An example of this may be the way in which the 'face in the sky' he experienced in the early 1960s resonated in his younger self to create at least one novel and one short story.

In 1953, he wrote a short story called *Fair Game*. He struggled to sell this and it finally appeared in *If Magazine* in 1959. It is a typical 'twist-in-the-tail' story involving a nuclear scientist who believes that aliens are after him to steal his knowledge when, in fact, they want to eat him. What is of significance is that in the story the central character, Anthony Douglas, sees a huge eye looking at him through the window of his house. Douglas explains what he saw to his wife, Laura.

> '"The damn thing was looking at me. It was me it was studying." Douglas's voice rose hysterically. "How do you think I feel—scrutinized by an eye as big as a piano! My God, if I weren't so well integrated, I'd be out of my mind!"'

In early 1955, PKD was consumed by a burst of creative energy. In just two weeks he wrote a full novel. He called this *With Open Mind* and delivered the completed manuscript to the Stuart Meredith Agency on 15 February 1955. It was given a series of extensive re-writes before being published by Ace in 1957. There is a powerful sequence in the book that led to a change of title. *With Open Mind* became *Eye in the Sky* (1957). In this section, two of the characters, McFeyffe and Hamilton, find themselves holding on to an umbrella that is rapidly ascending from the Earth and into space. They rise into the void and discover that the Sun actually does revolve around the Earth in the way described by the Medieval philosophers. This is a universe of Ptolemy not Copernicus. The other planets are discovered to be tiny and of no consequence. The Earth is found to be the centre of the universe. Beneath the Earth they see the red embers of Hell and above them the lights of Heaven. They then encounter an infinite semi-transparent wall that surrounds the universe. Looking above them and through the protective wall they see what they first think is a huge lake floating in space. Hamilton then notices that the centre of the lake was made of a denser, more opaque substance:

> 'A land of lake within a lake. Was all Heaven just this titanic lake? As far as he could see, there was nothing but lake. It wasn't a lake. It was an eye. And the eye was looking at him and McFeyffe! He didn't have to be told Whose eye it was.'[251]

Here again we have an image very similar to the face that PKD was to see seven years later in the skies above Marin County.

Of course, one could just as reasonably suggest that PKD was recalling the imagery from his 1953 story as a way of dramatizing what may have been a fairly mundane event. It is worth recalling the description of the 'face in the sky' that he gave to the reporter from the UK's *Daily Telegraph* in July 1974.

> 'There flooded in the perception of something in the sky. I wasn't on LSD or any other drug, not at the time; just this deprivation of the sense of other living things about me. What I saw was some form of evil deity. . . not living but functioning; not looking so much as scanning, like a machine or monitor. It had slotted eyes and always hung over one particular spot. I've used it for the title of my next-but-one story, *A Scanner Darkly*.'[252]

In 1978 he wrote that he was of the opinion that *Eye in the Sky* (1957), *Time Out of Joint* (1959), *The Three Stigmata of Palmer Eldritch* (1965), *UBIK* (1969) and *Maze of Death* (1970) were all the same novel written over and over again. For him these novels were somehow back-written in that at the time of their writing he was subliminally aware of the revelations of 2-3-74.

1972: We Can Build You – The Lincoln Simulacra

There is intriguing, and corroborated, evidence that PKD may have precognized the Lincoln simulacrum ('Mr. Lincoln') at Disneyland. PKD first presented the manuscript of his novel *We Can Build You* (then entitled *The First in Your Family*) to his agency on 4 October 1962. It was subsequently rejected by Putnam, Doubleday and a series of other publishers. It finally appeared in the *Amazing Stories* magazine in November 1969 under the title of *A Lincoln Simulacrum*. It was eventually picked up by publisher Don Wollheim for his own imprint DAW Books and appeared under the title of *We Can Build You* in July 1972.

The first audio-animatronic version of Abraham Lincoln made its debut on 22 April 1964 at the New York World's Fair. On 18 July 1965, another version of the Lincoln simulation was unveiled at Disneyland to mark the tenth anniversary of the opening of the park. It is therefore beyond doubt that PKD had created the idea of a talking animatronic version of Lincoln eighteen months before the first version was presented to the public in New York. Is this simply coincidence? One could argue that Lincoln's status as one of the most iconic of American presidents suggested that he would feature in an exhibition launched during the centenary of the American Civil War. But there are many ways that this president could have been depicted. Furthermore, PKD had written *First in Your Family* in 1961/62, just when the commemorations of the 100th anniversary of the start of the American Civil War (12 April 1861) would have been regularly featured in the mass media. Throughout these years, centenary events commemorating battles and political events would have continued as each date was reached. As such, Abraham Lincoln would have been very much in the news.

However, PKD would have quickly refuted this analysis. In the Apel interview he states that he saw a notice in a newspaper that Disney was planning to build the Lincoln simulacrum and he posted it on the wall of his study as a reminder of his precognitive abilities.

1973: *Rolling Stone* Magazine and 'The World Jones Made'

In a letter dated 21 July 1980, PKD describes to his agent, Russell Galen, how he might have an ability to perceive information from his own future. As he described it, he 'perturbed time in such a fashion that I drew information from the future into the present.'[253] This was stimulated by a series of discussions he had had with Patricia Warrick regarding the 'observer effect' of quantum mechanics. Later he states quite categorically that 'I am, ordinarily, a precog, as Paul Williams pointed out in his article in *Rolling Stone*.' What follows is an extremely important observation regarding the plot of his 1956 novel *The World Jones Made*. In this, PKD suggests that, unlike what happened to Jones, his own precog abilities were used to save his life. 'However, in 1974 I found out otherwise; my precog talent discerned that I would very soon die of a stroke from high blood pressure. At this point my precog talent, which normally operated on the margins of my conscious mind, took full control, assumed full volitional power of my motor centers. In other words it surfaced.' However he earlier asks a very intriguing question; 'Now what happens when a precog sees via his talent that in the very near future he will die?' This letter was written in July 1980. In March 1982, less than two years later, PKD was to die of a stroke brought about by his dangerously high blood pressure. Had PKD in some subliminal way sensed the contents of his own future and knew that this time his fate could not be escaped?

1974: The *Rolling Stone* Interview

This had been scheduled in late October 1974 but had to be postponed because of Christopher's surgery. In a letter dated 28 October 1974 (to Henry Ludmer), PKD confirms that it was planned to take place on the following Wednesday. This presents us with another mystery. In his interview with Gregg Rickman dated 22 April 1981, PKD claims that he precognized the *Rolling Stone* interview before he was aware that it was going to take place. He claims that '(in my revelation) I even saw portions of the text.'[254] This is intriguing in that Paul Williams had no idea that he was going to do an interview with PKD until August 1974, five months after PKD's VALIS experiences.

1974: *A Scanner Darkly*

It seems from a letter sent to his editor at Doubleday and Company, Diane Clever, PKD asked for an extension on the delivery of the manuscript of his novel *A Scanner Darkly*. The agreed date was to be 18 February 1974, but PKD wished to delay because he needed to include some recent research regarding 'split-brain phenomena' that he had read about in magazines such as *Psychology Today*. He insists that at the time of writing the original sections of *Scanner* he was totally unaware of this research. Indeed in his letter to Cleaver he states:

> 'Frankly, I had imagined that I had on my own discovered and observed this syndrome; hence I made it the topic of the novel. I am wrong. Certainly within the next year much more will be published about this syndrome, and certainly with such mass-media magazines as *Psychology Today* calling it to the attention of their readers I can't afford to shall we say fake it in regard to the scientific, empirical basis on which the decay of the novel's main character is put forth dramatically.'[255]

And later:

> 'I am sure you can imagine my surprise when, upon mentioning the theme of the novel to a scientifically inclined friend, he remarked casually, "Oh yes, I was reading about that just the other day; I'll bring over the article." What we must do here is turn a near-liability into an asset. Frankly, I'm lucky the novel did not come out as is – and *then* we discover the new material on split brain activity with all its bizarre details. Let us say I guessed close, but not quite close enough.'[256]

1974: *Flow My Tears, the Policeman Said*

In a letter dated 25 July 1974 to Jannick Storm, PKD describes how the section describing the rabbit that liked to play with cats and was attacked by a dog (pages 109-111) was influenced by a story that Ray Nelson's wife, Kirsten, had told him about her own rabbit. PKD knew the bare bones of this story but elaborated on it for the novel. He discovered later that the rabbit had died in almost identical circumstances to those described in the book, even though he had not been told about this.[257]

In his interviews with D. Scott Apel and Kevin Briggs,[258] PKD talks extensively about his precognitions, specifically a series of odd events involving his 1970 novel *Flow My Tears, the Policeman Said*. PKD suggested that much of this novel had appeared to him in dreams and that he used his memories of the dream images to create the novel itself. He decided that one of the characters would be called Kathy and she would have a husband called Jack. Initially, the reader is led to believe that Kathy works for the criminal underground but, as the novel progresses, it is discovered that, in fact, she is an undercover agent working for the police. How much of this plot was drawn up from half-forgotten dreams is difficult to say, but whatever their source they subsequently proved to be disturbingly precognitive.

PKD met Kathy on Christmas Day 1970. This was the same Kathy who was to have a profound influence on PKD's life throughout 1971. Through her, PKD meets her boyfriend, Jack, and then discovers that she is a drug dealer. This real-life echo of his novel disturbed PKD, but what happened next stunned him. In *Flow My Tears* the fictional Kathy has an affair with a police officer who always wears a grey coat. In 1972, PKD describes how he and the real Kathy were about to enter a restaurant when:

> 'Kathy stopped dead and said, "We can't go in there; Inspector So-and-so is in there." And in my book, he wears a gray coat, or something like that, and there he was, sitting there in a gray coat.'[259]

Later in the novel, there is an incident in which one character, Felix Buckman, grief stricken over the death of his twin sister, experiences an intensely vivid dream.

> 'He rode a horse, and approaching him on his left a squad of horses nearing slowly. On the horses rode men in shining robes, each a different color; each wore a pointed helmet that sparkled in the sunlight. The slow, solemn knights passed him and as they traveled by he made out the face of one: an ancient marble face, a terribly old man with rippling cascades of white beard. What a strong nose he had. What noble features. So tired, so serious, so far beyond ordinary men. Evidently he was a king.'

PKD was later to associate the images of this dream with his precognition of the lyrics of a cover version of the Neal Young song *After the Gold Rush* by the band Prelude. The narrator of the song describes how he 'dreamed I saw the knights in armour coming' adding later 'there was a fanfare blowing to the sun that was floating on the breeze'. PKD also felt huge recognition with regard to the final line of the song, 'To our new home in the sun'.[260]

Also in *Flow My Tears*, Felix Buckman is distraught at the death of his twin sister, Alys. He finds himself in an all-night gas station and there he meets up with a black stranger. Buckman and the black man start up a conversation. When PKD explained this scene to his local Episcopalian priest the cleric became very agitated and pointed out to PKD that he had written up a scene taken from the Book of Acts. PKD had never read this section of the New Testament but, on returning home, he was amazed to discover that the priest was right. In Acts Ch. 8 verses 26-28, a person called Philip meets an Ethiopian eunuch sitting in a chariot.

> 'But an angel of the Lord spoke to Philip saying, "Arise and go south to the road that descends from Jerusalem to Gaza." (This is a desert road.) And he arose and went; and behold, there was an Ethiopian eunuch, a court official of Candace, queen of the Ethiopians, who was in charge of all her treasure; and he had come to Jerusalem to worship. And he was returning and sitting in his chariot, and was reading the prophet Isaiah.'

Not only had PKD seemingly precognized a section of the Bible, but also intuited that the central character is somebody called Philip. PKD read on and discovered that Acts also includes a high-ranking Roman official called Felix who arrests and interrogates St Paul. In *Flow My Tears*, Felix Buckman is a high-ranking police official who arrests and interrogates the central character, Jason Taverner. By this stage PKD was feeling quite strange. He wondered if there was a link with the name Jason. He got out his Bible Index and found one single reference to the name Jason, a character in the Book of Acts.

In his essay *How to Build a Universe That Doesn't Fall Apart Two Days Later*, PKD makes the following observation:

> 'A careful study of my novel shows that for reasons which I cannot even begin to explain I had managed to retell several of the basic incidents from a particular book of the Bible, and even had the right names. What could explain this? That was four years ago that I discovered all this. For four years I have tried to come up with a theory and I have not. I doubt if I ever will.'[261]

But this story got even stranger. In the summer of 1978, PKD, uncharacteristically, decided to go out late at night to post a letter. In the darkness he noticed a man loitering by a parked car. PKD posted his letter and on the way back the man was still there. In a second uncharacteristic impulse PKD walked over to the man and asked if anything was the matter. The man replied that he was out of gas and he had no money with him. Much to his surprise, PKD found himself digging in his pocket and giving the man some cash. The man asked for PKD's address and said that he would return later and pay him back. As PKD entered his apartment, he realized that the money would be of no use to his new friend. There were no gas stations within walking distance. PKD went back out, found the man and offered to drive him to the nearest all-night gas station. As he stood watching the man fill up his metal gas can he had an alarming sensation of déjà vu-like recognition.

> 'Suddenly I realized that this was the scene in my novel—the novel written eight years before. The all-night gas station was exactly as I had envisioned it in my inner eye when I wrote the scene—the glaring white light, the pump jockey—and now I saw something which I had not seen before. The stranger who I was helping was black.'[262]

PKD drove the black man back to his car, they shook hands and PKD never saw him again. He finishes off his description of this event with a slightly chilling comment:

> 'I was terribly shaken up by this experience. I had literally lived out a scene completely as it had appeared in my novel. . . What could explain all this?'[263]

PKD answers his own question with the simple statement, 'Time is not real'.

1974: The Budding Grove Dream

On 5 July 1974, PKD wrote to Claudia Bush to inform her that he had been experiencing the same dream over and over again. The dreams had started three months earlier but within the 'the last few days' the dream had taken on a particular focus involving a specific book. PKD states in the letter that on 4 July he dreamed that he was at home with two mysterious men. They had asked him for a specific book from his collection. He selected his copy of Robert Heinlein's *I Will Fear No Evil*. He describes this as being a large blue-bound hardback book. He showed this to the men who stated that this was not the book they wanted. It was clear to PKD that the required book was a blue hardback. However, there is a problem here. As PKD wrote:

> 'In a dream a month ago I managed to see part of the title; it ended in the word "Grove." At the time I thought it might be Proust's *Within a Budding Grove*, but it was not; however, there was a long word similar to "Budding" before "Grove."'[264]

Now, if the dreams are in chronological order this seems, initially, to make no sense. It seems on first reading that this second dream came *after* PKD's

5 July dream. However, as PKD is keen to stress in earlier letters that time may be running backwards, maybe the dreams were in the order PKD describes. Indeed, in his next section he states that the information gleaned from the 5 July dream was added to the title information from a month earlier.

> 'So I knew by the first part of the day yesterday that I was looking for a large blue hardback book—very large and long, according to some dreams, endlessly long, in fact—with the final word of the title being "Grove" and a word before it like "Budding."
>
> In the last of the four dreams yesterday I caught sight of the copyright date on the book and another look at the type-style. It was dated either 1966 or possibly 1968 (the latter proved to be the case). So I began studying all the books in my library which might fit these qualifications. I had the keen intuition that when I at last found it I would have in my hands a mystic or occult or religious book of wisdom which would be a doorway to the absolute reality behind the whole universe.'[265]

In several of the earlier dreams PKD found himself in bookshops trying to find a copy of the mystery book. In one dream he saw the book held open in front of him with singed pages. From this he concluded that the book was sacred in some way. However, with the new information he was able to return to his book collection and, much to his amazement, he found what he was looking for.

> 'The book is called *THE SHADOW OF BLOOMING GROVE*, hardback and blue, running just under 700 huge long pages of tiny type. It was published in 1968. It is the dullest book in the world; I tried to read it when the Book Find Book Club sent it to me but couldn't. It is a biography of Warren G. Harding.'[266]

As PKD jokingly adds, 'It goes to show that that you should never take your dreams too seriously.'

1974: Precognition/Hypnagogia – Barrio Dream

On 9 May 1974, PKD wrote another of his frequent letters to Claudia Bush. He describes how, after the November 1971 'break-in', he stayed in bed for a whole week. During this period he had a recurring dream involving a Mexican city with 'square arrangements of streets and Yellow Cabs'. The yellow cabs suggest a location in the USA rather than Mexico or Latin America. At that time he was living in Marin County, north of San Francisco. In 1974 he was living in Fullerton, a city just south of Los Angeles. Right next to Fullerton is a place called Placentia, which is a strongly Hispanic area. PKD was convinced that this was the place he saw in his dreams.[267]

1974: Barbara Hershey and Blade Runner

In May 1968, PKD was delighted when a film company bought the option for his novel *Do Androids Dream of Electric Sheep?* There was no progress with this until some time around 1973 when the option was transferred to movie producer Herb Jaffe. However, after reading the initial screenplay, PKD was very disappointed and the project ground to a halt. Fortunately for PKD, ambitious actor-turned-screenwriter Hampton Fancher had recently come into some money and was keen to invest it in a movie project. As a huge fan of PKD's writing, Fancher saw *Do Androids Dream of Electric Sheep?* as the perfect story to apply his own developing screen-writing skill.

Fancher made contact with PKD in the autumn of 1974. Unfortunately, the option was still owned by Jaffe. This did not deter Fancher and, over a period of a few months, he and his associates became regular visitors to PKD's home in Fullerton. Although Tessa doesn't name him as such in her book *Remembering Firebright* (2009), she does mention how a. . .

> '. . .regular group, which included an independent film producer whose name I have forgotten, began coming round once a week.'[268]

It is clear that Fancher was keen to develop his relationship with PKD and these regular visits included the showing of pre-release movies in PKD and Tessa's living room. Over Christmas 1974 Fancher brought with him his close friend the actress Barbara Hershey, then going by the name of Barbara Seagull. Tessa describes an enjoyable evening in which PKD suggested that Barbara should play the role of Rachael in a forthcoming movie version of *Do Androids Dream of Electric Sheep?* before the actress helped her with the washing-up.[269]

This is a curious statement. At that time, the rights to the novel were owned by Jaffe and nothing had been agreed with regard to any future sale to Fancher. Indeed, as Tessa informed me in a personal message, PKD was pretending that he didn't know that Hershey was a famous actress and as such the whole comment was a bit of a joke.

In 1977, the option for the novel was eventually secured for $2,000 by Fancher's friend Brian Kelly and it was Kelly who subsequently approached Hollywood-based British producer Michael Deeley with the project.[270]

Although Deeley loved the novel he felt that its storyline would not lend itself to a movie makeover. But Kelly was not a man to give up easily. He approached Fancher and asked him to create a plot outline. This was submitted to Deeley who again turned it down. This upset Fancher who walked away from the project. However, Kelly felt that Fancher was the only screenwriter who could do PKD's story justice and continued to encourage his involvement. The person who eventually convinced Fancher to start writing a screenplay was Barbara Hershey. A year later, the script was finished and this time Deeley agreed to produce the film.

Deeley and his assistant, Katy Haber, started work on the new project in early 1979. This is over four years after Barbara Hershey visited PKD's Fullerton home. Some months later, casting started and one of the three actresses screen-tested for the role of Rachael Rosen was Barbara Hershey. Although the role eventually went to Sean Young, the decision was made purely on the fact that Deeley and his team were looking for an unknown actress to play the role.[271] Is this another example of PKD's precognitive skills? Remember PKD did not say that she would play the role, simply that she should.

As soon as he had the opportunity to see pre-release excerpts from the completed movie, PKD was keen to point out that the visuals were exactly as he had imagined them when actually writing the book. With regard to Rachel (Rachael) Rosen being played by Sean Young, PKD made the following comment:

> 'It's like they took my brain out and did sight stimulation on my brain, so it projected an image on the screen. That's exactly how I pictured her. If you'd laid out a hundred photographs of a hundred women I could have unerringly picked that one out, because that's Rachel. She's perfect.'[272]

Was this again because PKD had used his subliminal precognition skills to write *Do Androids Dream of Electric Sheep*? Had the future images of the *Blade Runner* movie played in his head like a private hypnagogic screening? I know what PKD would have said about this.

There is also a very curious synchronicity linking *Blade Runner* to another of PKD's books, *VALIS* (1981).

PKD began writing *VALIS* in October 1978. On 29 November 1978, he sent the manuscript to Russell Galen at the agency. The first edition was published by Bantam in February 1981. In an interview with John Boonstra on 22 April 1981, PKD states that the delay was because there had been a change of editors at Bantam. However later he gives a different explanation owning up to the fact that he had written two different versions of the same book. He was simply not happy with the first version. He did not wish to discard it altogether so, in a clever literary twist, he incorporated the first novel into the second as a movie that the central characters go to see in the middle section of the second version.[273]

PKD told Boonstra that the *VALIS* movie section was greatly influenced by Nicholas Roeg's *The Man Who Fell to Earth* (1976). PKD had seen the movie and he considered it to be one of the 'greatest experiences of my life'. His use of the film-within-a-novel was his homage to this movie. The producer of *The Man Who Fell to Earth* was non-other than Michael Deeley who was, a few years later, to produce *Blade Runner*. Was this another subliminal association or simply a curious coincidence?

So what, if anything, can we make of all these precognitions. Can they simply be considered to be a mixture of PKD's penchant for the embroidery of events to make them more interesting and simple coincidences or is there more to it? It may be of significance that PKD described the outset of his precognitions in this way:

> 'I feel them inexorably approaching, not generated from the present, but somehow already there but not yet visible. If they are somehow "there" already, and we encounter them successively.'[274]

PKD was keen to understand exactly what was happening during such events and through his extensive reading he was able to suggest a quasi-scientific model to explain such backwards-causation in time. We will now turn our attention to how PKD explained what was happening to him.

Time Theory
PKD's Time Theories

Philip K. Dick would happily dismiss the existence of any form of psychic phenomenon as nonsense if he felt that his audience disapproved of such beliefs. Yet his private letters and personal writings such as his *Exegesis* are full of ideas and theories to explain why he could preconceive actual events.

He was aware that most, if not all, his precognitions were dream-related. However, PKD's dream precognitions seem to be sourced mostly from his regular experience of the liminal states between wakefulness and dreaming. These are known as the hypnagogic state if experienced at the on-set of sleep and hypnagogia if perceived on awaking.[275]

In a letter written to Peter Fitting on 28 June 1974, PKD describes the power of his hypnagogic precognitive images.

> 'I got more: actual information about the future, for during the next three months, almost each night, during sleep I was receiving information in the form of print-outs: words and

sentences, letters and names and numbers — sometimes whole pages, sometimes in the form of writing paper and holographic writing, sometimes oddly, in the form of a baby's cereal box on which all sorts of quite meaningful information was written and typed, and finally galley proofs held up for me to read which I was told in my dream "contained prophecies about the future," and during the last two weeks a huge book, again and again, with page after page of printed lines.'[276]

This state has been described throughout history and it has long been regarded as the source of inspiration. In a letter sent to Terry Carr on 20 November 1964, PKD described the dream-like quality of his own creative process.

'When I do a novel, I am "there," within that world, among its people, involved in its idiosyncratic customs, etc. I am not thinking about it: I am participating . . . Like they say, my books don't signify anything. They simply are.'

This imagery is powerfully reminiscent of how a dream enfolds you and you become the observer of events that surround you. Indeed is it possible that PKD's creative muse was facilitated by waking hypnagogic images? The images populated his mind and he wrote what he saw in his mind's eye. If dreams are precognitive, then PKD's writings, fired by these waking dreams, would also be similarly precognitive.

In 1977, PKD informed his interviewers, D. Scott Apel and Kevin Briggs, that 'the more time passed, the more I was forced to face the actuality of the precognitive elements.'[277] Later PKD suggested that the future can be seen because it is like a groove on a long-playing gramophone record. The future is already recorded, it is just that the needle has yet to get to it. These days we have a much better analogy, digital video games. Every outcome of every game-decision made by the player is already digitally encoded within the medium. When the decision is made, the already-recorded outcome is uploaded on to the screen.

Although PKD never mentions this in any of his writings, this dream-precognition model was first proposed by British writer J.W. Dunne in his hugely influential book *An Experiment with Time* (1927). Dunne suggested that all of our dreams contain precognitive elements, the skill being to remember these elements and to isolate them from the dream symbolism created by the subconscious mind. Dunne also concluded that the information contained in precognitive dreams is taken from future personal experiences. In other words, the precognitions will involve elements of future personal experiences. Could these be the source of PKD's precognitions?

PKD had long been aware that what we presume to be the flow of time is simply our interpretation of other phenomena. In his short time at UCAL, he had been introduced to the philosophy of David Hume. Hume suggested how it is not always axiomatic that cause precedes effect. PKD was to refer back to this discovery of Hume in an unpublished paper from the late 1960s entitled 'The Day the Gods Stopped Laughing'. In this he refers to Hume's philosophy of causality.

> 'In one of the most brilliant papers in the English language Hume made it clear that what we speak of as "causality" is nothing more than the phenomenon of repetition. When we mix sulphur with saltpeter and charcoal we always get gunpowder. This is true of every event subsumed by a causal law – in other words, everything which can be called scientific knowledge. "It is custom which rules," Hume said, and in that one sentence undermined both science and philosophy.'

In other words, we confuse time flow with repetition. However, this did not really answer PKD's burning question as to how information from the future can be 'transmitted' into the past. In an article in *Harper's* magazine in July 1974, PKD discovered a theory that fitted in perfectly with his own experiences. Written by the Hungarian-British author Arthur Koestler, the article discussed the possible existence of enigmatic sub-atomic particles known as tachyons. Tachyons are theoretical particles that can only travel at speeds greater than light. In effect, this would mean that such a particle would travel backwards in time. The implications are mind-boggling. As Koestler wrote:

> 'They would thus carry information from the future into our present, as light and X-rays from distant galaxies carry information from the remote past of the universe into our now and here. In the light of these developments, we can no longer exclude on an a-priori grounds the theoretical possibility of precognitive phenomena.'[278]

Clearly, such particles, if they were discovered, would bring about a total revision of our present paradigm of science. They may be theoretical but they are, for the time being anyway, theoretically impossible. However PKD was not interested in the science as much as the implications. PKD took this as evidence that the universe was moving backwards from our point of view. This is a theme he was to associate with schizophrenia and autism in his earlier novels such as *Martian Time-Slip* (1965). Of course the classic Dick novel that deals with time running backwards is *Counter-Clock World* (1967). For PKD, this suggested that the universe is moving from chaos back into order. But more importantly his 'discovery' of the tachyon theory in 1974 gave him a mechanism by which his own earlier novels may have been created from future information. As we shall discover, PKD was to create a whole new model of time that could also facilitate this back-creation of plots.

During the summer of 1974, PKD had also discovered the existence of a substance known as gamma-aminobutyrc acid, or GABA for short. All neurotransmitters are responsible for facilitating or inhibiting communication between neurons, the cells of the brain. GABA is the chief inhibitory neurotransmitter of the mammalian brain and it does this by manipulating the electrical potential of individual neurons.

PKD believed that if GABA was rendered less effective, the brain could be open to perceiving messages contained in the tachyon field and, in doing so, open up the mind to information being transmitted from the future to the past. For PKD, the big question was, what was the source of the tachyonic messages; who was sending the information and why?

He quickly decided that the messages were being sent by a future version of himself. He had, for some time, felt that something else was writing his novels. Like many creative individuals, he believed that he was simply a medium for another source of creativity. He called this force, not surprisingly, Ubik. He considered that this force reveals its own truth in the novel, which is not a novel at all but a statement of fact.

> 'Ubik talks to us from the future, from the end state to which everything is moving; thus Ubik is not here — which is to say now — but will be, and what we get is information about and from Ubik, as we receive TV or radio signals from transmitters located in other spaces in this time continuum.'[279]

PKD explains that the novel *UBIK* was simply a future version of himself attempting to rationalize the truth behind a series of incidents in his life that, up until that time, made no real sense:

> 'I see no objection to interpreting the meaning of the force Ubik this way. Nor in interpreting the purpose of the novel Ubik by saying that in it I was trying in a dim and unconscious way to express a series of experiences I had had most of my life of a directing, shaping and assisting — and informing — force, much wiser than us which we in no way could perceive directly; where it was or what it was called I did not know; I knew it only by its effects: in Kant's terms, it is (or as I understand now will be) a Thing-in-Itself.'[280]

PKD then goes on to call *UBIK* the 'future total gestalt of Purpose and Meaning' and that the book's cover could just as accurately be shown as '*Philip K. Dick* by Ubik' as '*Ubik* by Philip K. Dick'.[281]

However, being PKD, if one theory was good then two are even better. He suggested, in support of his tachyon-Ubik model, that the time-theories of Soviet astrophysicist Nikolai Kozyrev created a model of time that facilitated such communications.

PKD makes the point that he encountered the work of Kozyrev after he wrote such time-reversal stories as *UBIK* and *Counter-Clock World*. Indeed he is quite correct in this regard: Dr. Kozyrev's papers were first published in the USA in May 1968 and first appeared in a Soviet academic journal in September 1967.[282] [283] We know that the completed *UBIK* manuscript was submitted to PKD's literary agency on 7 December 1966 and was based on the short story 'What Dead Men Say' written in 1963. Similarly *Counter-Clock World* was written in 1965.

In his 1967 paper, Kozyrev proposed that time is a form of energy that enters material systems and that can transmit information anywhere. As such, PKD concludes that the source from which he based his own plots was from information drawn out of time (in this case his own future). This information was subliminally understood and acted as the stimulus for plot devices. In other words he perceives something, an article for example, when he is 49 years old, and this idea immediately appears in his 46-year-old mind. The idea is so powerful that the 46-year-old PKD writes a story based upon its premise, or premises. Indeed PKD postulates that his future-reading of Kozyrev's work created the model for the Ubik spray can idea.

PKD proposed that there are two variations of time, both of which exist at right-angles to each other. We are usually only aware of 'vertical time', but there is another that runs at right angles to our space-time. He calls this 'orthogonal time'. If we could perceive both times simultaneously it would look cubical, hence his term *cubic time*. He proposed that events are actually located within this cubic time. As such, the idea of cause and effect cannot be applied within this model. Causality can run in reverse or act simultaneously with an event in the past or the future. In other words, within orthogonal time all past and future states exist at this moment.

This allows PKD a degree of speculation as to the true nature of time. PKD suggested that the basic premise of his short story *The Adjustment Team* (1954) – that there exists a way in which the past can be 'adjusted' to change the present – may be another of his fictionalized accounts of something that really takes place.[284] He applies this idea to his ability to recall the name Olive Holt the night after receiving the Xerox Letter.

> 'In my life, this would be why I always remembered the name
> of my babysitter, Olive Holt, when the names of most teachers

afterwards were forgotten. It was because that "name" in divided form would crop up in the Xerox letter, by accident — it could to a certain vague but real extent be found there; I would see it in the Xerox letter and my mind would work in a retrograde way, which is the direction the retention was impressed at the time, when I was 4 years old, because it would come up later — because that would clue me in, in 1974.'[285]

Later, in *Exegesis*, he implies that what he 'saw' in his hypnagogic state was the words 'Olive Holt' 'printed out on the far wall', suggesting that he was perceiving an external projection of his hypnagogic images. But what is stranger is that he states, quite specifically, that the letters were not Latin, but Hebrew.[286]

In support of PKD's Tachyon-Ubik-GABA theory, as I term it, one can cite his novel *Now Wait for Next Year*, another intriguing time-reversal story. This was written before December 1963 and was published in May 1966.

The central premise of *Now Wait for Next Year* is a drug called JJ-80. This is a hallucinogenic that can take the subject backwards and forwards in time. It also allows access to parallel time tracks existing in different universes. The central character, Gino Molinari, can also see into people's souls. Molinari uses JJ-80 to bring back other versions of himself from different time tracks. These are used to replace him whenever he dies through assassination or through the illnesses he acquires because of his special abilities.

A second character, Molinari's physician Eric Sweetscent, also uses JJ-80 to communicate with future versions of himself. Although there are myriad alternative futures that he could check out using JJ-80, and also the opportunity to bring back to this universe different versions of himself, he decides not to do so. He has already checked out a future in which he is divorced and, although he has a problematic relationship with his wife, decides to reject it. In this way, he accepts his fate.

Molinari seems to enjoy being ill. He uses this as an escape mechanism. Indeed because of the effect of JJ-80 he can actually die in order to escape awkward or difficult circumstances. We know that PKD suffered from recurring illnesses, some of which seemed to be psychosomatic in nature, particularly in his youth. Could this be a wish-fulfilment scenario for PKD, to be able to escape from difficult circumstances by going back and starting again? Indeed, this is the case with Molinari. Sweetscent is informed by the dictator's mistress that her older lover 'wants to be a baby again so he won't have grownup responsibilities'.[287]

In yet another intriguing piece of evidence in support of PKD's

Tachyon-Ubik-GABA theory we can return to PKD's encounter with the psychotropic drug 2,5-dimethoxy-4-methylamphetamine (DOM) on the night of the 25 February 1975.[288] By taking this drug, PKD believed that he was able to create a far more powerful model of orthogonal time than he had first envisaged. He experienced the 'orthogonal time axis' as the real form of time-flow. He also came to understand that each person is a single version of a greater entity that exists in orthogonal time:

'It is really true that billions of you exist, and billions of me exist — outside. But for utility, there must be (1) identifying; (2) recognition; (3) creating of continuity and the concept of Identity, of perseverance (a key word in this) of Being. "Being" is a kaleidoscope. I've seen it. It's fun, but you can't add up your checkbook; worse, you can't tell if it's your checkbook; worse, you can't tell if you exist as a continuing entity.'[289]

Was it this model for the many versions of Eric Sweetscent all existing in their own slices of orthogonal time? If so then the whole plot was facilitated by GABA inhibiting the brain's ability to block Tachyon-Ubik communications. It certainly is an intriguing thought.

In the whole of the *Exegesis*, PKD makes one passing reference to a physicist by the name of Herman Minkowski, the teacher of the much more famous Albert Einstein. With reference to his own precognitions PKD wrote:

'This is a disturbing new view but oddly enough it coincides with my dream experiences, my precognition of events moving this way from the future; I feel them inexorably approaching, not generated from the present, but somehow already there but not yet visible. If they are somehow "there" already, and we encounter them successively (the Minkowski block universe; events are all already there but we have to encounter them successively.'[290]

Minkowski suggested that space and time were aspects of the same underlying phenomenon, something he called 'Space-Time'. In a 1908 lecture he said:

'The views of space and time which I wish to lay before you have sprung from the soil of experimental physics, and therein lies their strength. They are radical. Henceforth space, by itself, and time, by itself, are doomed to fade away into mere shadows, and only a kind of union of the two will preserve as an independent reality.'[291]

We live in a world of three dimensions, breadth, height and length. By introducing time as a dimension Minkowski radically changed the way scientists perceive reality. So what do scientists actually mean when they talk about four dimensions? Look at a pencil and the shadow it casts on to a flat surface. In our three-dimensional world, the pencil has a defined length that you can measure with a ruler. This length is consistent at all times. However, if you twist the pencil and watch the shadow, the shape and length of the pencil's shadow on the two-dimensional flat surface changes. Indeed by changing the angle of the pencil you can make the shadow zero, or as long as the pencil itself, or any length in between. The length of the shadow in two dimensions depends upon the orientation of the shadow in three dimensions.

Minkowski said that the pencil also has a fourth dimensional length, which he termed its 'extension'. This extension, however, is not in space but in spacetime. This is the pencil as it exists in time. As it progresses through time it follows what is termed its 'worldline'. For example, if I chose to take a photograph of the pencil using a slow shutter speed of, say a tenth of a second, and I move the pencil backwards and forwards, the pencil, when photographed, will cease to be a pencil shape but will be an oblong with a length corresponding to how far I moved the pencil from side to side. It will have a depth equivalent to the width of the pencil and it will be seen as a solid object. The photograph will show the timeline of the pencil in four dimensions.

Imagine that you can actually hold this four-dimensional pencil. You could cut it laterally at any point and end up with a slice of the pencil as it was at any point in that tenth of a second period. According to Minkowski, all things really exist in this four-dimensional state, including you and me. We move through spacetime perceiving reality as a slice of this fourth dimension. Up until this revolutionary view of the universe, time was seen to be flowing from the future, into the present, then into the past. Like a river flowing around a rock. Minkowski and Einstein changed all this. Past, present and future do not exist; they are introduced by human consciousness. It is we who do the moving, not time. The slice of spacetime that the observer consciously perceives defines the present moment for that observer.

Each individual consciousness travels like a spotlight moving over a dark landscape. Those bits of the landscape that the spotlight has already picked out we term the 'past'; those that are yet to appear in the spotlight we term the 'future'. The four-dimensional block universe is static and unchanging. However, consciousness is under the illusion that things 'happen' in the same way that a traveller on a night train journey sees an illuminated station platform rush past and disappear. To the traveller, the station was somewhere in the future, 'happened', and then disappeared into the past. In reality, the station was static and has an on-going, and unchanging, existence that will be 'perceived' by another train as it travels along its own timeline.

The idea that your future is already out there waiting for you to arrive is a very disconcerting concept. This idea can be expanded to assume that your own past, although experienced, is also, in a very real sense, still here. The 19th-century German mathematician Hermann Weyl proposed this curious idea when he wrote:

> 'Every world-point (as suggested by Minkowski) is the origin of the double-cone of the active future and the passive past. Whereas in the special theory of relativity these two points are separated by an intervening region, it is certainly possible in the present case for the cone of the active future to overlap with the passive past; so that, in principle, it is possible to experience events now that will be in effect part of my future resolves and actions. Moreover, it is not impossible for a world line (particularly that of my body), although it has a time-like direction at every point, to return to the neighbourhood of a point that it has already passed through. The result would be a spectral image of the world far more fearful than anything the weird fantasy of E.T.A. Hoffmann has ever conjured up.'[292]

Interestingly enough, on two occasions in his *Exegesis*, PKD refers to Hoffmann's use of time in his stories. (Hoffmann was a writer of fantasy and horror of the Romantic school who was influential in the nineteenth century. He was also a composer.)

Now let us imagine a camera set up to simulate how the things will appear for an observer located outside of Minkowski's 'block' time. In effect this observer will be existing in what PKD termed 'orthogonal time'. To do this, the camera's period of exposure level (the time the lens is open to allow light on to the light-sensitive film inside) would be set to fifty-three years rather than the normal level of, say, one twenty-fifth of a second. The camera is set up to film PKD's life from the moment of his birth that cold Chicago day in December 1928 to his death in Los Angeles in March 1982. PKD would not be a single snapshot, but millions of individual images joined together like slices in a loaf of bread. This would show an extremely long, snake-like figure that would start very small, slowly grow bigger and bigger, maximizing at 5ft 11in in height and then suddenly disappearing.

At any point in space, the snake-like 'long body' can be sliced and an image of PKD at that moment in time can be seen. If a series of these slices are viewed one after another then the illusion of motion-in-time is seen. However, this is an illusion as each individual 'image' is motionless and timeless.

So, from the viewpoint of our orthogonal being, which slice is PKD? The answer is all of them. Could this help explain a handful of very curious incidents that took place in PKD's life? For example in October 1977 Richard Lupoff conducted an interview with PKD at the Berkeley radio station KPFA FM. This was broadcast in November 1977 and the transcript of this interview eventually appeared in the August 1987 edition of *Science Fiction Eye*. In this, PKD made a startling revelation regarding an incident that took place in 1951.

> 'Back at the time I was starting to write science fiction, I was asleep one night and I woke up and there was a figure standing at the edge of the bed, looking down at me. I grunted in amazement and all of a sudden my wife, woke up and started screaming because she could see it too. She started screaming, but I recognized it and I started reassuring her, saying that it was me that was there and not to be afraid. Within the last two years – let's say that was in 1951 – I've dreamed almost every night that I was back in that house, and I have a strong feeling that back then in 1951 or '52 that I saw my future self, who had somehow, in some way we don't understand – I wouldn't call it occult – passed backward during one of my dreams now of that house, going back there and seeing myself again. So there really are some strange things. . .'[293]

If PKD's interpretation can be taken at face value, we have here evidence that in some way his mind from the mid-1970s was manifesting itself back within its own Minkowskian 'timeline'. We know that PKD was busily writing his *Exegesis* at this time and it is possible that he saw this as evidence of his own 'orthogonal time' theory or, also possible, his own application of the tachyon hypothesis that he had read about in the Arthur Koestler article.

What may be of significance in this regard is that Kleo also reported that on two or three occasions when they were together PKD told her that he had experienced incidents where he found himself outside his body and viewing himself from an external vantage point. She recalled that 'once it happened upstairs and once downstairs' adding that 'he must have been asleep, or almost asleep.'[294]

There is another reference to this, or a similar incident, in a letter written to Claudia Bush dated 9 May 1974. He again cites examples of blackout periods where he could remember nothing. He then tells the story about waking up one night and seeing a figure at the end of his bed. He goes on:

> 'I recognized it as me. My wife suddenly woke up too and
> began screaming. I tried to soothe her, kept saying over and
> over "Ich bin's," which the next day I looked up in my German
> dictionary. It is the German idiom for "it is I," but I don't
> know that.'[295]

Interestingly, Gregg Rickman, in his *To the High Castle: Philip K. Dick: A Life,
1928-1962* (1989), links PKD's out-of-body experiences with him seeing
himself standing at the end of his bed. This incident is reproduced in a
fictional format in *Radio Free Albemuth* (1985) where the central character,
Nicholas Brady is visited by a ghostly figure that he interprets as being his
own future self guarding him.[296]

Among PKD's many influences one name comes up again and again,
Johann Wolfgang von Goethe, particularly his play *Faust*. Like many German
writers of the Romantic period, Goethe was also fascinated by the concept
of the *Doppelgänger* or Double. Like PKD, this interest was based on experience rather than mere intellectual curiosity.

In his autobiography, *Poetry and Truth*, Goethe described the following
curious event:

> 'I was riding on the footpath towards Drusenheim, and
> there one of the strangest presentments occurred to me. I
> saw myself coming to meet myself on the same road on
> horseback, but in clothes such as I had never worn. They
> were light grey mixed with gold. As soon as I had aroused
> myself from the daydream the vision disappeared. Strange
> however, it is that eight years later I found myself on the
> identical spot, intending to visit Frederika once more, and
> in the same clothes which I had seen in my vision, and
> which I now wore, not from choice but by accident.'[297]

As with PKD's own encounter with his younger self, this experience was
inextricably tied up with time and its circularity. It is not a flow but a
personally perceived circularity in which the tail of the 'snake' is swallowed
by its mouth. As suggested by the Minkowskian 'Block Universe' time really
does not flow anywhere. Everything just is. As such, everything that has
happened and can happen should be accessible to a mind opened up to
its full potential. Indeed, if we apply our earlier analogy regarding a 'time
lapse' photograph of fifty three years, why not extend that to a few thousand years because, as we have discovered, within the Minkowskian model
time and space are the same thing?

If this is the case then, under certain circumstances, we should be able to tune into the full information field and experience the thoughts and feelings of human beings from the deep past and the far future as well as all locations in between. Is this how PKD was able to perceive the thoughts and perceptions of ancient Roman Christians?

PKD first became aware of his 'alter-ego' from Roman Times during a particular vivid dream-sequence when PKD became convinced that he had been 'garrotted in the goddamn cave under the (Roman) Amphitheater'.[298]

The garrotting dream was the start of the manifestation of the entity PKD came to know as 'Thomas'. PKD woke up from this first dream and started talking to Tessa.

> 'I woke her up, and sat up, and she told me that I was another personality talking to her. That I discussed people and events that she had never heard of, and I never heard of when she told me about them.'[299]

PKD then claims that Tessa and 'Thomas' had direct conversations in which Tessa tried to convince Thomas that Rome had been gone for 1600 years. In fact, Thomas became so dominant in PKD's mind that for a time he had to give up driving. In *Exegesis*, PKD postulates that Thomas was a version of himself sharing the same location in orthogonal time but divorced from his alter-ego by around sixteen centuries in linear time.

During December 1964 PKD's old school friend, fellow science fiction author Ray Nelson, facilitated two LSD 'trips' at PKD's house. In the first, PKD seemed to take on the personality of an ancient Roman, possibly an early manifestation of this 'Thomas' character and even spoke to Ray in flawless Latin. PKD later concluded that this was strong supporting evidence that 'Thomas' had been manifest in his life for decades.

> 'No wonder I could read and write Latin under LSD. That was not — I repeat not — a former life but my real life and real time, place, self. It anticipated the Xerox missive; that was no incidental matter but the crux of my mission here.'[300]

So was this a real encounter with a fluent Latin speaker from across the centuries or simply PKD enjoying the moment and having a bit of fun at Ray's expense? There is evidence from other sources that PKD had a basic knowledge of Latin from his school years. Indeed in an interview with Arthur Byron Cover that was published in *Vertex* magazine in February 1974, PKD stated that he did have a Latin language experience under the influence of LSD but this involved writing rather than speaking.

> 'I did one page once while on an acid trip, but it was in Latin. Whole damn thing was in Latin and a little tiny bit in Sanskrit,

and there's not much market for that. The page does not fall
in with my published work.'[301]

Curiously Ray does not mention PKD writing anything, but of course, it
is possible that this incident happened on another occasion.

During his second trip, again facilitated by Nelson, PKD reported to
his friend that he had re-lived the final few minutes in the life of a Roman
gladiator and felt a spear being thrust through his body. However, in a
later letter to Claudia Bush dated 15 July 1974 PKD was to describe a
totally different dream sequence in which he was not back in ancient Rome
but experiencing visions based upon a much older tradition, that of
Zoroastrianism. Of course it is possible that within the time-dilation of an
LSD experience many, many perceptions can flow through the mind.

In a 1967 letter, PKD gives more information regarding the 'gladiator'
LSD experience.

> 'Fortunately I was able to utter the right words, "Libera me,
> Domine," [Free me, God] and hence got through it. I also saw
> Christ rise to heaven from the cross, and that was very inter-
> esting too (the cross took the form of a crossbow, with Christ
> as the arrow; the crossbow launched him at tremendous velocity
> – it happened very fast, once he had been placed in position).'

In one of her interviews with Lawrence Sutin, Tessa describes a curious
event that took place in late February 1974, after PKD had had his 'pink
light' experience but before the manifestation of VALIS. Tessa woke up to
a snake-like hissing noise. PKD was in a deep sleep but was hissing loudly.
Finally the hissing stopped and then:

> 'He cried a little and started praying in Latin. "*Libera me
> Domine*". It was something he had learned from an opera.'[302]

But PKD was insistent that it was more than simple subliminal memories
from his present life. Much later, in September 1981, PKD wrote a letter
to Patricia Warrick in which he expands on his orthogonal time model and
attempts to explain why all the information located within orthogonal
time can be made available to a consciousness open to it. Here is what
PKD wrote over 30 years ago:

> 'The universe is an information retrieval system; which is to say,
> everything that has ever happened, ever been, each arrangement
> and detail – all are stored in the present moment as informa-
> tion; what we lack is the access or entry mechanism to this
> stored information. You can see how UBIK fits in; what I call
> the Platonic forms axes, where the past of each object – all its

prior manifestations along the Form axis – this is all stored in
the present object and can be retrieved.'[303]

Although PKD seems not to have made the link, this idea had been with
him for some time. In the first chapter of *The Divine Invasion* (1981) PKD's
central protagonist, Herb Asher, discusses how it came about that James
Joyce 'precognized' audiotapes in his novel *Finnegan's Wake*. Asher points
out that Joyce called them 'talk-tapes'. Using his character as a cipher PKD
writes:

> 'I'm going to prove that *Finnegan's Wake* is an information
> pool based on computer memory systems that didn't exist
> until a century after James Joyce's era; that Joyce was plugged
> into a cosmic consciousness from which he derived the inspi-
> ration for his entire corpus of work.'[304]

PKD's experiences led him to believe that the creative process involves the
acquisition of information from an underlying field that can be accessed
by the brain under certain 'altered-states of consciousness'.

This is again astounding evidence that PKD seemed to be actually
doing what he suggests Joyce did; accessing information from some
form of infinite data-field. This is in keeping with the work of modern-
day researchers such as Ervin Laszlo and Bernard Haisch, both of whom
have suggested that this 'library' is, in fact, something known as the
Zero-Point Field.[305]

He warms to this theme and, in a subsequent letter to Warrick dated
2 October 1981, PKD links the information field with Gnosticism. He
suggests that 'the Gnostic receives the total picture of reality; the non-
Gnostic receives only a mere fragment.'[306] PKD described this full reality
as being the 'Palm-Tree Garden' as he termed it. The illusory world that
is presented to us by our crude senses PKD called the Black-Iron Prison.
We are trapped in this prison-of-the senses and only occasionally, through
epiphanies, theophanies or other induced altered-states, do we perceive
the 'real' reality', what the Gnostics called the 'Pleroma'.

As we have already discovered, PKD used the analogy of a long-playing
record to explain his model. The music 'encoded' within the groves is not
accessible under normal circumstances. A stylus and an amplifier are needed
to actually draw the music out of the groove. PKD suggested that the
Gnostics were able to access the 'music' encoded within reality.

To the Gnostics, access must have seemed to be divine revelation, and
in a sense it is, for this information lies on a radically different plane to
normal reality: it is truly supernatural just as music might be regarded as
'supernatural' in relationship to the record-groove.

At that time, many of PKD's associates thought that this analysis of reality was evidence that he was going crazy. In a sense he was, in that he was using early 1980s technology as an analogy for what his hypnagogic revelations were telling him. He simply did not have the reference material at hand to describe in any understandable way what he was uploading from the Zero-Point Field. Imagine if he had survived into the 21st century. Suddenly his analogies would not only be far more powerful, but also far more understandable. Most of us are well aware of how digital recording works. We are used to using CDs and lasers to draw up music from a series of binary codes.

Nowadays we have artificial reality computer games within whose three-dimensional worlds we can wander at will. These first-person role-playing games involve the player in a fully sensory experience. Indeed with the next generation of 3D games they will be able to duplicate our everyday experience of the universe in a digital format. This is what PKD was trying to describe. Perhaps he was not crazy, just prescient.

If PKD really was able to perceive information from his own future encoded in the Zero-Point Field then what was processing this information for him? It was clear that he could only access this information during altered-states of consciousness, usually within a semi-dream state known as hypnagogia. It was here that his everyday, waking consciousness could 'meld' with another being that co-existed within his mind. This being seemed to have access to all areas of PKD's life. It seemed to exist like a 'long body' and could manifest anywhere along PKD's personal Minkowskian timeline.

An example of a visitation from his future self may have occurred in December 1972. At that time, PKD's health took a distinct turn for the worse. He contracted double pneumonia and became seriously ill. There is a period during the development of pneumonia known as the 'crisis'. This was first described by Hippocrates and it is the point in which the fever becomes so high that the patient either dies or recovers. This is usually accompanied by hallucinations. It comes as no surprise that with PKD the hallucinations were particularly powerful. It seems that he suffered this illness at home, that is, in the apartment that both he and Tessa were convinced was haunted. It is therefore not surprising that PKD had one of his classic 'bedside' visions during his 'crisis'. In this, PKD believed that he was visited by Death himself. He described him as a figure wearing a single-breasted plastic suit and carrying a sample case full of psychological tests.

> 'Death pointed to a rising road, up a long twisting hillside,
> and indicated to me that there was a mental hospital at the
> top of the hill there where I could go and take it easy and

not have to try anymore. He led me up the winding road toward it, higher and higher.'[307]

At that point Tessa came into the bedroom to see if he was okay. PKD found himself 'instantly back in bed sitting up against my pillow'.[308]

This sounds like a classic 'near-death experience' (NDE). This phenomenon is associated with the out-of-body experience (OBE), something that PKD had described happening to him a few times in his life. For example when his was living with Anne at Port Reyes Station he reported to Anne at least two out-of-body experiences. The first involved walking into the living room and seeing himself 'already there'.[309] Of possibly greater significance when we review his 'Doppelgänger' experiences is the following curious event.

> 'I was lying in bed and I saw myself standing by the bed getting dressed. Suddenly I was in the body that was getting dressed, looking down on the body that was in bed.'[310]

So if PKD's model is correct, then a version of himself existed within orthogonal time and could appear, as if from nowhere, to assist his other self existing in linear time. Indeed, if this 'Orthogonal-PKD' had access to all the outcomes of every decision that 'Linear PKD' will make throughout his life, then this being would seem to be a form of 'guardian angel' or, as PKD termed it in *Exegesis*, his 'Daimon'.

> 'Eureka! I've been reading Rollo May's *Love and Will*. He describes Eros, the spirit of life, mediator between men and gods, partaking of the human and the divine; it is the *élan vital* of Bergson, Dionysos, it is especially Socrates' daimon – this is the voice I hear; this is what "possessed" me in 3-74.'[311]

The first manifestation of this entity took place during a physics examination when PKD was a teenager. The environment of the examination hall was obviously threatening to PKD and he found that he could not recall the principles he needed to answer the questions correctly.

> 'I sat for almost two hours staring at the page and my college entrance depended on getting that test right. It was the final test . . . I didn't understand the principle. I didn't even remember the principle let alone know how to apply it. I prayed and prayed and prayed and prayed and then this voice clicked in and said . . . "the principle is really very simple." And then it went on and stated the principle and it explained how it was applied . . . I got (the test) back with an "A".'[312]

Unfortunately, his overall exam results were such that he was not, at that stage, to progress further in his education. Indeed, the voice seemed to go quiet for a few years. However, there was one very curious event that took place in 1950 when PKD and Kleo moved into their new home at 1126 Francisco Street. In her biography of PKD, Anne recalls a throwaway comment that PKD made to her many years later.

> '"One day, a fly buzzed and buzzed, circling around in the living room. I watched it for a while and then I began to hear a tiny voice talking." He didn't tell me what it said, and I was so amazed at his experience I didn't ask.'[313]

Here we have PKD 'hearing voices'. Clearly this was a very different set of circumstances to the supportive 'A.I.' voice that had assisted him in his physics exam. It is unfortunate that Anne did not ask PKD exactly what the 'tiny voice' was talking about. Of possible significance is that in the June 1957 edition of *Playboy* magazine was a short story by George Langelaan called *The Fly*. In one sequence a character thinks he hears a fly speak to him in a tiny, human voice. Could this have been what influenced PKD's tale?

In an interview by Gregg Rickman in October 1981, PKD was asked if the 'Voice' had continued throughout the 1950s. PKD replied that it disappeared only to re-appear under very prosaic circumstances in the 1960s. He described how he had been watching a TV programme about the Galapagos turtles. The fight for survival of one particular female turtle had really upset him. After laying her eggs she had turned in the wrong direction and instead of going towards the sea she crawled inland. Soon the heat had brought about extreme dehydration. She was dying. As she began to fade, her legs were still seen to be moving. The film had been edited to give the impression that the dying turtle was imagining she was back in the ocean. He went to bed with this tragic image in his mind. He woke up in the night to hear the same voice that he had heard many years before during his physics exam. It explained to him that the turtle actually believed that she was in the water.

> 'I was just terribly amazed and dumbfounded to hear that voice again. It wasn't my own voice because one of the sentences the voice said was "And she shall see the sea" and I would not use the two words "see" and "sea" in the same sentence. It tends to do that, use word choices I don't use. One time it used the expression "a very poisonous poison" which I would not use.'[314]

In *Exegesis* he also terms this voice to be the 'A.I. Voice', 'Diana', 'Sophia' or the 'Shekinah'. All these are divine female principles. Although it is not clear from PKD's description, it is reasonable to conclude from the female archetypes that he linked to 'the voice' that it was the voice of a young woman. In his 1981 interview with John Boonstra, he added that he thought the voice to be *ruah*, the 'Spirit of God'.

> 'I only hear the voice of the spirit when I am falling asleep or waking up. I have to be very receptive to hear it. It's extremely faint. It sounds as though it is coming from a million miles away.'[315]

This is again evidence that this 'Voice' was inextricably related to PKD's hypnagogic states.

He finally concludes that this voice is that of his 'daimon', a guide that is located in the non-dominant hemisphere of the brain. He drew this conclusion not through pure subjective experience but by a decades-long search for answers to his own peculiar psychology. He wanted scientific answers and his search was to uncover some fascinating possibilities.

2. Daimonic Duality – The Science

By the mid-1940s, brain surgery had advanced to such an extent that a very radical operation could be considered, something known as a commissurotomy. This involved severing something known as the corpus callosum, a wide, flat bundle of neural fibres found beneath the cortex. In effect this structure facilitates communication between the right and left hemispheres of the brain. By cutting it surgeons believed that they could restrict epilepsy to one of the hemispheres, thus allowing a patient to remain conscious during a seizure.

The pioneer of this radical form of surgery was Roger Wolcott Sperry. Together with his associate Joseph Bogen and student Michael Gazzaniga, Sperry carried out a series of operations that were to bring about a stunning truth about the human brain – we all have two personalities co-existing in our head. In 1974, Sperry made his thoughts on this crystal clear.

> '. . .It is our own interpretation . . . that the minor hemisphere is indeed a conscious system in its own right, perceiving, thinking, remembering, reasoning, willing, and emoting, all at a characteristically human level, and. . . both the left and the right hemisphere may be conscious simultaneously in different, even in mutually conflicting, mental experiences that run along in parallel.'[316]

And, in 1976, Sperry made this amazing statement:

> 'In our split-brain studies of the past two decades, the surgically
> separated hemispheres of animals and man have been shown
> to perceive, learn, and remember independently, each hemi-
> sphere evidently cut off from the conscious experience of the
> other. In man the language dominant hemisphere further
> reports verbally that it is not consciously aware of the concom-
> itant or immediately preceding mental performances of the
> disconnected partner hemisphere. These test performances of
> which the speaking hemisphere remains unaware obviously
> involve perception, comprehension, and in some cases non-verbal
> memory. Reasoning and concept formation of different kinds
> depending on the nature of the test task. In these and many
> other respects, the split-brain animal and man behave as if each
> of the separated hemispheres had a mind of its own.'[317]

As we have already found, PKD's discovery of these operations, also in
1974, was to bring about another of his own curious precognitions in that
he had already written about two personalities in one mind in the initial
manuscript of *A Scanner Darkly*, asking for an extension to the submission
date so that he could include the supporting material. We also know that
he applied a similar model in his novel *VALIS* (1981) when he presents the
dualistic Phil Dick/Horselover Fat.

It is clear that 1974 was a year of neurological and neuro-chemical
discoveries for PKD. In March he had read a book entitled *The Nature of
Human Consciousness* (1974) edited by Stanford University psychologist
Robert Ornstein. Ornstein had taught at the Langley Porter Neuropsychiatric
Institute in San Franscisco, a research facility that PKD had visited many
times as a patient. What the book had to say about the nature of human
cerebral bicamerality had intrigued PKD. The book suggested that most
people only use their left brain hemisphere, leaving the right to be terra
incognita. PKD felt that by using the ortho-molecular vitamin formula he
would be able to bring about radically improved neural firing in the brain.
He felt that this had caused his 'unused right hemisphere to wink on as
Ornstein says it ought to'.[318] Indeed, PKD was clearly delighted with
Ornstein's comment that in 1969 humanity sent 'half a man to the moon'.[319]

PKD was even more pleased when, in late December 1974, he was visited
by Tony Hiss and his associate Henry Korman of the *New Yorker* magazine.
Although the reason for the visit was to interview PKD about his writing,
they quickly turned to more esoteric matters. PKD was delighted to discover
that both Hiss and Korman were extremely knowledgeable about Ornstein
and his intriguing theories. PKD took the opportunity to discuss his own

2-3-74 experiences with two individuals keen to apply leading-edge psychology to PKD's visions. PKD and his guest concluded that through PKD's use of vitamins he had, for a short period of time, made both his brain hemispheres work as a single unit. This allowed PKD's everyday consciousness to perceive the universe as it really was. Unfortunately, as he explained in a letter to Malcolm Edwards in January 1975, this also brought about a massive increase in his blood-pressure levels that led to his hospitalization.[320]

For PKD, this was evidence that he had over-ridden what French philosopher Henri Bergson called the 'reducing valve', something that limits the amount of 'reality' that enters consciousness. Indeed, in 1911, Bergson wrote that 'the brain is the organ of attention to life' and its role is that of 'shutting out from consciousness all that is not of practical interest to us'.[321]

Later in the year, probably in the early autumn, PKD came across the work of Canadian psychiatrist Richard Maurice Bucke. In a letter dated 3 November 1974 to his old friend Ursula Le Guin, PKD talks excitedly about Bucke's writings. Bucke had encountered something very similar to PKD's 2-3-74 experiences and, published a book, *Cosmic Consciousness: A Study in the Evolution of the Human Mind* (1901), in which he painstakingly describes how such experiences are harbingers of a new evolutionary step for human consciousness. It was this book that was to stimulate PKD into another frenzy of activity. In the letter to Le Guin, he excitedly lists some of the historic individuals who, according to Bucke, shared similar experiences to his own. This included Balzac, Pascal, Saint Paul and Mohammad.

But what really intrigues him is what Bucke terms 'The Duplex Personality' which is acquired when this leap of consciousness takes place. PKD describes how, since his experience he has been aware of a second entity within his mind. He considers it be neither male nor female. He also points out that the 'Voice' occasionally lapses into Greek when it speaks to him at night. Here again we have PKD's hypnagogic state coming to the fore. He adds that the origin of this entity is a mystery. Even Bucke would suggest no answer. PKD adds:

> 'None to whom this happened ever had a theory either, but many of them named the other inner companion; Mohammed called him Gabriel. To Dante it was woman. What has happened, I think, is that completeness takes place suddenly and from then on a dialogue exists. I've found that in me this Other seems to know everything. I, like Dante, sense her to be a woman.'[322]

Indeed, PKD describes 'her' as having 'blonde pigtails' and 'exactly resembles Ella Runciter at the end of my novel *UBIK*'.

PKD was very taken with Bucke's Fourth Stage of human evolution, *Cosmic Consciousness*. For Bucke, a civilization is directly influenced by the number of human beings that have reached this stage of evolution. PKD clearly believed that his 2-3-74 experiences had placed him at this stage of development. Indeed, PKD considered that Bucke's Cosmic Consciousness was synonymous with St Paul's comment that 'The Kingdom of Heaven which is within'. However, in order to link Bucke's model to his own experiences, PKD needed something more than a hypothetical model such as Cosmic Consciousness. He needed something that would place such an idea both within an evolutionary model and within a historical context. He would have to wait three years for this link, but, as far as PKD was concerned, it was worth the wait.

On Monday March 14th 1977 *Time* magazine carried an article entitled *The Lost Voice of the Gods,* describing a revolutionary new theory of human consciousness proposed by Princeton University psychologist Julian Jaynes. Jaynes' book, *The Origin of Consciousness and the Breakdown of the Bicameral Mind*, had been published the year before and very quickly became a best-seller. This was somewhat unusual for a book with such a cumbersome title and even more obscure subject matter. It is clear from a letter dated 17 March 1977 written by PKD to a correspondent called 'Mark' that this article had really stimulated PKD's interest. Within three days, PKD had acquired a copy of the book and read it from cover to cover.

In general terms, Jaynes suggested that human consciousness is 'bicameral'. By this he meant that the two hemispheres of the brain work independently of each other. In effect this means that inner thoughts would have been sensed as verbal instructions by our distant ancestors. They heard the gods speaking to them. Jaynes believed that the source of these 'instructions' was the right temporal lobe.

As more complex language developed, so did the corpus callosum, the band of nerve fibres that link the right and left hemispheres of the brain. In doing so, mankind became 'unicameral' in that both sides of the brain worked in deeper association. Jaynes argued that sometimes chemical imbalances, head injuries or illness can replicate this bicamerality so the subject again starts to hear voices.

In the 1977 letter, PKD makes direct comparisons between the theories of Jaynes and his novel *VALIS* (1981) and his encounters with Zebra.

> 'Well, now, consider my novel *VALIS*. Here is an ancient teaching satellite which is also an ancient invisible "godly" life form. Look at what I can add to my book based on Jaynes' book—which due to the *TIME* article is probably being widely read and discussed, now. Obviously, VALIS/Zebra is the source of these

inner godly voices; the right hemisphere is a transducer-receiver for VALIS/Zebra, and at one time VALIS/Zebra spoke to man in exactly the way that Jaynes describes. I therefore in *VALIS* am saying what the source of those now-silent voices is, which Jaynes does not for the simple reason that he cannot and hence does not try. I say, there was VALIS long ago, talking with man as I talk with other men now.'[323]

Indeed PKD then states that he had written to Jaynes outlining his own interpretation of the bicameral theory. Unfortunately I can find no reference to any reply by Jaynes.

PKD was clearly stunned by this book. It suggested to him an additional explanation that he could add to his readings of Ornstein and Bucke. Indeed PKD believed that Jaynes' hypothesis explained fully his own experiences of his 'Daimon'. In an interview with Gregg Rickman recorded in October 1981, PKD discusses his own 'daimonic encounters'.

'I have that. I have that right hemisphere intuition thing occur. Unless you know what it is it does seem like psychic power. That's the way the right hemisphere works. It's got to work like that. . .. And it seems as if it knows the future. What it sees is in the way of a pattern, and part of a pattern is still yet to come. It is actually seeing part of a pattern that is not fully emerged. It can tell from the section it has what the total pattern will be like. It can fill in the missing part.'[324]

In an *Exegesis* entry he pulls together the work of Ornstein and Jaynes with regards to bicamerality and the implications of split-brain operations.

'My theory: the loss of bicamerality is what we call "the Fall." We could no longer "walk and talk" with God. Well, to restore bicamerality is now theoretically again possible — cf. Ornstein and Bogen on bilateral hemispheric parity. This forthcoming event will mark the end of the period of the Fall. Our sin is self-centered monocamerality.'[325]

PKD called the next step in human evolution the 'Ditheon mind'. He was presented with this term in a dream he experienced on the night of 11 June 1981. In this dream, he is presented with a carton containing a medication that he must take. Written on the carton was the word 'Ditheon'.[326] In *Exegesis* PKD explains how he understood this to mean two minds in one. Later, he concludes that this concept is the 'complete, absolute, total, accurate, definitive, final, ultimate explanation of 2-3-74'. He then adds:

'This one word conveys it all, and the concept may be

unknown in religious and theological history. It is a concept that I would never have reached on my own; I have had over 7 years to work on my *Exegesis*, and never arrived at it.'[327]

He was clearly of the opinion that this term had been given to him through a form of revelation.

PKD suggested that over the centuries many mystics had reached this stage through meditation and other occult techniques whilst others receive fleeting flashes of enlightenment, usually termed the 'oceanic experience'. He believed that what happened to him during his 2-3-74 experiences was brought about by him becoming a Ditheon.

PKD couldn't wait to write a novel based upon this intriguing concept. It seems that he had started on such a work by the middle of 1981.

In a letter sent to David Hartwell, his editor at Timewell Books, in May 1981, PKD describes the plot of a story that he had provisionally entitled *The Owl in Daylight*. In his classic work *Commedia*, Dante created three realms, *Inferno*, *Purgatorio* and *Paradiso*. In his new work, PKD intended to take this idea and have one central character experience all three worlds within his own mind. He called this the 'three coaxial realms' view, a concept he had first discussed in his Metz speech of September 1977. His initial idea was to make James Pike the central character,[328] but after thinking about this for a month or so decided his new 'ultra-complex' novel, as he termed it, would have a totally fictional central character. This person would be a 'double-psyche entity'. He describes this as a person with two minds, one of which is human and the other an alien entity. The two minds see the world in two totally different ways. The human psyche perceives only the middle realm, the equivalent of Dante's *Purgatorio*. For the alien psyche, the universe consists of the lower realm, that of *Inferno*. However, there is the third realm, that of *Paradiso*. This can only be perceived when the two minds are united as one single consciousness. This is the realm of the Ditheon.[329]

What we have here is an amazingly complex novel in which PKD applies the theories of Julian Jaynes and Robert Ornstein with the findings of Roger Sperry and Michael Gazzaniga to the psychological model of human behaviour suggested by Ludwig Binswanger.

Binswanger was the chief medical director of the Belleview Sanatorium in Kreuzlingen in north-eastern Switzerland. In the 1930s he had been greatly influenced by the philosophy of Martin Heidegger, specifically Heidegger's concept of *Dasein*, German for 'being there'. By this, Heidegger meant that we exist in one place. We are trapped within our body. But at the same time we interact with the world that is not us. Where 'we' end and the external world 'starts' is a matter of viewpoint. We just found ourselves in this world. This world seems to be indifferent to our fate. Even worse, we lack real control over our environment. Death can strike at any time and it is, in a very real sense, the only certainty that life offers us. Heidegger called our awareness of our own mortality 'being-towards-death'. Binswanger took these philosophical concepts and applied them directly to psychiatry using them as a way of not only understanding the complexities of human psychology but also as presenting psychiatrists with a model by which certain mental issues can be cured.

Binswanger's model became known as Existentialist Psychiatry. Like all forms of therapy, this is an attempt to cure a person of psychological problems. To do this an existentialist psychiatrist must seek out the 'lived world', the *Lebenswelt*, of his or her client. This is, in simple terms, a person's view of how the world functions for them.

Central to this is the belief that all human beings exist in two places simultaneously. We all know that we exist in the world, but we are also not part of the world. In other words our body is in the world but our thoughts and feelings are not. We share the external world with others whereas in our internal world we are totally alone. These two worlds are known by the Greek terms, the *idios kosmos* and the *koinos kosmos*. In 1975, PKD attempted to explain his understanding of these concepts.

> 'I have been very much influenced by the thinking of the European existential psychologists, who posit this: for each person there are two worlds, the *idios kosmos*, which is a *unique* private world, and the *koinos kosmos*, which literally means *shared* world (just as *idios* means private). No person can tell which part of his total worldview is *idios kosmos* and which is *koinos kosmos*, except by the achievement of a strong empathetic rapport with other people.'[330]

In his 1968 novel *A Maze of Death*, PKD introduced these esoteric concepts into what seems to be, on the surface anyway, a very standard, if somewhat oddly plotted, science fiction story. In a telling line, the central character, Seth Morley, observes that his fellow colonists are exhibiting a 'kind of idiocy. Each of you seems to be living in his own private world'. Critic Eugene Warren points out that here we have PKD playing on the word 'idiocy' from the Greek root 'idios', meaning private.[331]

Binswanger grafted onto this structure of the inner and outer perceptions the idea that we all also exist in three different worlds; the *Umwelt*, the *Mitwelt* and the *Eigenwelt*. These are, respectively, the physical world of external things, the social world and a person's inner, private world.

In *Exegesis*, PKD defined his interpretation of these three worlds.

'These categories obviously correspond to the three persons of the Trinity. Historically, god-above-the-universe is encountered first (the *Umwelt* of the European Existential psychiatrists), then god-with-us as a human (the *Mitwelt*, which for us would be the second period of man-god encounter: the encounter with Christ), then the third and final: God within, the Holy Spirit (the *Eigenwelt*).'[332]

In his letter to Hartwell, PKD outlines the plot of *The Owl in Daylight* in some detail. In this intriguing story-line the central character, a scientist, finds himself trapped in a computer program in which he is experiencing the simulation through the senses of a high school student. All his memories have been wiped clean so that he believes his is, to all intents and purposes, a real boy locked in an amusement park. The computer that is running the simulation gives the boy a series of tasks and challenges that he has to solve or overcome. However, on to this scenario – hugely reminiscent of modern, first-person video games – PKD adds another factor: that there is another time-axis that is vertical to the inner, horizontal one experienced by the scientist.

PKD's idea of 'orthogonal time' is referenced many times in the *Exegesis*. Peter Ouspensky and John William Dunne both suggested very similar models. Indeed, in his novel, *The Strange Life of Ivan Osokin* (1915), Ouspensky has a very similar story-line to that of *The Owl in Daylight*. Unfortunately I can find no evidence that PKD was aware of the work of either writer.

In a twist that can only be taken from PKD's own life experiences, for example, in his own encounters with the 'A.I. Voice', VALIS and the 'Shekinah' (the female guiding principle within the Kabbalah), the scientist's daughter communicates with him from 'outside the park' – outside the simulation – as a disembodied voice that he simply hears in his head. So, as far as the scientist/young boy is concerned, he is being guided by some form of disincarnate entity that seems to have limitless knowledge regarding the environment he finds himself within.

The boy grows up within the simulation, experiencing many of the incidents that actually took place in PKD's life. It is clear that PKD was planning to present another thinly disguised biography similar to *VALIS* (1981) and *Radio Free Albemuth* (1985). In the letter to Hartwell, PKD describes this.

'The subcultures that he is involved with will include: the Bay Area homosexual community of that period; the artistic-intellectual community (which overlaps with the first), political people; the store he goes to work at and the fellow employees and boss; an enigmatic venerable figure based on Tony Boucher who encourages the boy to become an SF writer.'[333]

The boy then marries a woman who is, in fact, an incarnation of his own daughter. With her guidance he is able to solve all the problems thrown up by the computer and 'ascends', as PKD terms it, 'all the way to what is called "The Eighth Level"' when he will be:

> 'Sprung from the Park; he will not just be rewarded by Paradiso – he will remember his true identity and return to the real world.'[334]

Sadly, *The Owl in Daylight* was never published. Indeed, it also appeared in various differing plot-lines in PKD's letters. However, in his very last completed novel, *The Transmigration of Timothy Archer* (1982), PKD did manage to pull together many of the themes and concepts regarding his recently acquired understanding of human psychic duality. The curious title reflects the fact that, towards the end of the book, the dead spirit of one of the characters, the eponymous Bishop Timothy Archer, manifests itself in the mind of the schizophrenic character Bill Lundborg. In effect, Timothy Archer's personality 'transmigrates' from one brain to another. This was a fictional rendering of what PKD finally believed happened to him during his 2-3-74 experiences. The fictional character of Bishop Timothy Archer is a thinly disguised version of the real-life Bishop James Pike. Indeed, at one stage during his 2-3-74 experiences, PKD became convinced that the entity that had taken over his mind was a manifestation of Pike.

However, on further consideration, PKD postulated that the being that had appeared in February and March 1974 was, in fact, his own Higher Self communicating from a location in orthogonal time. This being had been in occasional contact throughout his life but the pink light, whatever its source, either reflected off the fish pendant or else off the sticker on the living room window, had facilitated fully open communication channels with his own Higher Self in the guise of VALIS, A.I., The Shekinah or possibly even James Pike. PKD was keen to understand what had been 'opened' at that time and whether this could be explained using modern science. He wouldn't have to wait long. In April 1975 an article appeared in *Psychology Today* that was to introduce PKD to a whole new area of enquiry, one that lead him to some astounding conclusions.

3. The Pineal Gateway

PKD and Tessa subscribed to *Psychology Today*, which allowed PKD access to the latest research into the brain and its functions. An article in the March 1974 issue stimulated PKD's interest in the roles of the right and left hemispheres, so it was not at all surprising when an article on biorhythms caught his attention in the April 1975 edition. Written by

Berkeley-based psychologist Gay Gaer Luce, this short piece discussed the role of a chemical substance called melatonin in the modulation of sleep cycles and maturation.[335] What caught PKD's attention was Luce's description of the role of the pineal gland in these processes. She described how this small organ, located in the centre of the brain, was sensitive to light and used this sensitivity to control the production of melatonin, the chemical that regulates the human 'body clock'. PKD immediately linked this pineal light sensitivity to his own 'pink light experience' the year before. He excitedly comments upon this discovery in a fascinating *Exegesis* entry:

> 'This news (in Psy. Today) about the pineal body being a light receiving organ or gland is so exciting to me because it means that the chromatic phosphene source I experienced did not merely go to the light-sensitive part of my brain, but also to my pineal gland . . . My brain saw the phosphene activity and was dazzled and delighted; however, probably as far as the brain itself went, it ended there. Not so for my pineal body; it responded to what it received from the optic nerve, accepting it not as entertainment but as signal.'[336]

Phosphenes are a form of light perceived when there is no actual light entering the eye, sometimes called 'seeing stars' when we bang our head, or created when we rub or press our eyes with the lids shut. It must be noted that this was not PKD's first awareness of the role of the pineal gland. For example in his 1970 novel *A Maze of Death*, one of the characters wishes to pray for assistance.

> 'So he had during the previous week gone to the ship's transmitter and attached conduits to the permanent electrodes extending from his pineal gland. The conduits had carried his prayer to the transmitter, and from there the prayer had gone into the nearest relay network; his prayer, during these days, had bounced throughout the galaxy, winding up—he hoped—at one of the godworlds.'[337]

It is clear from this that PKD had already regarded the pineal gland as a conduit that links a person to a higher being who responds to prayer. However, it is also fair to conclude that this article had certainly focused PKD's attention on to this small organ. According to Tessa, PKD subsequently believed that the woman from the pharmacy was actually the Sybil and that the pink light had shot out of her forehead to hit his own.[338]

When using the term 'Sybil', PKD was referring to an entity, or a group of entities, that he had encountered in his dreams. In his two interviews with D. Scott Apel and Kevin Briggs, in June and July 1977, PKD gave some amazing descriptions of his encounters with these beings. He believed that the opening of his 'third eye' had allowed his ego to descend into the collective unconscious. In one particularly disturbing example, PKD described to his young interviewers how he had found himself in a mysterious place where he encountered a humanoid figure. In his description, the singular entity suddenly becomes a group. As such, it is very difficult to tell from the transcript whether PKD encountered one or many of these entities. He describes 'them' as having 'avocado-shaped' skulls. But what was really striking was that these beings:

> 'Had a third eye right in the middle of their foreheads. But it was not a pupil-type eye; it was a lateral lens. It was definitely electronic, not organic, and was removable.'[339]

Kevin Briggs immediately makes the link to the beings that allegedly abducted Betty and Barney Hill in September 1961.[340] In response to this, PKD confirms that Betty's drawing of the entities that abducted her and her husband were identical to those that PKD encountered in his deep hypnagogic state. PKD claims that he knew nothing about the Hill case at the time of his encounter with the three-eyed beings. If this is to be believed, then the similarities are, indeed, uncanny. Is this evidence that PKD's 2-3-74 experiences and, indeed, many other odd events in his life, can be explained by the fact that he was an 'abductee'?

Alien Abduction
1. The Special Child

PKD had long been interested in the idea of being 'special'. George Koehler, a long-time friend of PKD's throughout his childhood and early teenage years described how PKD was fascinated by the Rorschach 'ink blot' tests from the age of eleven. These are created by splashing ink on to a sheet of paper and then folding the paper in half to create a symmetrical, but abstract pattern. Patients say what the shape reminds them of and the psychologist interprets their comments. PKD also seemed to know all about the Thematic Apperception Test. This test uses actual pictures in which the events depicted are open to several interpretations. Patients are asked to describe what is going on in the pictures and, again, the psychologist interprets their answers. He was keen to give the impression that this knowledge had been gained because he had been part of a special, and presumably secret, programme for 'gifted' children. Intriguingly, his last wife, Tessa, also believes that she was involved in such a programme.[341] Even before the events of 2-3-74, PKD had felt that his life had been manipulated by outside 'powers'. He called this shadowy organization 'Solarcon'. If this was the case, and

Tessa and PKD were both part of a similar programme, then was their chance meeting in the summer of 1972 more than mere chance? PKD did not believe so. In his book *The Dark-Haired Girl* (1989) he claims that Ginger was an agent for Solarcon and through her this secret organization was responsible for his meeting with Tessa. In another very peculiar section of this semi-autobiographical book, PKD suggests that Tessa was a reward given to him for being a 'good person'. He describes Solarcon's purpose.

> '. . .trying to learn enough about me to determine whether I should be punished, if I have been a criminal going unpunished, or if I have been a good person wronged and deprived, then rewarded. They studied me and found me to be a good person wronged.'[342]

Here was PKD at his most paranoid. He was being permanently watched by mysterious individuals who were judging him and manipulating his world in order to reward or punish him.

PKD never really identified the origins of Solarcon. In an October 1972 letter to the FBI, he described them as being a shadowy neo-Nazi organization, but he readily admits that this is simply supposition on his part. If we analyse his descriptions of Solarcon in the light of his later 2-3-74 experiences and his subsequent beliefs that he had been abducted at various times during his life, we suddenly see Solarcon to be part of a much broader conspiracy involving non-human manipulation of PKD's 'reality'. Indeed it is important to realize that, although it was published in 1988, PKD's manuscript for *The Dark-Haired Girl* was submitted to his literary agent in November 1972 and so was written well over a year before the 2-3-74 events.

So what exactly was Solarcon, why was PKD of such interest to them and what gave them the power to judge him and ultimately reward or condemn him? A clue may lie in a very curious event PKD described to Apel and Briggs in his 1977 interview with the two young researchers. After PKD had finished recording the first interview, PKD's then girlfriend, Joan Simpson, insisted that PKD tell his guests 'the important part' as she described it. It was only then that PKD divulged this intriguing coda.

He explained that, just after the diagnosis of Christopher's birth ailment, he received a mysterious letter, supposedly from a group of Soviet scientists. In this letter they explained that they had read *UBIK* and that they had:

> 'Already formulated theories that the afterlife was remarkably close to what I had theorized in that novel. They wanted me

to come over so they could find out what I knew – and probably experiment on me to find out *how* I knew.'[343]

After giving it some serious consideration, he decided not to take up the offer. He wrote back with a fabricated excuse for not travelling. He then claimed that things took a very sinister turn. A few months later, a black limousine turned up outside his apartment and three men dressed in trench coats got out and walked to his door. They were a delegation from the Soviet Embassy. They wished to know more about *UBIK*. PKD invited them in and chatted with them for about an hour. As he told his young interviewers, 'I didn't tell them nothin'. . .just played stupid.' His 'Soviet' visitors left and he never heard from them again.[344]

At the start of PKD's 2-3-74 experiences, he recalled, during a powerful hypnagogic state, that he had been abducted by persons unknown in Vancouver in 1971. These individuals were in a large limousine and were dressed in black suits. He told Tessa that he experienced this 'vision' in real-time and that he was remembering an actual event that took place in early 1972, just before his suicide attempt.[345] PKD wondered if he had been trying to escape these mysterious people when he attempted suicide.

So who exactly were these mysterious abductors? PKD's description has an uncanny resemblance to the 'Men-in-Black' of flying-saucer lore. According to UFO researcher John Keel, these beings are a modern-day manifestation of a historical phenomenon that has been reported throughout the centuries. In his book *UFOs: Operation Trojan Horse*, Keel makes the following comment:

> 'Those mysterious "men in black" who travel around in unlicensed Cadillacs have reportedly been seen wearing lapel pins bearing (a) symbol. They have identified themselves directly as being from "The Nation of the Third Eye".'[346]

The Men-in-Black are always associated with UFO events, usually visiting witnesses after a sighting or close encounter. So why were they so interested in PKD and, indeed, was this 'Nation of the Third Eye' in any way related to Solarcon? The modus operandi of both groups seem very similar. But there is another, somewhat disturbing, link and that is the relationship between the Men-in-Black and another aspect of the UFO/Abductee phenomenon: the 'Greys'.

These are entities that are small in stature with long, elongated faces, insect-like eyes and a grey-coloured skin. The most iconic image of a 'grey' is found on the cover of Whitley Strieber's book *Communion* (1987). I recently discovered, from Whitley himself, that PKD and he had been in direct contact in the early 1980s. So what is the link? In PKD's novel *Radio Free Albemuth* (1985), the central protagonist, Nicholas Brady, is explaining to his friend 'Phil Dick' how he has been experiencing vivid dreams involving strange humanoid creatures. These creatures have three eyes.

> 'The normal two, and then one with a lens and a pupil. Dead center in the forehead. That third eye witnessed everything. They could turn it on and off, and when it was off it was entirely gone. Invisible. . . .. Their craniums were enlarged . . .. To accommodate the third eye. Massive craniums. A wholly different shape from ours, very long. The Egyptian Pharaoh had it – Ikhnaton. And Ikhnaton's two daughters, but not his wife. It was hereditary on his side.'

So here we have Grey-like entities with three eyes. Are these 'The Nation of the Third Eye' whose representatives on Earth are the mysterious Men-in-Black? But how can this be linked to science fiction writer Philip K. Dick?

This was not the first time PKD had written about these curious creatures with three eyes. In mid to late 1975, PKD wrote a strange short story entitled *The Eye of the Sibyl*. This is considered to be the first work influenced directly by his 2-3-74 experiences. If so, then it is likely to be the most accurate reflection of how PKD interpreted what was taking place soon after the actual events. We know that, as an author, PKD would naturally embroider a story and add elements to make the narrative interesting. *Eye of the Sibyl* was not like this. It was only one step removed from its source.

According to the Philip K. Dick Fans Site, it was written soon after a visit in the spring by Art Spiegelman, editor of an illustrated magazine called *Arcade*. It is suggested that the story was written for inclusion in this magazine. However, the story proved too complex for conversion into a comic-format. In its finished form, the story was sent to SMLA, arriving on 15 May 1975. It did not find a publisher until after PKD's death when Paul Williams, PKD's literary executor, sent it to D. Scott Apel for inclusion in his book *Philip K. Dick: The Dream Connection*. This book was published in March 1987, exactly five years after PKD died. It has also appeared in Volume Five of *The Collected Stories of Philip K. Dick*, also first published in 1987.

The story starts in ancient Rome soon after the assassination of Julius Caesar. The narrator is Philos Diktos of Tyana, a priest in the service of the Cumean Sibyl. His wife, Xantipe, is a typical 'Bitch Wife'. Philos makes his way to the temple. As he enters the sacred area, he sees the Sibyl sitting with a round bubble in front of her. In the bubble are two 'immortals', as he calls them.

> 'They resembled men but each of them had an additional—I am not sure even now what they had, but they were not mortals. They were gods. They had slits for eyes, without pupils. Instead of hands, they had claws like a crab has. Their mouths were only holes, and I realized that they, gods forbid, were mute.'[347]

They all turn to look at Philos and allow him to listen in to their conversation. It seems that the Immortals are describing the future for the Sibyl. They tell her that a new cult will arise around a 'Light Creature' who will be murdered. They then look forwards two thousand years to the 21st century. She is told that the situation will be very bad by then. The Immortals then vanish. Philos watches as the Sibyl takes out an eye from beneath her robes and places it in the centre of her forehead, whereupon she cries out and faints. Philos runs forward, touches the Sibyl and suddenly sees what she saw – a city of narrow, high buildings – and then he senses that he is falling into a void.

When he comes to, he is a child playing with a puppy in a yard. He has been transported to 20th century Berkeley and his name is Philip. After a short interlude, he flashes forwards in time to the fifth grade at school. He has forgotten who he really is but has occasional 'flash-back' recognitions of current events having been experienced in an ill-defined past. Many of these memories are to do with snake-like creatures.

> 'I seemed to have memories, and yet they had nothing to do with growing up in Berkeley at the Hillside Grammar School, or my family, or the house we lived in. . . they had to do with snakes. I know now why I dreamed of snakes: wise snakes, not evil snakes but those that whisper wisdom.'[348]

He then has a vivid dream.

> 'One night I had an odd dream. I was maybe in junior high school, getting ready to go to Berkeley High next year. I dreamed that in the deep of night – and it was like a regular dream, it was really real – I saw this person from outer space behind glass in a satellite of some kind they'd come here in. And he couldn't talk; he just looked at me, with funny eyes.'[349]

We can date the chronology of this story from a comment made by Philip referencing that in a precognitive dream, he saw the assassination of President Kennedy. This suggests that the reincarnated Philos was born in the mid-1950s.

Philip fulfils his ambitions set in train after the 'spaceman' dream and becomes a science fiction writer. One day he sees a photograph of somebody wearing a caduceus bracelet. This triggers more lost memories of coiled snakes and a visual 'hallucination involving 1139 activity in both his eyes'. We discover that the date is 16 March 1974. He then speaks to his wife in Latin. The two beings who were advising the Cumean Sibyl reappear. They make his wife forget what she witnessed to protect Philip's true identity but this helps PKD to remember.

> "'I remember,' I said, pressing my hands to my head. Anamnesis had taken place; I remember that I was from ancient times, and, before that, from the star Albemuth, as were these two Immortals.'

This theme of 'benign forgetting' can be found in many of PKD's short stories and novels. For example, in 1953 he wrote '*Piper in the Woods*'. This is the re-telling, in an off-Earth setting, of the beautifully atmospheric chapter in Kenneth Grahame's famous children's story *The Wind in the Willows* called 'The Piper at the Gates of Dawn', in which the central characters, Rat and Mole, meet the god Pan. They are allowed to revel in the enchantment of their encounter for only a short time, however, and cannot be allowed to retain their memories. At the end of the encounter, Grahame describes the slow loss of the memory.

> 'As they stared blankly in dumb misery deepening as they slowly realised all they had seen and all they had lost, a capricious little breeze, dancing up from the surface of the water, tossed the aspens, shook the dewy roses and blew lightly and caressingly in their faces; and with its soft touch came instant oblivion. For this is the last best gift that the kindly demi-god is careful to bestow on those to whom he has revealed himself in their helping: the gift of forgetfulness. Lest the awful remembrance should remain and grow, and overshadow mirth and pleasure, and the great haunting memory should spoil all the after-lives of little animals helped out of difficulties, in order that they should be happy and lighthearted as before.'[350]

For Grahame, this hidden memory is 'the wind in the willows' that we all sense sometimes in our lives. A modern-day variation is the sense that something is not quite right with reality, as described by Morpheus in the profoundly phildickian movie *The Matrix*.

> 'Let me tell you why you're here. You're here because you know something. What you know you can't explain, but you

feel it. You've felt it your entire life, that there's something wrong with the world. You don't know what it is, but it's there, like a splinter in your mind, driving you mad. It is this feeling that has brought you to me.'

We have already discussed PKD's interest in the Platonic concept of 'anamnesis', the recovery of lost memories. He felt that this is exactly what had happened to him during his 2-3-74 experiences. In his 1976 interview with Daniel DePrez he describes the background to this concept.

'In the Greek Orphic religion, they – that was the mystery that you learned. You recovered your memory. It's called anamnesis, which was the loss of amnesia. You remembered your origins, and they were from beyond the stars.'[351]

Note that he states quite categorically that we discover that our origins are 'beyond the stars'. This is why the *Eye of the Sibyl* story is so important. It can tell us about PKD's personal interpretation of 2-3-74. Unlike his later semi-fictionalized accounts of his 2-3-74 experiences, *Eye* suggests that the beings that PKD called VALIS, or more accurately, Zebra, were aliens and that PKD himself was one of them, a 'star-seed'.

PKD was sure this was the case. In his collection was the Jefferson Starship album *Dragonfly*. When he showed Doris Sauter the cover he pointed to the alien creature and told her that he was not of this earth.[352]

What can we make of this? Is it just evidence of PKD being dramatic and trying to impress a new girlfriend or was there something more to these claims?

A possible answer may be found in an intriguing interview with PKD's close friend William Sarrill that took place in January 2013. In this web-based broadcast, Sarrill stated that PKD believed himself to be a 'star child', that is, an alien hybrid who had been placed on Earth.

Sarrill lived with PKD for a total of around five weeks in 1968. Around 1980 he visited PKD and PKD informed him about a book by Brad and Francie Steiger called *'The Star People'* published in 1981. He had been interviewed by Brad in 1980. PKD pointed out that on page 41 it mentions PKD without identifying him. In this PKD states that he is one of the 'star people'. These are people who have had extra-terrestrial experiences, people who are waking up to their extra-terrestrial memories; in effect 'star seeds'. PKD claimed that the gist of his 1966 short story *We Can Remember It for You Wholesale* was true and that the events outlined in the story had actually happened to him. If this was the case then it may help explain another odd and surprisingly little-known interview that PKD did with his close friend Brad Steiger.

3. The Homoplasmate

In Brad Steiger's book *Gods of Aquarius: UFOs and the Transformation of Man* (1976), he introduced the concept of 'Star People'. Steiger defined them as human beings who have within their genes memories of interactions with extraterrestrials. PKD wrote to Steiger stating that he suspected that he was one of these people. He explained that his 2-3-74 experience had opened up his own DNA packet. However, there was another reason for this communication. In one of his hypnagogic episodes, the Sybil had shown PKD the cover of Steiger's book *Revelation: The Divine Fire* (1973) and told him that in this book he would find the explanation of what was happening to him.

In the letter to Steiger, he explained that he was soon to publish a novel that would present his experiences in a fictional format. PKD informed Steiger that he wished to:

> '. . .hide behind the veil of fiction. I can claim that I made the whole thing up. The revelations that I received were so astounding that it has taken me five years to arrive at a place where I will even put forth the concept as fiction.'[353]

According to Steiger, PKD was told that he had been a member of a highly advanced civilization which was responsible for dispersing 'phylogenic memory' across the galaxy. In the vision, he saw himself in a stricken spacecraft heading towards the Earth. He knew that this had taken place millions of years ago. He explained that these phylogenic memories were encoded within DNA information packages. In the letter to Steiger, PKD gives a detailed description of the process. I now quote this in full.

> 'These dominant DNA information packets would be disinhibited—induced to fire—in due time, depending on either synchronized inner biological clocks or pure chance stimuli. Or a combination of both, ideally. Thus even thousands of years later, the primordial civilization will be 'released' in the minds of the astonished descendants who suppose themselves autochthones [*aboriginal inhabitants*] of the planet they now inhabit.
>
> The DNA packets in a given individual will tell him: 1) Where he is from; 2) What made up that original civilization, his civilization; 3) His true nature and faculties; 4) What he must do. Ideally, he will act out a series of responses based on the packet, the purpose of which is to create on his planet, insofar as it is possible, the civilization which his ancestors maintained. I evaluate the current widespread firing of these phylogenic memory packets in those you call the Star People as a matter of supreme importance.

In February, 1974, my own DNA memory packet was disin-
hibited, either by an inner biological clock, which synchro-
nized it with disinhibitions in other people, or by accident.
It fired for one complete year.[354]

Steiger's book *The Star People* (1981) elaborated on the hypothesis first
presented in *Gods of Aquarius* and included a series of quotes from a 'well
known science fiction writer'. PKD's alternative understanding of his VALIS
experience had been published, albeit anonymously. PKD arranged to visit
Brad on his birthday at home in Phoenix in February 1982. Sadly, PKD
was not to make that visit. We can only conjecture what ideas and theories
would have been produced had fate not intervened.*

It is clear from his interview with Steiger, PKD believed that in some
deeply significant way that DNA was responsible for his experiences. He
made this clear in a quotation cited by Sutin *in Divine Invasions*.

> 'This is to do with the DNA because the memory is located
> in the DNA (phylogenic memory). Very ancient memories,
> predating this life are triggered off. (. . .) You remember your
> real nature. Which is to say, origins (from the stars) *Die Zeit
> ist da!)* (The time is here) The Gnostic Gnosis. You are here
> in this world but you are not *of* this world.'[355]

PKD concluded that he had bonded in some way with an immortal part
of himself. He had, in effect, become an amalgamation of two entities; the
Philip K. Dick who existed before February 1974 and a being that carried
a vast store of memories and perceived reality from a totally different
vantage point. He called this 'life-form' a *plasmate*.

> I term the Immortal One a plasmate, because it is a form of
> energy; it is living information. It replicates itself – not
> through information or in information – but as. . .information.
> The plasmate can crossbond with a human, creating what I
> call a homoplasmate. This annexes the mortal human perman-
> ently to the plasmate. We know this as the 'birth from above'
> or 'birth from the Spirit'. It was initiated by Christ, but my
> Empire destroyed all the homoplasmates before they could

---

* In an interesting aside, Brad Steiger writes: 'I had a revelation to share with Phil: The
essence of *The Divine Fire* had been given to me in 1969 during a late night encounter with
a hooded, monk-like entity. To silence my inquisitive—and startled—mind, the mysterious
visitor had placed me into a deep sleep, but in the morning I arose with the complete outline
of *Revelation: The Divine Fire* in my awakened consciousness. The book was published in 1973,
about a year before Phil received the vision from the Ruah advising him to read it.'

replicate. . . As living information, the plasmate travels up the optic nerve of a human to the pineal body. It uses the human brain as a female host in which to replicate itself into its active form. This is an interspecies symbiosis.'[356]

Being a homoplasmate with a very active, all-knowing element to his consciousness PKD's life-long but somewhat dormant precognitive skills started to come into their own.

In many ways, PKD's model of the human-plasmate bonding was an updating of Bucke's 'Ditheon Mind' for a late 20th-century audience. However, unlike Bucke, PKD does not see this in an internal spiritual context but in one which involves an external source whose location is outer, not inner, space. The plasmate is an alien life force that has come to Earth from elsewhere in the universe and its ultimate aim is the evolution of the human species. The plasmate itself embodies what PKD called 'the logos' – the ground-state of everything. PKD believed that this entity had existed at least as far back as ancient Sumer and that it is:

> 'Moving in a retrograde direction through time; i.e. from the future to the past, carrying with it an enormous organizing potential, as well as information of all sorts not yet available to us . . . It is capable of infusing persons and even groups almost in a sort of intoxifying form. This might explain the ancient account of "being possessed by the god," whether the god is Apollo, or Dionysus or even the Christian god, that is, the Holy Spirit. In present-day terms it might take account for paranormal powers and so-called UFO experiences, taking the form of involuntary holograms.'[357]

This is a fascinating quote. It suggests that the plasmate carries through time and, under certain circumstances, literally 'enthuses' individuals and groups. This model has echoes of Julian Jaynes' hypothesis. However, PKD adds an intriguing addition to the model by suggesting that the pineal gland was central to this process of 'cross-bonding'.

> 'As living information the plasmate travels up the optic nerve of a human to the pineal body. It uses the human brain as a female host.'[358]

In other words, PKD believed that the opening up of his pineal gland had, in some way, facilitated 'inter-species bonding' between a human being and a 'plasmate', which brings about a new life-form, the Ditheon, or, as he was later to call it, the Homoplasmate.

Could this be the explanation for PKD's belief that he was a 'star seed'?

Is this why he believed that he was being watched at all times by mysterious organizations like Solarcon? Does the plasmate model of an entity 'moving in retrograde motion through time' explain PKD's precognitions? Or could it be that PKD had certain easily explained neurological conditions that facilitated such beliefs?

We will now turn our attention to a more prosaic and less romantic interpretation of PKD's experiences: that they were all in his head.

PART THREE
A NEUROLOGICAL EXPLANATION

Self-aware consciousness is singularly the greatest mystery of modern science. How does a collection of neurochemicals, electrical impulses and billions of cells create the concept of 'selfhood'. At what point do inorganic chemicals become organic and at what point do these chemicals become sentient? Is consciousness simply an accident of evolution or is it something more? Is consciousness located within the brain or is the brain simply a form of receiver tuning in to a field of sentience? All these are huge questions that modern science has yet to answer. The experiences of Philip K. Dick may be explained by the application of known neurological abnormalities but taking account of something is not the same as explaining it. However, it is our responsibility to present a full review of the evidence so let us begin.

We shall start by reviewing the initial pink-beam incident the day that the young woman delivered medication.

1. The Pink Beam

PKD dates this event as 20 February and in VALIS he described that the light came directly out of the pendant. As we have already seen, this is not how Tessa remembered it. Tessa also has a far less mysterious explanation for the source of PKD's 'pink light'.

> 'What really happened was that the rays from the setting sun had hit our west-facing window, where we had stuck a small rectangular bumper sticker. That sticker showed a silver fish sign on a black background, and the silver part of it reflected the sunlight into Phil's eyes as he turned round.'[359]

What it seems had actually taken place was that the reflecting light had triggered phosphene activity. Phosphenes are a form of light that is perceived when there is no light actually entering the eye. As previously described, we can all reproduce phosphene activity by simply closing our eyes and either rub them or apply pressure on them through the closed eyelid. We also experience them as 'seeing stars' when we have a blow to the head or we sneeze violently. It is clear from the many references to phosphene activity found in *Exegesis* that PKD was very aware of this phenomenon. Of course, what we don't know at this time is whether the 'pink light' incident stimulated this interest. One reference in *Exegesis* may be of potential significance.

'The phosphenes — optic neurons — are a primordial sense system by which the "archetypal ideas or eidei" were originally *a priori* perceived, but like the bicameral mind, it has atrophied. Why, the hallucinogenic mushroom bread and broth sets off phosphene activity! As mescaline, peyote, LSD, etc., do.'[360]

But here we have another mystery. Gregg Rickman interviewed Tessa for his book *Philip K. Dick: The Last Testament*. These interviews took place in April and May 1982. Tessa describes the events surrounding both the 'pink light' event and the mystery of the reflective bumper stickers. In her interview with Rickman, Tessa says:

'After he saw the fish necklace on the delivery girl from the pharmacist we went to a Christian bookstore and got a couple of bumper stickers with fish signs on them. We put one on the car and one on the living room window. They were kind of a silver-metallic and black.'[361]

I interviewed Tessa about this in March 2013 and she said that this was incorrect. PKD and Tessa had bought the reflective stickers some time in 1973 and the one on the west-facing window had become a permanent fixture since then. This explanation may have been confirmed by PKD himself. In one of his last *Exegesis* entries, from February 1982, he makes the following enigmatic statement:

'2-74: light (sunlight reflected off the golden fish sign). 3-74 (Valis) light ("beam of pink light") is what I always say, but it was sunlight, as in 2-74, only this time it was the sticker of the fish sign in the living room window.'[362]

Whatever the true source, PKD felt that the pink light had given him a way of accessing memories that had been long suppressed. He was later to call this process *anamnesis*. We shall return to this intriguing theme later. However, the initial pink beam was just the start of some very strange occurrences. The question that must be asked is, are these experiences spontaneous or facilitated by some neurological condition.

I will now review some of the possibilities, starting with the pharmacological and moving to the neurological and finally ending up with the seismological.

2. DOM

During the evening of 25 February 1975, PKD had tried desperately to phone his daughter Laura. This would have been her fifteenth birthday. He was so depressed at failing to get hold of her, despite multiple calls, that he went round to a friend, who gave him something to 'get ripped'.[363] According to a later folder described in the notes in *Exegesis*, PKD described this substance as 'DOM', 2,5-dimethoxy-4-methylamphetamine.[364] This is a powerful hallucinogen that was made illegal on 21 September 1973. So we have good evidence that PKD was taking a powerful, and illegal, hallucinogen during his 'theophany'. In his letter to Claudia Bush, dated the next day, he writes:

> 'Listen, Baby. I am still ripped and it is tomorrow (that was today, when he gave it to me); we talked, and I said, man I can't take it anymore. Later as I was still taking it (the garbage out) he stopped me and handed me the good message. I squirreled it away for like until later and then I did it. I did it. Claudia it hit me like a 1100 of brick fists.'[365]

Clearly PKD knew who to contact to acquire this substance and he does not say that this was his first experience of DOM. Tessa informed me that PKD used to spend time next door with two young men, possibly students. She recalls that, on that particular night, PKD had suddenly decided to pop next door, returning a few minutes later and disappearing into the toilet. Could this have been when he took his shot of DOM?

In the letter, he describes how he announced to Tessa that his 'consciousness was now accessible'. He was keen for Tessa to ask him what presence had taken him over the previous February. It seems that on this occasion the answer was Erasmus. PKD then describes how, later that night, during a hypnagogic episode, he saw a series of maths symbols and Greek letters. He awoke Tessa and asked her if she had heard of Erasmus. She stated that she hadn't. The next morning they looked up the name and were both stunned to discover that he was, as PKD stated in the letter to Claudia, 'one of the first Greek scholars'.

Tessa told me that she vaguely recalled the discussion regarding Erasmus but nothing about PKD being particularly odd or strange the evening before. Did PKD actually take DOM or was this simply a way of impressing his much younger graduate-student penfriend?

It is reasonable to suggest the possibility that the whole 2-3-74 experience was actually facilitated by easily available 2,5-dimethoxy-4-methylamphetamine. However, PKD would have to have been extremely careful to hide this from Tessa. What is of significance is that in none of his accounts does PKD associate this substance with his experiences. I am sure that, had he believed DOM to be responsible, he would have commented upon this in his *Exegesis*, which was, after all, written purely for himself and not for eventual publication. The only time DOM is mentioned in the whole of PKD's *Exegesis* is in the letter to Claudia cited above, which was added by the editors and is not technically part of the main body of the writings.

3. Vitamin Overdose

In March 1974, the magazine *Psychology Today* featured an article written by a psychiatrist called Harvey Ross. Usually the articles were of passing interest but Ross's particularly caught PKD's attention. It described how the condition of a young boy with severe schizophrenically induced visions was improved by the introduction of a high-protein, low-carbohydrate diet supplemented by a cocktail of vitamins. Ross gave the recipe for the cocktail including that 500mg of vitamin C should be taken in the first month, with an increase to 1000mg for the second month onwards. Ross argued that the large dose of vitamins brings about a marked improvement in the firing of brain cells (neurons) which, in turn, facilitates the synchronization of the two hemispheres of the brain.[366]

PKD was very excited by this discovery. As the cocktail of vitamins were all water soluble and easily available from any pharmacist, he decided that he would try this himself. He was already aware of the developments in neurology suggesting that the right and left hemispheres of the brain function independently and that most 'normal' people only use their 'dominant' hemisphere. For PKD, it was logical to conclude that by using Ross's recipe human consciousness could be raised to another level of awareness.

> 'It occurred to me that maybe in a normal person with normal, which is to say, average synchronization, it might cause firing to take place so efficiently that both hemispheres of the brain might come on together.'[367]

He then goes on to describe how, after taking the dose, he found that his two hemispheres did, indeed, 'came on together' as he termed it. According to Lawrence Sutin, PKD actually got the recipe wrong and ending up taking seven grams more vitamin C than he should have done.[368] It is clear from the dates that PKD encountered the *Psychology Today* article after his experience with the pink light. However, we know from Tessa's recollections that there may be a far more prosaic explanation of the 'pink beam' in that it may have been the rays of the sun reflecting off a car bumper sticker. Is it possible that the hallucinations and visions may have been caused by something more than simply PKD's overdosing on vitamin C? After all, many of PKD's subsequent 2-3-74 'visions' took place before PKD read Ross's article. So the vitamin overdose may have accentuated the sensations in the late spring of 1974 but the major visions and auditory hallucinations took place in early February. Therefore we have to look elsewhere for our explanation.

4. Migraine

Let us review what took place during PKD's 2-3-74 experiences. Tessa informed me that he started to spend hours, and sometimes days, in bed at a time. She was expected to supply him with food and drink during these periods. One of the symptoms of hypokalaemia, which is brought about by the lack of potassium, is that the sufferer finds that no amount of sleep can relieve the fatigue. This is why he never fully went to sleep but existed in a liminal, semi-sleep state known as hypnagogia. In this state, something called REM-intrusion can take place. Here dream-images are drawn up from the subconscious and perceived by a mind that is in a semi-waking state. In other words, the person is self-aware and can perceive the dream as part of a waking reality. Sometimes intense visions and hallucinations can be perceived.

While in a hypnagogic state one day, PKD was presented with a series of stunning images that lasted for an hour or two. He was looking down at himself sitting in a large black limousine with two burly figures either side of him. These men were dressed in black suits and were very intimidating. He watched as a series of questions was fired at the PKD trapped in the car. He could see out of the car window and he was aware that the car was driving through the back streets of a large city, which he identified as Vancouver.

On awaking fully from this bi-located state, PKD concluded that, in February 1972, he had been abducted and then brainwashed. He concluded that this would explain his suicide attempt in Vancouver. This was, in his opinion, an attempt to avoid doing whatever it was that these mysterious figures wished him to do. Something was certainly opening up his neurons to a much wider field of perception, be it his hypokalaemia, his overdose of vitamin C or, as he believed, the pink light.

It will be recalled that in one amazing eight-hour extended hypnagogic experience, PKD saw thousands of abstract images flash across his visual field. As a precursor to this he had, on 16 March, experienced a series of brightly coloured geometric shapes and flashing lights of various colours and intensities. In *Exegesis* he describes the experience.

> 'One night I found myself flooded with colored graphics which resembled the nonobjective paintings of Kandinsky and Klee, thousands of them one after the other, so fast as to resemble 'flash cut' used in movie work. This went on for eight hours.'[369]

PKD later describes this as being phosphene activity within the eyes. For him, the mystery was what had stimulated such activity. There is a simple answer, classic migraine. Not once in the whole of the *Exegesis* does PKD reference this illness. In her review of my book *The Daemon, A Guide to Your Extraordinary Secret Self*,[370] Tessa Dick made the following comment, 'Phil did not have migraines – he had bad teeth that gave him pain.'[371] This opinion must be taken into account in any analysis of PKD as a migrainer. However, and this is to me a very important point, classic migraine is much more than simply a pain in the head. It is a whole spectrum of symptoms, one of which is a headache. As a classic migrainer myself, I have experienced only one migraine headache in the last ten years, but frequent migraine 'auras'.

In a letter sent to his friend, Carol Carr on 7 July 1967 and reproduced by Anne Dick in her biography *The Search for Philip K. Dick*, PKD stated that he experienced that year what he was to describe as a 'breakdown'. This is how he describes it:

> 'Vivid horrible tastes and pain of a tri-geminal sort. Inability to spell words or to type. Loss of memory—found snuff tin mysteriously in kitchen cupboard. Lost important IRS documents which I had previously carefully assembled (they still haven't turned up). . . .Bees in head. . . My prolepsis factor [*time sense*] went out completely.'[372]

I can readily identify with these sensations. It is part of what is known as the 'aura state' and it is well documented in the literature. Trigeminal pain is felt along one side of the face and is regularly associated with migraine. Migraine auras are also distinguished by peculiar tastes in the mouth (gustatory aura), a buzzing in the ears, usually accompanied by vertigo, a sense that time is slowing down or stopping, and a feeling of dislocation from reality as if falling down a large hole or looking at the world through the wrong end of a telescope.

There is evidence from PKD's youth that he had experienced all of these sensations. For example in an interview with his friend Tim Powers, PKD described how, when he was in his early teens, or maybe slightly younger, he found himself experiencing a form of frozen time. Powers explains:

> 'One time he walked out on the street and there was nobody up and down the street. Nothing was moving. He waited a few minutes and still nothing was moving. So he ran back inside the house and started filling up any kind of bottles he could get with water. He figured some dreadful calamity had struck and he figured he had better get drinkable water while it was still in the pipes.'[373]

This is a very curious incident. Did PKD simply misunderstand the atmosphere of a quiet Californian day or was there more to this? It is reasonable to conclude that this took place at a location that PKD knew very well. For him there was something distinct about this time. Did he mean that there were no people around, no traffic moving, and an absence of activity? If so, then one can only come to two conclusions; either everybody had disappeared or else time had subjectively stopped for the young PKD. Of course, if this was the case, how could he get water to pour out of the taps?

It is possible that PKD may have used this incident as the inspiration for one of the most famous descriptions of disorientation in the whole of science fiction. This is when Ragle Gumm, the central character in PKD's 1959 novel, *Time Out Of Joint*, realizes that there is something very wrong with his universe.

> "'Got any beer?" he said. His voice sounded funny. Thin and remote. The counter man in white apron and cap stared at him, stared and did not move. Nothing happened. No sound, anywhere. Kids, cars, the wind; it all shut off.'[374]

This is a typical migraine aura sensation, as is a series of curious visual hallucinations that took place during PKD's teens. During these unusual states of consciousness, PKD felt as if the world around him was either drawing in or expanding out. He described one incident as follows.

> 'The walls seem to crush you and then all of a sudden the walls open out like a bellow and suddenly you have nothing to stand up against and support yourself and hold onto". My special sense would get impaired. So I experienced first spaces too small and then spaces too large.'[375]

We also know that a similar attack took place during PKD's short period at UC Berkeley in the late 1940s. These may have been brought about by an attack of claustrophobia triggered by the atmosphere of the lecture theatre. However, PKD's reaction seems somewhat extreme. In his biography *Divine Invasions*, Lawrence Sutin quotes a friend of PKD's at that time, Iskander Guy. Guy states that PKD discussed with him in detail the 'horrible experiences' he had to endure at UC Berkeley.

> 'The whole bloody world collapsed on him psychologically as he was walking down a classroom aisle. It was something of such pain – not hyperbole, but extreme pain that we are talking about – like the whole world disappeared in front of him and he was turned into this painful, vulnerable, embat-tled thing, and where at any moment the floor might open up and he might be cancelled out as a living entity. Those were the kind of statements he would make.'[376]

One can reasonably assume from the two dates that whatever PKD was experiencing it was not related simply to adolescence but can be seen as an ongoing neuro-psychological issue. There is a condition that accurately reflects what PKD experienced. It is called 'Alice in Wonderland Syndrome' (AIWS).

AIWS takes its peculiar name from the children's novel written by Charles Lutwidge Dodgson under the pseudonym of Lewis Carroll. Dodgson suffered from powerful migraine auras and he used these experiences as material for his writings. In the book the heroine, Alice, experiences a sensation of falling down a rabbit hole, growing huge and then shrinking back again. It was first categorized as a symptom of migraine by John Todd in 1955 and is also known as Todd's Syndrome. The visual effects that accompany it are known as 'Lilliputian hallucinations' or micropsia. When things seem to become large and confine the experiencer, the effect is known as macropsia. Of possible significance in PKD's case is that AIWS can also bring about a perception of time slowing down. [377]

According to Sutin, PKD experienced another peculiar sensation in his senior year at Berkeley High School. He was walking down the aisle of a classroom when suddenly 'the floor seemed to be tilting away from him.'[378] Compare this with an article published in the UK's *Guardian* newspaper in 2008.

> 'It wasn't long, however, before I started experiencing more extreme spatial distortions. Floors either curved or dipped, and when I tried walking on them, it felt as though I was staggering on sponges. When I lay in bed and looked at my hands, my fingers stretched off half a mile into the distance.'[379]

Later in the article, the writer, Rik Helmsley, also describes another symptom related to AIWS:

> 'Whatever the reason, my AIWS is now at a level that enables me to lead a relatively normal life, so I've learned to accept it. Undoubtedly the syndrome has made my life infinitely more challenging, but there is one part of it that I really enjoyed: sometimes, especially shortly after waking up, I would experience a kind of binocular vision. Lying in bed, I would find myself staring out of the window, watching crows flying over trees 100m away, but able to see the details on each bird and treetop as if they were at arm's length.'[380]

Anne Dick described a conversation with PKD regarding an incident that took place in his second year at Berkeley High. PKD had been talked into being an usher at a performance of the San Francisco Symphony. He explained to Anne that something very frightening happened to him that evening.

> 'Phil told me that he had a terrible vertigo attack; something irreversible happened to his psyche when he was ushering at the symphony with Dick. He said that his being had sunk down into itself—from then on, it was as if he could only see out into the world with a periscope, as if he were in a submarine. He felt that he had never recovered his ability to perceive the world directly.'[381]

Migraine auras also involve spectacular visual disturbances in which objects seemingly disappear and reappear and a section of the visual field just ceases to exist. On 17 July 1981, PKD wrote a letter to science writer John I. Yellott after reading his article about the illusion of depth perception.[382] PKD felt that it partly explained a peculiar visual issue that he had experienced after taking his cat to the vet. PKD's all-black cat was inside a wire-mesh cage placed on the seat next to him. PKD was looking at the cat through the mesh in an effort to re-assure it when something strange happened.

> 'All at once the mesh receded so that it became ground; that is, it was as far back as my focus-point allowed. Immediately – although there was a bright overhead light in the room – the cat simply disappeared. I sat there, still staring, not changing my focus-point, realizing that my eyes had accidentally performed that Necker cube reversal, but what I was wondering was, what is my brain now going to do with the cat? Well, it – or my eyes – did something extraordinary. Very gradually an image of the cat formed *this side of the mesh*, so that the wire mesh was no longer between me and the cat.'[383]

PKD then describes how the cat appeared as a 'hologram-like image, projected directly at me, as if only a few inches from my eyes'.[384] Unfortunately, PKD fails to then describe how his vision went back to normal with the cat back inside the mesh.

This can be interpreted as a migraine aura in which PKD's visual field was disrupted. The cat's sudden disappearance suggests a classic white-out scotoma. It is of possible significance that PKD was aware of the bright light overhead. The cat appearing the other side of the mesh is more difficult to explain, but it was clearly something to do with PKD's visual system. This may be diagnosed as a 'negative scotoma'. In his classic study of migraine, Dr Oliver Sacks describes this as 'suddenly observing the bisection of a face, or the disappearance of certain words or figures on a page'.[385]

However, I believe there is evidence that PKD had experienced migraine auras and associated headaches for most of his life. In his youth, PKD experienced severe attacks of vertigo together with a sensation of his body shrinking or expanding. Both vertigo and AIWS are symptoms of a classic migraine aura. In his early novel *Confessions of a Crap Artist* (1975), the main character, Jack Isidore, is visited by a strange woman called Claudia Hambro. She is the leader of a flying saucer cult who believed the world was about to end. After initial pleasantries, Hambro asks Isidore a very strange question, 'Have you been having any pains in your head lately? Around your temples?' The woman explains that this pain is 'the crown of thorns' that must be worn for a new world to come to pass. She then asks Isidore if he had experienced any strange sensations 'like silk being drawn across your stomach?' Or heard loud whistles, or people talking? Jack replies that 'for the past month I had had a terrible tight feeling around my head, as if my forehead were about to burst'.

This 'crown of thorns' effect is often referred to in the context of migraine. For example, the patron saint of migrainers, St Gemma Galgani, referred to her migraine attacks as a 'crown of thorns'.[386]

When PKD returned from the dentist having had his impacted wisdom tooth removed he began seeing coloured lights dancing across the white walls and ceiling of the bedroom. Dots and lines and circles of various colours appeared as he lay in bed. He couldn't stand to have the lights on because they hurt his eyes.

Of possible significance here is that the external light hurt his eyes. This again suggests a migraine attack, possibly brought on by the painkillers he was taking. Percodan, otherwise known as Aspirin Oxycodone, should not be taken by anybody with any form of heart rhythm disorder, such as tachycardia, or kidney disease, both of which PKD suffered from. It is also recognized that Oxycodone can bring about something known as a 'narcotic headache'. Indeed, Oxycodone is an 'opioid' with the known side-effect of causing hallucinations. It is therefore reasonable to conclude that PKD's 'images' were either related to a migraine-related reaction to the Oxycodone or simply caused by the fact that Oxycodone is an opioid.

Soon after the arrival of the Xerox letter, PKD began to notice a flickering effect in his extreme peripheral vision. This again suggests a visual disturbance brought about by classic migraine. For PKD, this suggested that the apartment had a mysterious visitor that was camouflaging itself and merging into the background. As we already know, as an acknowledgement of this ability, PKD decided to call this entity 'Zebra'.

There is a parallel to be drawn between PKD's 2-3-74 'visions' and those described by 12th century nun and mystic Hildegard of Bingen. Hildegard kept meticulous accounts of her 'visions' and these give us an intriguing insight into exactly what she experienced during these altered states. According to psychiatrist Oliver Sacks, Hildegard is a classic example of a migrainer. In his book *Migraine* he states:

'A careful consideration of these accounts and figures leaves no room for doubt concerning their nature; they were indisputably migrainous, and they illustrate indeed, many of the varieties of visual aura earlier discussed.'[387]

This is how Hildegard described her own 'theophany':

'And it came to pass in the eleven hundred and forty-first year of the incarnation of Jesus Christ, Son of God, when I was forty-two years and seven months old, that the heavens were opened and a blinding light of exceptional brilliance flowed through my entire brain. And so it kindled my whole heart and breast like a flame, not burning but warming... But although I heard and saw these things, because of doubt and a low opinion (of myself) and because of the divine sayings of men, I refused for a long time the call to write, not out of stubbornness but out of humility, until weighed down by the scourge of God, I fell onto a bed of sickness.'[388]

In his essay *The Speaking Light*, Robert Mapson asks us to compare Hildegard's description above with PKD's experience as he perceived it.

'Then... while lying in bed unable to sleep for the fifth night in a row, overwhelmed with dread and melancholy, I suddenly began seeing whirling lights which moved away at such a fast speed — and were instantly replaced — that they forced me into total wakefulness. For almost eight hours I continued to see these frightening vortexes of light... I felt as if I were racing along at the speed of light, no longer lying beside my wife in our bed. My anxiety was unbelievable.'[389]

In my opinion, it is fair to conclude that PKD had experienced classic migraine auras throughout his life and that these auras became more intense in the first half of 1974. The question is why? It is known that migraines are triggered by chemical changes in the brain: specifically a decrease in the neurotransmitter serotonin, the release of protein fragments called peptides or, of possible significance in PKD's case, inflammation of the maxillary nerve brought about by swelling of the gums.

We know for certain that PKD was in extreme discomfort after recent surgery for the removal of his impacted wisdom teeth. It is highly likely that this pain was related to the inflammation of his maxillary nerve. It is also known that a drop in the amount of magnesium in the brain causes the neurons to misfire, bringing about the classic aura hallucinations described above. Could PKD's 2-3-74 experiences been triggered by a mixture of his gum inflammation and his concoction of pain-killers or was there another possibility that can indirectly be linked to classic migraine?

5. Hypokalaemia/ hypomagnesaemia

In March 2013, Tessa informed me that PKD's suicide attempt in February 1976 bizarrely ended up saving his life. While he was in hospital under observation, it was noticed that PKD had dangerously low levels of potassium in his body. If this had not been picked up, his heart would have stopped beating.

This was not a new problem. We know from Tessa's account that in early 1974 the family physician, Dr Morrison, had been concerned about PKD's increasing levels of hypertension, or high blood pressure, a dangerous condition and can lead to heart attacks and strokes. This is usually treated by a class of drugs known as diuretics. Diuretics instruct the kidneys to extract excess water and salts from the blood and excrete these in the urine. Morrison decided that an increase in PKD's intake of diuretics was needed. However, a side effect of large doses of diuretics is that other chemicals are also excreted, including potassium and magnesium. This, in turn, can lead to an illness known as hypokalaemia, caused by extremely low levels of potassium. PKD had been taking large amounts of diuretics since at least January 1974, so by February 1976 his cellular levels of potassium were, as Tessa states, 'approaching zero'.[390]

This low level of potassium is directly related to an illness brought about by the effect of diuretics on the body's magnesium levels. A diagnosis of hypokalaemia is nearly always linked with a similar diagnosis of hypomagnesaemia, a low level of magnesium in the blood. This is because of the direct relationship between potassium and magnesium in metabolic processes. Potassium is an electrolyte, a crucial chemical for cell function. In order to cross cell membranes and enter the cells it needs magnesium. Insufficient magnesium, therefore, is associated with hypokalaemia and hypomagnesaemia.

Research has shown that individuals who suffer from recurrent migraine attacks have lower intercellular magnesium levels.[391] So we can reasonably conclude there is a link between PKD's hypertension medication and his powerful migraine auras during the first half of 1974.

6. Transitory Ischaemic Attacks

Many neurologists consider migraine attacks and a phenomenon known as a TIA or transitory ischaemic attack may be related. TIAs are mini strokes, a larger version of which led to PKD's death in March 1982. Research has suggested that TIAs can be directly linked to migraine[392]. Indeed, TIAs are sometimes indistinguishable from a migraine 'aura'. In a 2004 paper, physician Nina J. Solenski made the following comment:

> 'Distinguishing TIA from migraine aura can be difficult. Younger age, previous history of migraine (with or without aura), and associated headache, nausea, or photophobia are more suggestive of migraine than TIA. In general, migraine aura tends to have a marching quality; for example, symptoms such as tingling may progress from the fingers to the forearm to the face. Migraine aura also is more likely to have a more gradual onset and resolution, with a longer duration of symptoms than in a typical TIA.'[393]

Of possible significance is that the common symptoms of a TIA include a difficulty in swallowing, true vertigo (spinning sensations rather than simple dizziness), agitation or psychosis and somnolence and high blood pressure.

The similarities between TIAs and migraine auras came to the public notice on 13 February 2011 when CBS TV reporter Serene Branson suddenly started speaking incoherently during a live broadcast of the 2011 Grammy Awards. After a series of tests it was concluded that Serena had experienced a classic migraine attack, not, as it was initially thought, a TIA.

It may be of significance that one of the major symptoms of TIAs is somnolence. This is defined as a state of drowsiness or 'near sleep'. Is this not another term for hypnagogia and hypnapompia? In her book *Remembering Firebright*, Tessa comments that PKD used to take 'frequent naps'[394] and, indeed after one of these he woke up knowing that Christopher had a dangerous birth defect that required urgent attention. It is clear that this information had been 'received' during a hypnapompic state.

So, did PKD experience a TIA or a migraine aura? The evidence seems to suggest the latter rather than the former. It has been assumed that because PKD died of a stroke in 1982, the March 1974 experiences were precursor TIAs. However the subsequent full stroke after a TIA usually occurs within a week, not eight years. Indeed, in 2008, a research paper was published in the journal *Cerebrovascular Diseases* that showed that of 100 emergency room incidents that initially suggested a TIA, 60 per cent of the cases were actually classic migraine auras.[395] What distinguished the two was the speed of onset of symptoms. In an interview for *Neurology Today*, research team leader, Dr Prabhakaran, explained how it works.

> 'This is a very telling marker for differentiating between the two. With neurological problems like migraine and seizures

that can mimic a TIA, the onset of symptoms is progressive. With migraine, symptoms march along the cerebral cortex over minutes, unlike TIA, which happens within seconds.'[396]

Until now, I have focused on either drug-related or internally created explanations for PKD's perceptions in early 1974. However these cannot explain how Tessa shared some of the experiences. From her own account it is clear she was aware of poltergeist activity in their first apartment as well as the mystery of the unplugged radio. Could it be that the explanation can be found in the environment in which these two sensitive people lived? One possible line of enquiry is a phenomenon known as temporal lobe lability.

7. Temporal Lobe Lability

PKD considered that his encounters with VALIS and the other entities were real events. Furthermore, there is evidence that he believed these entities may have been extraterrestrial in origin and that he may, at some time in his past, have been abducted by these beings. Of specific interest are the beings that PKD described by the term 'Zebra'. These seem to be very similar to the aliens known as the 'Greys' in UFO literature. Why is it that so many people report similar beings? It is as if these beings are in some way archetypes representing something deeply ingrained within the human subconscious. Psychologists call this underlying knowledge, *transliminality*.

It is believed that transliminality is facilitated by the temporal lobes of the brain. According to psychiatrist Vernon Neppe these are:

'Well situated for their major physiologic function of integrating polymodal perceptual inputs of all kinds, including those from the sense organs. For example, smell, balance, hearing, and taste are processed by temporolimbic structures; and vision, touch, position sense, and pain by neighboring areas. In addition the temporal lobes are responsible for interpreting various aspects of affective, conative, and cognitive functions such as memory, learning, language interpretation, and sense of self. Thus, complex symptomatology results from firing within a temporal lobe or non-functional atrophic lesions of parts of a temporal lobe. This may be further complicated by alterations in states of consciousness.'[397]

It is also known that the temporal lobes seem to be very sensitive to many influences, both internal and external to the brain. This is technically known as lability. For example, lack of oxygen supply, fasting, meditation or localized electromagnetic fields all seem to affect how the temporal lobes function.

Michael Persinger of the Laurentian University, in Sudbury, Canada has spent his career evaluating the subjective experiences stimulated by lability in the temporal lobes. He suggests that these effects can be induced in everybody by artificial stimulation of the temporal lobes. At his laboratory Persinger has created an isolation chamber in which subjects wear a specially designed helmet containing three solenoids. When switched on these solenoids generate a pulsating electromagnetic field. The experiences differ from person to person but subjects frequently report the sensation of another 'presence' either in the room or, more intriguingly with regards to our line of enquiry, within the consciousness of the patient. Known as the 'sensed presence' this has intrigued Persinger for years.[398] Indeed Persinger has suggested that in people who have a naturally high temporal lobe lability such sensations, when encountered alone or in the middle of the night, could account for many alien abduction cases.

Of possible significance with regards to PKD's encounters with VALIS and the Zebra entities, Persinger and his team have discovered that the release of seismic energy within certain geographic areas has been associated with an increased number of alien encounters.[399]

We know that both Tessa and PKD experienced ghostly happenings in their Cameo Lane apartment before PKD had his 2-3-74 experiences. Fullerton is around 25 miles from the Newport-Inglewood-Rose Canyon Fault line which suggests that this part of Southern California is an area of high seismic activity.

According to Persinger and his associate Makarec individuals with high creativity, suggestibility, memory capacity and intuitive processing show higher levels of temporal lobe lability.[400]

PKD's own encounter with an alien presence is also linked to a profound religious experience. This is exactly how Persinger describes the effects of small electromagnetic fields or seismic activity on individuals with high temporal lobe lability.[401]

8. Blackouts

PKD was preoccupied with what he termed *anamnesis*, the recovery of lost memories. This particularly features in his later novels. However, it first appears in his earliest novel, *The Cosmic Puppets* (1957). It also appears in *The Man Who Japed* (1956) and is the central plot-device of *Time Out of Joint* (1959). He claimed that his memories of one whole year in the 1960s were missing (according to Tim Powers, this was 1969). There was also the curious memory loss in Vancouver in 1972 and again in 1973, coincident with the birth of Christopher.[402] This can be linked to his blackout(s) on the freeway.

In November 1973, PKD was visited by two different movie producers.

PKD drove one to the airport. On his way back he seemed to suffer a form of blackout on the freeway. In a letter to the English science fiction journalist Peter Nichols, dated 9 January 1975, he describes the incident in this way:

> 'When I got back home I told Tessa that in truth, in very truth, only God could have made that drive successfully; I think I did pass out, sort of, from fatigue and hypertension. For what it is worth God drives better than I do. Which seems reasonable.'[403]

What was this blackout? It is clear that PKD, or something that was not PKD, managed to get him home. This seems very similar to a petit-mal 'absence' as experienced by individuals suffering temporal lobe epilepsy or, more likely, a transitory ischaemic episode (TIA).

In mid-December 1974, he was asked to make a video recording at Cal State. Tessa drove him as far as the building but, while walking across the quad he was overcome by a powerful attack of vertigo. This was so bad that he had to cancel the recording.

In late September 1976, PKD found himself driving the wrong way down a freeway. It was only by turning into a petrol station that he avoided a head-on collision. Was this a 'blackout' and a precursor for his final stroke? Indeed it may again have been a classic transitory ischaemic event. He was also extremely depressed and, on 19 October 1976, he checked himself into the psychiatric ward of St Joseph Hospital, in Orange, California. According to what he told Tim Powers, the catalyst had been PKD's small breakdown while trying to buy cat litter in Trader Joe's.

It is possible that these 'attacks' returned in early 1981. According to Barry N. Malzberg in his introduction to the Taplinger *Writers of the 21st Century* collection of essays on PKD's work, at that time PKD wrote a lengthy letter to his literary agent, Russell Galen, in which he describes how he had experienced a terrifying blackout while driving on the freeway. His doctors put this down to exhaustion, but PKD was convinced that it was a serious warning. The letter seems to be a summing up of his life and the accumulated damages brought about by thirty years of overwork. He felt that he had already pushed himself too far and that he would soon pay the price.[404]

So where does this leave us? We have reviewed all of the more down-to-earth possibilities and each one of them could have been responsible for the experiences. Any permutation of the options could also be suggested as a cause. In the final analysis, I think that we can never really know the ultimate causes of PKD's experiences. Sadly, PKD is no longer with us to assist in this enquiry and I suspect that even if he was he would present us with so many contradictory accounts that we would struggle to differentiate between fact and fiction. However, there is one thing that he did leave behind that may help us gain a glimpse of the personality behind this complex individual – a psychometric profile.

EPILOGUE

THE MAN BEHIND THE MYTH

Having now spent nearly a year of my life reading every available biography on Philip K. Dick, having read all of his selected letters, listened to all of his interviews, presentations and lectures and spoken to as many of his friends and associates as was humanly possible, am I any closer to understanding the man behind the myth? I can honestly say that I know the chronology of his life in great detail. I have a fair idea of what those who knew him well made of him. I also think, to a certain extent, I understand his intellectual influences. However this has really not got me any closer to what Philip K. Dick thought of himself. He was a great analyst of his experiences and he wrote thousands of pages attempting to understand what had happened to him during his 'theophany'. However this analysis is not self-reflective in that his essays and his *Exegesis* analyses the significance of the experiences rather than the effect they had on PKD himself.

Fortunately, and quite by chance, I found that in the appendix of Gregg Rickman's outstanding biography *To the High Castle, Philip K. Dick: A Life 1928-1962* there can be found the results of a psychometric profile that PKD completed in the late 1950s

In April 1958, the *Journal of Clinical Psychology* published an academic paper entitled *Personality and Creativity in Artists and Writers*. The authors, John E. Drevdahl and Raymond B. Cattell, studied the personality characteristics of eminent artists and writers and compared them with a 'normal' group.[405] One of the fifty-eight science fiction writers who responded with a completed questionnaire was Philip K. Dick.. As a qualified psychometrician and having worked with such tools in a business capacity I am in the fortunate position of being able to interpret these results. This may give us the opportunity to understand the man behind the façade – the real Philip K. Dick.

As we have already discovered, from the age of eleven, PKD was fascinated by the Rorschach 'ink blot' and the Thematic Apperception tests. He was probably really delighted when, at the age of eighteen, he attended the Langley Porter Clinic, in San Francisco, for a series of psychological and psychometric tests. PKD was keen to put a gloss on these sessions. He claimed to some associates that they were part of a special study of students with particularly high IQs.

He believed that from these experiences and his own reading around the subject he would easily fool the psychiatrists. He added that he could always see through the tricks of the personality tests that were administered to him as a child and as a teenager. We know that he used psychometrics as plot devices in some of his novels, including the Voight-Kampff Empathy Test in *Do Androids Dream of Electric Sheep?* Was he right? Can psychometric tests really be manipulated by a knowledgeable, manipulative individual? Well, in order to decide if this is possible, we need to understand the history of psychometrics and the science behind them.

Measuring personality

In the early 1930s, Harvard psychologist Gordon Allport set up America's first university class offering a course in a subject known as personality psychology, which included something known as 'Trait Theory'. This suggests that each individual personality is composed of a series of dispositions. For example, if asked to describe the personality of a friend we may use the terms 'happy', 'outgoing', 'shy', 'emotional', for example. During his research Allport identified more than 4,000 words in the English language used to describe these traits.[406] In 1936 he published a paper describing these traits and suggesting that they should be termed 'personal dispositions'. He suggested that each person has a unique profile of 'dispositions' that are easily recognized.

American-based British psychologist Raymond Cattell saw Allport's 'Trait Theory' as a potential tool for the objective measurement of personality. In 1941, Cattell moved from Clark University to Harvard where he worked with Allport on developing the theory. By using a statistical technique known as factor analysis, Cattell was able to reduce Allport's 4,000 personality traits down to 16 key traits, or factors.[407] However, for Cattell this was not enough. He felt that if psychology was to develop as a science it needed to have tools that could consistently and objectively measure personality, one that would lend itself to statistical analysis and comparability between individuals. Cattell worked on developing such a tool and, in 1949, published his first version of a test that was to become known as the 16PF.

The 16PF questionnaire consists of 185 questions or statements such as 'I feel uncomfortable around others'. The subject then gives a response to the statement. They can 'strongly agree', 'agree', 'neither agree nor disagree', 'disagree' or 'strongly disagree'. A modern version of this test can be completed on-line at http://personality-testing.info/tests/16PF.php.

A subject's responses to the 185 questions or statements are evaluated against what is known as a 'norm group'. We know from the abstract that the responses to this particular test were measured against the general population of 1950s America.

Responses are then placed on a chart broken down into ten ascending points. These are known as 'stens', 'standard tens'. This is a statistical tool used by psychologists and statisticians to gauge responses against those of the norm group. In simple terms, and using general data around 2.5 per cent of the population will be at sten 10, 4.5 per cent at sten 9, 15 per cent at sten 8 and so on. As this follows a natural curve, the majority of people will be found in the middle stens of 6, 5 and 4, with 50 per cent scoring above a sten of 5.5 and 50 per cent below the 5.5 sten.

The sixteen factors of the 16PF can be grouped into what is known as the 'Big Five'. These are defined as 'Extroversion', 'Anxiety', 'Self Control', 'Independence' and 'Receptivity'. I am using these as the basis of my analysis of PKD's self-reported personality.

Philip K. Dick's personality profile

The first thing that struck me was the extremes within PKD's profile. It is unusual to have five sten 10 scores in a single profile together with one 9 and one 8. The profile also has one sten 2. In effect, this means that eight out of the sixteen factors were statistically unusual in that only 16 per cent or fewer of the general population would be in that group. Indeed a 10 sten score on any one factor would cover only 2.5 per cent of the general population. To have five factors within such a small minority is very unusual.

The 16PF is a 'self-reporting tool' in that subjects describe their own personality. They choose how to answer each statement or question and also the strength of their own agreement or disagreement. Of course, it can be manipulated by somebody who wishes to come across in a particular way. But, and this is really important, the very manipulation of the answers can also tell us a great deal in that this is what they feel is a positive way of responding. So, did PKD manipulate his 16PF profiles? Let's review his responses and see how he wished to come across in the mid-1950s.

Extroversion

Extroversion and its opposite, Introversion, are personality traits that most people immediately recognize in others. They indicate the level by which somebody comes across as a strong, confident, outgoing individual, or otherwise. Indeed, this is probably the best known psychometric and is regularly used in general discussions about friends and associates. In the 16PF, this major trait is based on the scores of five of the minor traits, Warmth, Boldness, Impulsivity, Privateness and Self-Reliance. Cattell was careful to make sure that each trait descriptor can be immediately understood by a layperson.

PKD's scores were outside the average in that he self-reported a sten of 4 for Boldness, 3 for Warmth, 8 for self-reliance, 7 for Impulsivity and 2 for Privateness. So here we have a person who sees themselves as being a fairly cold, stand-offish individual. This relates strongly to PKD's high level of self-reliance. He prefers his own company and is suspicious of the motivations of others. Somebody scoring low on these traits would usually be expected to have a low Impulsivity score. This is not so in PKD's case. I am suspicious that PKD may have tried to answer the questions on Impulsivity to come across in a positive way. We know that he attempted suicide many times in his life and this would normally suggest a low Impulsivity score.[408] It also fails to match the comparatively low score of 4 for Boldness.

Anxiety

Of all PKD's responses to the 16PF it is this group that promises to tell us a great deal about his personality. PKD was at the highest sten possible, 10, for Insecurity. He also scored a 10 on Irritability. Conversely he scored a low 3 sten on Emotional Stability. A high score on Insecurity is described in this way by Heather Birkett Cattell, Raymond's second wife, in her book *The 16PF: Personality in Depth*:

> 'Suffering dominates the inner life of O+ persons. By their endorsement of O scale items they are saying that they stay awake at night worrying, become dejected when criticized, act in a self-depreciating way and are self-reproaching.'[409]

As PKD recorded a sten of 10 on this trait, one can only conclude that at that time he was going through a particularly bad time in his life. But remember, that this was before he lived in Point Reyes Station, and was happily married to Kleo. Of course, he did have great money worries and received regular rejection slips for his mainstream novels. However, one can only wonder how strong his response would have been at later times in his life. His sten score for Irritability was also a 10. According to Karson and O'Dell in their *Clinical Use of the 16PF*, a high score on Irritability may be of great significance:

> 'Note that many of the items on Q4 are readily transparent, and hence easily faked. A high score usually implies that the person is under so much tension that he is overwhelmed by it. Apparently, at the moment of answering the questions, he cannot tear himself away from his problems for a sufficient length of time to give socially desirable answers, or else he subscribes to these items as a cry for help.'[410]

According to Raymond Cattell, an abnormally high score on Q4 suggests bi-polar disorder.[411] Was PKD so stressed at this time that this was, indeed, a 'cry for help'?

Perhaps unsurprisingly, the third trait contributing to the 'Anxiety' group, Emotional Stability, presents us with another extreme score. Here

PKD came out at a sten 3. Together with Scale O, Scale C is considered to be 'the most important indicator for the clinician searching for psychopathology.'[412] This is another factor that is easily faked. Yet, again, we have PKD seemingly deliberately trying to create an abnormal response. In general terms, a professional psychometrician encountering this anxiety profile would be extremely concerned and would probably suggest that the subject seek immediate psychiatric help.

Self-Control

This is made up of only two traits, Perfectionism and Conformity. PKD scored 3 and 4 respectively. His perfectionism was the same as his fellow sci-fi writers but somewhat higher with regards to Conformity, in which the sci-fi group scored an average of 3. In general, though, PKD's responses are what could be termed 'normal' for his profession. Indeed, if anything, this suggests a surprising level of conservatism for a writer who had, up until that time in his life, spent many years as a member of the bohemian fringe in Berkeley.

Independence

This consists of Suspiciousness and Dominance. PKD scored a 10 on Suspiciousness and a 9 on dominance. This was much higher than the average for his fellow science fiction writers with regard to Dominance (Sci-Fi writers averaged a 6) and slightly higher with regard to Suspiciousness. But remember, a 10 on any factor is abnormal, with fewer than 5 individuals in any 200 showing this extreme behaviour. The high score on Suspiciousness is yet another response that would have the warning-bells ringing in the mind of a professional psychometrician. According to Carson and O'Dell, 'Factor L (Suspiciousness) is one of the most indicative of disturbance of all the 16PF scales.' Somebody who scores high on this factor shows marked tendencies towards paranoia. As PKD scored a sten 10 on this factor, it is clear that at that time he felt under attack from various sources. We know from his subsequent behaviour that this paranoia continued throughout his life. Cattell called a high score on this factor 'protension', his short-hand term for 'projection and inner tension'.[413] He does not necessarily see this as being a negative indicator, particularly with regard to creative people. It may be of significance that the average sten of all sci-fi writers was 9. Indeed, of even greater significance is a high Factor L score is also indicative of 'childhood alienation, explaining the sense of deprivation that underlies this pole.'[414]

Receptivity

Here again is an abnormally high response reflected over the three sub-traits of Imagination, Sensitivity and Openness to Change. PKD scored two 10s and an 8 respectively. He was far higher on Imagination than his fellow Sci-Fi writers, who averaged a 6, and, the other two groups involved, artists and general writers, who averaged 7 and 5 respectively. PKD's very high positive response to the questions seeking out information on Imagination shows a person with an intense inner life. Heather Birkett Cattell considers that this trait suggests an attempt to escape into the inner life of imagination at the cost of everyday, external, existence.[415]

Her husband, Raymond, used the technical term 'Autia' to describe this trait, suggesting a possible link with autism. Of possible significance in this respect is PKD's similarly abnormally high response to the Sensitivity questions. A very high Sensitivity (Premsia, as it is technically known) when associated with a similarly extreme Autia, suggests a person who may have difficulty in differentiating perceptions generated by the internal world of the imagination and actual events that take place in the external world. PKD regularly used the terms *koinos kosmos* and *idios kosmos* to define the inner and outer worlds. However, and this may be of crucial importance, PKD considered both to be equally real. Is this why we have so many cases in which PKD's description of events seem to differ markedly from those of his associates? Is this why, as he grew older, his inner, fictional world of the *idios kosmos* became part of the external world that he shared with others, the *koinos kosmos*. It will be recalled that, on occasions, PKD felt as if he was living in a Philip K. Dick novel.

> 'My God, my life is exactly like the plot of any one of 10 of my novels or stories. Even down to fake memories and identity. I'm a protagonist from one of PKD's books.'

With regard to 'Openness to Change', PKD is, if anything, marginally more conservative than his fellow writers, but they are all, quite naturally, forward-thinking individuals. Could a science fiction writer be any other way?

Summary

So what does this tell us about the most fascinating writer of the twentieth century? One thing is for sure; PKD was a very complex individual. His extremes on many of the 16PF factors suggest a personality that was profoundly unusual, even when compared with his fellow science fiction writers. It is important to realize that any psychometric profile is based on the responses of the subject. It is the subject who decides how to answer the questions. As such, a knowledgeable and, dare I say it, manipulative subject, might spot what traits the questions are trying to isolate and answer them in a way that comes across in a positive or negative way. However, this also tells us a great deal about the subject. For example, if PKD deliberately manipulated his answers to come across in a certain way, why did he wish to be seen in that light? To put this another way, a person whose behaviour is odd behaves that way because that is the way they naturally behave. For them, such behaviour is 'normal', possibly even desirable. As such, I believe that even if PKD did try to manipulate his answers his profile is an accurate one.

However if this is the case then PKD's profile is not just unusual, it is virtually unique. In 1981 psychologist Samuel E. Krug wrote a manual entitled 'Interpreting 16PF Profile Patterns'.[416]A 'profile pattern' is simply a chart that links the various factor scores to create a line pattern. Professionals have used this pattern book since its publication to quickly match subjects to standard profiles, each of which is linked to success in a particular occupation or to a particular clinical state. The book contains around eighty of the most common profiles found in the general American population. I have looked through this in detail and I can find no profiles even vaguely similar to the one self-reported by PKD in the late 1950s. Is this seemingly unique profile what made PKD the special person he was?

One possible conclusion that can be drawn from PKD's curious profile is that he may have experienced a form of one of the various neurological states now grouped under the umbrella term Autism Spectrum Disorder or ASD. This conclusion can be drawn from PKD's low score on the factor for 'shrewdness' (M) together with his similarly low score on factor A, warmth and his abnormally high score for imagination (L). Indeed this profile suggests Asperger's syndrome. However we know that PKD could be sparkling in company and the general descriptions of his social life was that he was an extremely popular, possibly even charismatic, individual who easily moved from one social situation to another. However, it is clear that he did not see himself as a particularly warm or approachable individual. Indeed he felt that he was easily manipulated by others as reflected in his almost off-the-scale score of a sten 10 for lack of suspiciousness, and being 'tender-minded'. This suggests that he sometimes found it difficult to read the motivations of others. This may have been reflected in his own paranoia when he failed to interpret correctly these motivations. Indeed with his extremely high score on imagination, another sten 10, one can reasonably conclude that he 'imagined' motivations in others that were clearly obvious in their behaviour.

It has been commented many times by critics that PKD's stories were always excellent, but that his characterization was generally not that good. His characters tend to be used as vehicles to move the plot along rather than well-drawn studies of motives and psychological complexity. Indeed this may be why he failed to become a published writer of 'mainstream' fiction, which usually depends more on characterization than pure plotting. Of further significance may be the only 'mainstream' novel published in PKD's lifetime: *Confessions of a Crap Artist*. In this the central character, Jack Isidore, shows strong elements of ASD and it is reasonable to conclude that PKD felt particularly at ease describing the inner world of his narrator. Indeed the opening line of *Confessions* is pure ASD.

> 'I am made out of water. You wouldn't know it, because I have it bound in. My friends are made out of water, too. All of them. The problem for us is that not only do we have to walk around without being absorbed by the ground but we also have to earn our livings.'[417]

Isidore also describes how he had built his own radio receiver describing how his room was 'overflowing with earphones and coils and condensors along with plenty of other equipment.'[418] We know that PKD was similarly fascinated with electrical equipment so one can assume that this section is purely autobiographical.

Could it be that PKD's genius, frustratingly unrecognized by his teachers and peers, was part of his ASD? Indeed in recent years it has been recognised that 'High Functioning Autism' (HFA) and Asperger's Syndrome can be present in individuals who are, to all intents and purposes, active members of society. Of possible significance is that individuals with HFA have a very high risk of developing severe anxiety. PKD's 16PF shows yet another abnormally high (sten 10) score for anxiety (factor Q4). This may be of significance in this regard. However, it must be stated that one of the prime symptoms of HFA and Asperger's is a lack of a sense of humour. PKD's humour was wonderful and one of the most attractive elements in his writing.

However, there is evidence that PKD experienced a mild form of Asperger's. It is recorded that he had no interest in sport of any description. Indeed at school he actively avoided any form of games. This is known to be an Asperger's trait. Reinforcing this are the following identified Asperger's traits: panic attacks, difficulty with eating in public, poor spelling, having strong 'crushes', the creation of neologisms, the creation of imaginary worlds and depression. Indeed in his book, *Asperger's Syndrome: A Guide for Parents and Professionals*, clinical psychologist Tony Attwood cited a particular case.

> 'Liam spends hours drawing his own adventure comics about his hero, Supakid, who battles evil and promotes cricket.'[419]

It will be recalled that at fourteen PKD created his own super-hero, Future-Human, who used his powers to battle evil and placed this character in a cartoon strip. However, for me the most telling Asperger's trait with regard to PKD's own experiences is the high incidence of perceptual distortions found in Asperger's children. In his youth PKD regularly perceived micropsia and macropsia – sensations that the world was shrinking or growing in size.

Here a young Asperger's experiencer explains his perceptual distortions:

> 'I used to hate small shops because my eyesight used to make them look as if they were even smaller than they really were.'[420]

Indeed PKD regularly claimed that in his youth he had been diagnosed as a schizophrenic. When Hans Asperger first described the syndrome named after him in the mid-1940s, about the time of PKD's 'diagnosis', Asperger felt that it was a condition that could easily develop into schizophrenia. We now know this to be an outcome only slightly more likely with Asperger's experiencers than the general population. However, there is still a degree of diagnostic confusion. Attwood suggests that even today some cases of 'atypical schizophrenia' are actually misdiagnosed Asperger's Syndrome.[421]

I am of the opinion – and it must be stressed that this is based solely on my own impressions of this enigmatic genius – that Philip K. Dick was a unique individual and one that we will never fully understand. He perceived a universe so different from most of us that to even try and place him in a category, psychological or otherwise, is well-nigh impossible. For example, we can draw certain conclusions from his 16PF, but this was designed by psychologists working in the extremely materialistic worldview of mid-century science. Indeed psychology at that time was, and to a certain extent still is, influenced by the materialist reductionist worldview. Personality can be broken down into traits and these traits can be measured and quantified in the same way that all other elements of the physical world can be broken down. Consciousness is an illusion and that mind is simply an epiphenomenon of brain processes. For such a philosophy to accommodate the experiences of Philip K. Dick is an impossibility. PKD felt, probably with justification, that he was precognitive. He also believed that time was an illusion and that the world presented to consciousness was similarly a collective hallucination. Psychometric tests are not designed to accommodate a personality influenced by such concepts.

In the final analysis we may never know the exact causes of PKD's unique worldview. Indeed to speculate on neurological or psychological models can possibly lead us down blind alleyways. There is strong evidence that PKD did experience extraordinary events and that he was, in some yet-to-be understood way, a precognitive. Without these predilections PKD would have been a mediocre science fiction writer whose stories would have followed the same patterns as those of his peers. However PKD was an extraordinary science fiction writer and possibly one of the most original thinkers of the 20th century. Indeed, I genuinely believe that his fame and influence will only continue to expand as more of his stories are turned into movies and more and more people discover that Philip K. Dick actually described in detail the world we live in now. The state watches our every move through surveillance cameras and the monitoring of activity on the internet. Our eyes are scanned as we go through airport security and many of us now download our daily newspaper on to our tablets. PKD foresaw all of this. For example, here is PKD describing the downloading of the latest news on to a tablet:

> 'In a corner of the large room a chime sounded and a tinkling mechanical voice called, "I'm your free homeopape machine, a service supplied exclusively by all the fine Rootes hotels throughout Earth and the colonies. Simply dial the classification of news that you wish, and in a matter of seconds I'll speedily provide you with a fresh, up-to-the-minute homeopape tailored to your individual requirements; and, let me repeat, at no cost to you!"' (*UBIK* – 1969)

So is PKD now looking down from a location somewhere out in orthogonal time? Is he lying on his bed on a warm Californian day in 1975, dipping in and out of a semi-dream state and perceiving images of 2013?

If so, he's probably laughing, for these days we all seem to be living in a Philip K. Dick dream.

Endnotes

1. http://www.philipkdick.com/new_letters-nbc-spillane.html
2. Boonstra, John, *Rod Serling's The Twilight Zone Magazine*, Vol. 2, No. 3, June 1982, pp. 47-52 http://www.philipkdick.com/media_twilightzone.html
3. Boonstra, John, *Rod Serling's The Twilight Zone Magazine*, Vol. 2, No. 3, June 1982, pp. 47-52 http://www.philipkdick.com/media_twilightzone.html
4. Sutin, Lawrence, Biography of Philip K. Dick, http://www.philipkdick.com/aa_biography.html
5. http://1999pkdweb.philipkdickfans.com/The%20Android%20and%20the%20Human.htm
6. Sirois, A.L., SF Site, http://www.sfsite.com/10a/ubik90.htm
7. http://en.wikipedia.org/wiki/A._E._van_Vogt
8. http://en.wikipedia.org/wiki/The_Exegesis_of_Philip_K._Dick
9. Ziegler, Chris, 'A Very PhilDickian Existence', *OC Weekly*
10. Dick, Anne R., *The Search for Philip K. Dic*k, Kindle Loc: 3692 The Independent Publishers Group. Kindle Edition.
11. Sutin, Lawrence, *Divine Invasions: A Life of Philip K. Dick*, Page 12 Orion Books (2006).
12. Rickman, Gregg, *To The High Castle, Philip K. Dick: A Life 1928-1962*, Page 13 Fragments West (1989).
13. Sutin, Lawrence, *Divine Invasions: A Life of Philip K. Dick*, Page 12 Orion Books (2006).
14. Dick, Anne R., *The Search for Philip K. Dic*k, Loc: 722, The Independent Publishers Group. Kindle Edition.
15. Sutin, Lawrence, Philip K. Dick Biography, http://www.philipkdick.com/aa_biography.html
16. Dick, Anne R., *The Search for Philip K. Dic*k, Loc: 3790-3793, The Independent Publishers Group. Kindle Edition.
17. Dick, Anne R., *The Search for Philip K. Dic*k, Loc: 3764-3765, The Independent Publishers Group. Kindle Edition.
18. Vitale, Joe *The Aquarian*, No 11, October 11-18, 1978; PKD OTAKU, No. 4, 2002 http://www.philipkdick.com/media_aquarian.html
19. Dick, Philip K., *Self Portrait*, (1968) from *The Shifting Realities of Philip K. Dick*.
20. Rickman, Gregg *To The High Castle, Philip K. Dick: A Life* 1928-1962, Fragments West (1989).
21. Dick, Philip K., *We Can Build You*, Page 108.
22. Umland, Samuel J. http://www.60x50.com/2011/01/voder.html Jan 3 2011
23. Dick, Tessa B., *Philip K. Dick: Remembering Firebright*, Page 106, (2009).
24. Dick, Tessa B., *Philip K. Dick: Remembering Firebright*, Page 107 (2009).
25. Dick, Anne R., *The Search for Philip K. Dick.*, Page 228, The Independent Publishers Group. Kindle Edition.
26. Dick, Anne R. *The Search for Philip K. Dick*, Page 228, The Independent Publishers Group. Kindle Edition
27. Carrere, Emmanuel, *I Am Alive and You Are Dead: A Journey Inside the Mind of Philip K. Dick,* Page10 Bloomsbury (2006).
28. Dick, Philip K., *Self Portrait*, (1968) from *The Shifting Realities of Philip K. Dick*.
29. Vitale, Joe, *The Aquarian*, No 11, October 11-18, 1978; PKD OTAKU, No. 4, 2002

http://www.philipkdick.com/media_aquarian.html

30. The Selected Letters of Philip K. Dick, Vol.2 1972-1973, Page 50, Underwood-Miller (1993).

31. Rickman, Gregg, *Philip K. Dick: In His Own Words*, Page 166, Fragments West (1988).

32. Rickman, Gregg, *To The High Castle, Philip K. Dick: A Life 1928-1962*, Page 111, Fragments West (1989).

33. Dick, Anne R., *The Search for Philip K. Dick*, Page 230, The Independent Publishers Group. Kindle Edition.

34. Dick, Anne R., *The Search for Philip K. Dick*, Page 230, The Independent Publishers Group. Kindle Edition.

35. Butler, Andrew J., Philip K. Dick: The Pocket Essentials, Page 24, Pocket Essentials (2007).

36. http://www.philipkdickfans.com/mirror/websites/pkdweb/return%20to%20lilliput.htm

37. Rickman, Gregg, *To The High Castle, Philip K. Dick: A Life 1928-1962*, Page 129, Fragments West (1989).

38. Rickman, Gregg, *To The High Castle, Philip K. Dick: A Life 1928-1962*, Page 130, Fragments West (1989).

39. Sutin, Lawrence, *Divine Invasions: A Life of Philip K. Dick*, Page 58, Orion Books (2006).

40. Dick, Anne R., *The Search for Philip K. Dick*, Page 245, The Independent Publishers Group. Kindle Edition.

41. Rickman, Gregg, *To The High Castle, Philip K. Dick: A Life 1928-1962*, Page 184, Fragments West, (1989).

42. Rickman, Gregg *To The High Castle, Philip K. Dick: A Life 1928-1962*, Page 186, Fragments West (1989).

43. Rickman, Gregg, *To The High Castle, Philip K. Dick: A Life 1928-1962*, Page 183, Fragments West (1989).

44. Dick, Anne R., *The Search for Philip K. Dick*, Page 245, The Independent Publishers Group. Kindle Edition.

45. Sutin, Lawrence, *Divine Invasions: A Life of Philip K. Dick*, Page 59, Orion Books (2006).

46. Dick, Anne R., *The Search for Philip K. Dick*, Page 246, The Independent Publishers Group. Kindle Edition.

47. Dick, Philip K., *Five Great Novels*, Page 573, Gollancz (London) (2004).

48. Rickman, Gregg, *To The High Castle, Philip K. Dick: A Life 1928-1962*, Page 194, Fragments West (1989).

49. Purser, Philip *Even Sheep Can Upset Scientific Detachment*, Pages 27-30, *Daily Telegraph* 506. July 19 1974 – http://www.philipkdick.com/media_london_telegraph.html

50. Rickman, Gregg, *To The High Castle, Philip K. Dick: A Life 1928-1962*, Page 160, Fragments West (1989).

51. Dick, Anne R., *The Search for Philip K. Dick*, Page 249, The Independent Publishers Group. Kindle Edition.

52. Rickman, Gregg, *To The High Castle, Philip K. Dick: A Life 1928-1962*, Page 259, Fragments West (1989).

53. Boonstra, John, *Rod Serling's The Twilight Zone Magazine*, Vol. 2, No. 3, June 1982, Pages 47-52, http://www.philipkdick.com/media_twilightzone.html

54. Vitale, Joe, *The Aquarian*, No 11, October 11-18, 1978; PKD OTAKU, No. 4, 2002, http://www.philipkdick.com/media_aquarian.html

55. Rickman, Gregg, *To The High Castle, Philip K. Dick: A Life 1928-1962*, Page 236, Fragments West (1989).

56. Dick, Anne R., *The Search for Philip K. Dick*, Page 25, The Independent Publishers Group. Kindle Edition.

57   Dick, Anne R., *The Search for Philip K. Dick*, Page 25, The Independent Publishers Group. Kindle Edition

58   Dick, Anne R., *The Search for Philip K. Dick*, Page 57, The Independent Publishers Group. Kindle Edition.

59   Dick, Anne R., *The Search for Philip K. Dick*, Page 61, The Independent Publishers Group. Kindle Edition.

60   Dick, Philip K. *We Can Build You,* Page 22, Vantage ebooks.

61   DePrez, Daniel, *An Interview With Philip K. Dick, Science Fiction Review*, No 19, Vol 5, no 3, August 1976.

62   Rickman, Gregg, *Philip K. Dick: In His Own Words*, Page 139, Fragments West, (1988).

63   Dick, Anne R., *The Search for Philip K. Dick,* Page 67, The Independent Publishers Group. Kindle Edition.

64   Hayles, N.B., *Metaphysics and Metafiction in "High Castle"* in Greenberg, M.H & Olander, J.D, *Philip K. Dick,* Page 67, Taplinger Publishing Co, New York (1983).

65   Hayles, N.B., *Metaphysics and Metafiction in "High Castle"* in Greenberg, M.H & Olander, J.D, *Philip K. Dick,* Page 59, Taplinger Publishing Co, New York (1983).

66   Cover, Arthur Byron, *Vertex Interviews Philip K. Dick*, Vertex, Vol. 1, no. 6, Feb (1974).

67   Dick, Anne R., *The Search for Philip K. Dick*, Page 66, The Independent Publishers Group. Kindle Edition.

68   Purser, Philip, *Even Sheep Can Upset Scientific Detachment*, Pages 27-30, *Daily Telegraph* 506. July 19 1974 – http://www.philipkdick.com/media_london_telegraph.html

69   Rickman, Gregg, *Philip K. Dick: The Last Testament,* Page 13, Fragments West (1985).

70   Dick, Anne R., *The Search for Philip K. Dick*, Page 65, The Independent Publishers Group. Kindle Edition.

71   Dick, Anne R., *The Search for Philip K. Dick*, Page 66, The Independent Publishers Group. Kindle Edition.

72   Wintz, Henri, Hyde, David, *Precious Artifacts: A Philip K. Dick Bibliography*, Page 62, Wide Books (2012).

73   Warrick, Patricia S., *Mind in Motion: The Fiction of Philip K. Dick*, Page 95, Southern Illinois University Press (1987).

74   Dick, Anne R., *The Search for Philip K. Dick*, Pages 84-85, The Independent Publishers Group. Kindle Edition.

75   Dick, Anne R., *The Search for Philip K. Dick*, Pages 86, The Independent Publishers Group. Kindle Edition.

76   Boonstra, John, *Rod Serling's The Twilight Zone Magazine*, Vol. 2, No. 3, June 1982, Pages 47-52 http://www.philipkdick.com/media_twilightzone.html

77   Dick, Anne R., *The Search for Philip K. Dick*, Page 94, The Independent Publishers Group. Kindle Edition.

78   Dick, Anne R., *The Search for Philip K. Dick*, Page 98, The Independent Publishers Group. Kindle Edition.

79   Vitale, Joe, *The Aquarian*, No 11, October 11-18, 1978; PKD OTAKU, No. 4, 2002 http://www.philipkdick.com/media_aquarian.html

80   Dick, Anne R., *The Search for Philip K. Dick*, Page 111, The Independent Publishers Group. Kindle Edition.

81   Dick, Anne R., *The Search for Philip K. Dick*, Pages 117-18, The Independent Publishers Group. Kindle Edition.

82   Sutin, Lawrence, *Divine Invasions: A Life of Philip K. Dick*, Page 18, Orion Books (2006).

83   Dick, Anne R., *The Search for Philip K, Dick*, Page 116, The Independent Publishers Group. Kindle Edition.

84   Sutin, Lawrence *Divine Invasions: A Life of Philip K. Dick,* Page 140, Orion Books, (2006).

85   Dick, Anne R., *The Search for Philip K. Dick*, Page 121, The Independent Publishers Group. Kindle Edition.

86   Carrere, Emmanuel, *I Am Alive and You Are Dead: A Journey Inside the Mind of Philip K. Dick*, Page 123, Bloomsbury (2006).

87   Larre, Emiliano, Vega, Patricio Philip K. Dick – The Penultimate Truth DVD. 47 min-50 min in : http://www.youtube.com/watch?v=CfTCZCvgy3E

88   Vitale, Joe, *The Aquarian*, No 11, October 11-18, 1978; PKD OTAKU, No. 4, 2002 http://www.philipkdick.com/media_aquarian.html

89   Dick, Anne R., *The Search for Philip K, Dick*, Page 130, The Independent Publishers Group. Kindle Edition.

90   Sutin, Lawrence, *Divine Invasions: A Life of Philip K. Dick*, Page 150, Orion Books (2006).

91   Pike, Bishop James, *The Other Side*, Page 145, Abacus (1975).

92   Pike, Bishop James, *The Other Side*, Page 159, Abacus (1975).

93   Pike, Bishop James, *The Other Side*, Page 169, Abacus (1975).

94   Sutin, Lawrence, *Divine Invasions: A Life of Philip K. Dick*, Page 149, Orion Books (2006).

95   Dick, Anne R. *The Search for Philip K. Dick,* Page 135, The Independent Publishers Group. Kindle Edition.

96   Dick, Anne R. *The Search for Philip K. Dick*, Page. 135, The Independent Publishers Group. Kindle Edition

97   Dick, Anne R. *The Search for Philip K. Dick,* Page 138, The Independent Publishers Group. Kindle Edition.

98   Sutin, Lawrence, *Divine Invasions: A Life of Philip K. Dick*, Page 166, Orion Books (2006).

99   Dick, Anne R., *The Search for Philip K. Dick*, Page 142, The Independent Publishers Group. Kindle Edition.

100   Sutin, Lawrence, *Divine Invasions: A Life of Philip K. Dick,* Page 178, Orion Books (2006).

101   Dick, Anne R., *The Search for Philip K. Dick*, Page 144, The Independent Publishers Group. Kindle Edition.

102   Dick, Anne R., *The Search for Philip K. Dick* , Page 145, The Independent Publishers Group. Kindle Edition.

103   Personal correspondence between the author and Ray Nelson, 15 March 2013

104   Personal correspondence between the author and Ray Nelson, 15 March 2013

105   Massagli, Andrew & Steensland Mark, *The Gospel According to Philip K. Dick* (18:50 mins), First Run Features (2001).

106   Rickman, Gregg, *Philip K. Dick: In His Own Words*, Page 184, Fragments West (1988).

107   Rickman, Gregg, *Philip K. Dick: In His Own Words*, Page 184, Fragments West (1988).

108   Vitale, Joe, *The Worlds of Philip K. Dick*, (*The Aquarian*, 11 Oct. 1978) reproduced in PKD Otako 04 (Page 9).

109   Sutin, Lawrence, *Divine Invasions: A Life of Philip K. Dick,* Page 182, Orion Books (2006).

110   Sutin, Lawrence, *Divine Invasions: A Life of Philip K. Dick,* Page 183, Orion Books (2006).

111   Dick, Anne R., *The Search for Philip K. Dick*, Page. 158, The Independent Publishers Group. Kindle Edition.

112   Cover, Arthur Byron, *Interview With Philip K. Dick* Vertex, Vol. 1, no 6, Feb (1974).

113   Dick, Anne R., *The Search for Philip K. Dick*, Page 158, The Independent Publishers Group. Kindle Edition.

114   Cover, Arthur Byron, *Interview With Philip K. Dick*, Vertex, Vol. 1, no 6, Feb (1974).

115   Spinrad, Norman, *Science Fiction In The Real World*, Page 211, Southern Illinois University Press (1990).

116   Apel, D Scott, *Philip K. Dick: The Dream Connection*, Page 43, Permanent Press (1987)

117   Dick, Anne R., *The Search for Philip K. Dick*, Page 177, The Independent Publishers Group. Kindle Edition.

118   http://totaldickhead.blogspot.co.uk/2008/06/letter-from-dark-haired-girl.html

119   http://totaldickhead.blogspot.co.uk/2008/06/letter-from-dark-haired-girl.html

120   http://www.thedark-hairedgirl.com/PKDCorrespondenceModified.pdf

121   Dick, Anne R., *The Search for Philip K. Dick*, Page. 166, The Independent Publishers Group. Kindle Edition.

122   http://ubikcan.wordpress.com/2008/11/28/linda-levy-story-about-philip-k-dick/

123   Ziegler, Chris, 'A Very PhilDickian Existence', *OC Weekly*

124   *Selected Letters of Philip K. Dick*, Vol Two 1972-73, Page 31, Underwood-Miller (1993)

125   Sutin, Lawrence, *Divine Invasions: A Life of Philip K. Dick*, Page 169, Orion Books (2006).

126   Petrunio, Nita J., An Interview with Philip K. Dick http://www.philipkdick.com/media_petrunio.html

127   http://www.thedark-hairedgirl.com/PKDCorrespondenceModified.pdf

128   http://ubikcan.wordpress.com/2008/11/28/linda-levy-story-about-philip-k-dick/

129   http://ubikcan.wordpress.com/2008/11/28/linda-levy-story-about-philip-k-dick/

130   http://www.thedark-hairedgirl.com/PKDCorrespondenceModified.pdf

131   Dick, Philip K., *The Dark-Haired Girl,* Page 82, Mark V. Ziesing (1988).

132   Ziegler, Chris, 'A Very PhilDickian Existence', *OC Weekly* (2002).

133   Ziegler, Chris, 'A Very PhilDickian Existence', *OC Weekly* (2002).

134   *Selected Letters of Philip K. Dick*, 1974, Page 176, Underwood-Miller (1991).

135   Dick, Tessa, *Philip K. Dick: Remembering Firebright*, Page 40 (2009).

136   Dick, Tessa, *Philip K. Dick: Remembering Firebright*, Page 138 (2009).

137   *Selected Letters of Philip K. Dick*, 1972-73, Page 72, Underwood-Miller (1993).

138   Ziegler, Chris, 'A Very PhilDickian Existence', *OC Weekly* (2002).

139   *Selected Letters of Philip K. Dick*, 1972-73, Page 77, Underwood-Miller (1993).

140   *Selected Letters of Philip K. Dick*, 1972-73, Page 77, Underwood-Miller (1993).

141   Dick, Tessa, *Philip K. Dick: Remembering Firebright*, Page 50 (2009).

142   *Selected Letters of Philip K. Dick*, Vol Two 1972-73, Page 45, Underwood-Miller (1993).

143   Dick, Philip K., *The Dark-haired Girl* , Pages 86-87, Mark V. Ziesing (1988).

144   *Selected Letters of Philip K. Dick*, Vol Two 1972-73, Page 210, Underwood-Miller (1993).

145   Dick, Tessa, *Philip K. Dick: Remembering Firebright*, Page 46.

146   *Selected Letters of Philip K. Dick*, Vol Two 1972-73, Page 370, Underwood-Miller (1993).

147   *Selected Letters of Philip K. Dick*, 1974, Page 28, Underwood-Miller (1991).

148   Purser, Philip, *Even Sheep Can Upset Scientific Detachment*, Pages 27-30, *Daily Telegraph* 506. July 19 1974 – http://www.philipkdick.com/media_london_telegraph.html

149   Dick, Tessa, *Philip K. Dick: Remembering Firebright* , Page 173 and 46

150   Dick, Philip K., *The Exegesis of Philip K. Dick*, (Kindle Loc: 523-24), Hachette Littlehampton. Kindle Edition.

151   *Selected Letters of Philip K. Dick,* 1972-73, Page 295, Underwood-Miller (1993).

152   *Selected Letters of Philip K. Dick,* 1972-73, Page 321, Underwood-Miller (1993).

153   Dick, Tessa, *Philip K. Dick: Remembering Firebright*, Page 77, Create Space (2009).

154   Dick, Tessa,. *Philip K. Dick: Remembering Firebright*, Page 77, Create Space (2009).

155   Dick, Tessa, *Philip K. Dick: Remembering Firebright*, Page 78, Create Space (2009).

156   Dick, Philip K., *The Exegesis of Philip K. Dick*, (Loc:3326-28), Hachette Littlehampton. Kindle Edition.

157   *Selected Letters of Philip K. Dick,* 1974, Page 44, Underwood-Miller (1991).

158   Dick, Tessa, *Philip K. Dick: Remembering Firebright*, Page 82, Create Space (2009).

159   Rickman, Gregg, *Philip K. Dick: The Last Testament,* Page 24, Fragments West (1985).

160   Apel, D Scott, *Philip K. Dick: The Dream Connection*, Page 98, Permanent Press (1987).

161   Dick, Tessa, *Philip K. Dick: Remembering Firebright*, Page 119, Create Space (2009).

162   Dick, Tessa, *Philip K. Dick: Remembering Firebright*, Page 119, Create Space (2009).

163   Dick, Philip K., *The Exegesis of Philip K. Dick* Kindle Loc: 6554-6558, Hachette Littlehampton. Kindle Edition.

164 Rickman, Gregg, *Philip K. Dick: The Last Testament*, Page 43, Fragments West (1985).

165 Rydeen, Paul, *Philip K. Dick: The Other Side*, (http://www.gnosis.org/pkd. biography.html) (1994)

166 *Selected Letters of Philip K. Dick*, 1974, Page 244, Underwood-Miller (1991).

167 *Selected Letters of Philip K. Dick*, 1974, Page 246, Underwood-Miller (1991).

168 *Selected Letters of Philip K. Dick*, 1974, Page 264, Underwood-Miller (1991).

169 Apel, D. Scott, *Philip K. Dick: The Dream Connection*, Page 98, Permanent Press (1987).

170 *Selected Letters of Philip K. Dick*, 1974, Page 268, Underwood-Miller (1991).

171 *Selected Letters of Philip K. Dick*, 1974, Page 272, Underwood-Miller (1991).

172 *Selected Letters of Philip K. Dick*, 1974, Page 272, Underwood-Miller (1991).

173 Rickman, Gregg, *To The High Castle, Philip K. Dick: A Life 1928-1962*, Page 236, Fragments West (1989).

174 Sutin, Lawrence, *Divine Invasions: A Life of Philip K. Dick*, Page 102, Orion Books (2006).

175 Williams, Paul, *The True Stories of Philip K. Dick, Rolling Stone*, Page 46, 6 Nov, (1975).

176 *Selected Letters of Philip K. Dick*, 1975-76, Page 4, Underwood-Miller (1992).

177 Dick, Tessa, *Philip K. Dick: Remembering Firebright*, Page 139, (2009).

178 Dick, Tessa, *Philip K. Dick: Remembering Firebright*, Page 25, (2009).

179 Dick, Tessa, *Philip K. Dick: Remembering Firebright*, Page 142 (2009).

180 Sutin, Lawrence, *Divine Invasions: A Life of Philip K. Dick*, Page 240, Orion Books (2006).

181 Dick, Philip K., *VALIS*, Pages 10-11, Vintage Books (1991).

182 Sutin, Lawrence, *Divine Invasions: A Life of Philip K. Dick*, Page 241, Orion Books (2006).

183 Dick, Tessa, *Philip K. Dick: Remembering Firebright*, Page 143 (2009).

184 Sutin, Lawrence, *Divine Invasions: A Life of Philip K. Dick*, Page 241, Orion Books (2006).

185 Dick, Tessa, *Philip K. Dick: Remembering Firebright*, Page 142 (2009).

186 Dick, Tessa *Philip K. Dick: Remembering Firebright*, Page 141 (2009).

187 Dick, Philip K., *VALIS*, Page 45, Vintage Books (1991).

188 Dick, Anne R., *The Search for Philip K. Dick*, Page 178, The Independent Publishers Group. Kindle Edition.

189 Lee, Gwen & Sauter, Doris Elaine, *What if our World Was Their Heaven?: The Final Conversations of Philip K. Dick.*, Page 9, Duckworth (2006).

190 Ziegler, Chris, 'A Very PhilDickian Existence', *OC Weekly*

191 Lee, Gwen & Sauter, Doris Elaine, *What If Our World Was Their Heaven?: The Final Conversations of Philip K. Dick*, Page 9 (2006).

192 Lee, Gwen & Sauter, Doris Elaine, *What If Our World Was Their Heaven?: The Final Conversations of Philip K. Dick*, Page 8 (2006).

193 Lee, Gwen & Sauter, Doris Elaine, *What if our World Was Their Heaven?: The Final Conversations of Philip K. Dick.*, Page 9, Duckworth (2006).

194 Dick, Tessa, *Philip K. Dick: Remembering Firebright*, Page 145 (2009).

195 Sutin, Lawrence, *Divine Invasions: A Life of Philip K. Dick*, Page 239, Orion Books (2006).

196 Dick, Anne R., *The Search for Philip K. Dick*, Page. 203, The Independent Publishers Group. Kindle Edition.

197 Dick, Tessa, *Philip K. Dick: Remembering Firebright*, Page 146 (2009).

198 Boonstra, John, *Rod Serling's The Twilight Zone Magazine*, Vol. 2, No. 3, June 1982, Pages 47-52 http://www.philipkdick.com/media_twilightzone.html

199 Apel, D. Scott, *Philip K. Dick: The Dream Connection*, Page 17, Permanent Press (1987).

200 Apel, D. Scott, *Philip K. Dick: The Dream Connection*, Page 17, Permanent Press (1987).

201 Morgan, Jamelle, *PKD:TDC – A Second Take on Scott Apel's Dream Connection* in PKD OTAKU 22 (2011)

202 Butler, Andrew M., *Philip K. Dick*, Page 105, Pocket Essentials (2007).

203 Sutin, Lawrence (Editor), *The Shifting Realities of Philip K. Dick*, Pages 233-258, Vintage (1995).

204   Sutin, Lawrence, *Divine Invasions: A Life of Philip K. Dick*, Page 253, Orion Books (2006).

205   Dick, Anne R., *The Search for Philip K. Dick*, Page. 202, Independent Publishers Group. Kindle Edition.

206   Dick, Anne R., *The Search for Philip K. Dick*, Page 202, The Independent Publishers Group. Kindle Edition.

207   *Selected Letters of Philip K. Dick,* 1980-82, Page 5, Underwood-Miller (1991).

208   *Selected Letters of Philip K. Dick,* 1980-82, Page 43, Underwood-Miller (1991).

209   *Selected Letters of Philip K. Dick,* 1980-82, Page 43, Underwood-Miller (1991).

210   Boonstra, John, *Rod Serling's The Twilight Zone Magazine*, Vol. 2, No. 3, June 1982, Pages 47-52 http://www.philipkdick.com/media_twilightzone.html

211   Boonstra, John, *Rod Serling's The Twilight Zone Magazine*, Vol. 2, No. 3, June 1982, Pages 47-52 http://www.philipkdick.com/media_twilightzone.html

212   Boonstra, John, *Rod Serling's The Twilight Zone Magazine*, Vol. 2, No. 3, June 1982, Pages 47-52 http://www.philipkdick.com/media_twilightzone.html

213   Rickman, Gregg, *Philip K. Dick: In His Own Words*, Page 172, Fragments West (1988)

214   Boonstra, John, *Rod Serling's The Twilight Zone Magazine*, Vol. 2, No. 3, June 1982, Pages 47-52 http://www.philipkdick.com/media_twilightzone.html

215   Boonstra, John, *Rod Serling's The Twilight Zone Magazine*, Vol. 2, No. 3, June 1982, Pages 47-52 http://www.philipkdick.com/media_twilightzone.html

216   *Selected Letters of Philip K. Dick,* 1980-1982, Vol. 6, Page 18, Underwood Books (2009).

217   *Selected Letters of Philip K. Dick,* Vol 6, Page 127, Underwood Books (2009).

218   Rickman, Gregg, *Philip K. Dick: The Last Testament,* Page 73, Fragments West (1985).

219   *Selected Letters of Philip K. Dick,* 1980-82, Pages 257-259, Underwood-Miller (1991).

220   Dick, Philip K., *The Exegesis of Philip K. Dick* (Kindle Loc: 17607-08), Hachette Littlehampton. Kindle Edition.

221   Dick, Philip K., *The Exegesis of Philip K. Dick* (Kindle Loc: 17784-89), Hachette Littlehampton. Kindle Edition.

222   Sutin, Lawrence, *Divine Invasions: A Life of Philip K. Dick*, Pages 284-85, Orion (2006).

223   Dick, Tessa, *Book Review, The Daemon by Anthony Peake* July 17th 2009: http://pkdmemoir.blogspot.co.uk/2009/07/book-review-daemon-by-anthony-peake.html

224   *Selected Letters of Philip K. Dick,* 1980-1982, Vol. 6, Page 290, Underwood Books (2009).

225   *Selected Letters of Philip K. Dick,* 1980-1982. Vol. 6, Page 292, Underwood Books (2009).

226   *Selected Letters of Philip K. Dick,* 1980-1982, Vol. 6, Page 294, Underwood Books (2009).

227   Dick, Philip K., *The Exegesis of Philip K. Dick* (Kindle Loc: 17791-92), Hachette Littlehampton. Kindle Edition.

228   *Selected Letters of Philip K. Dick,* 1980-1982, Vol. 6, Page 294, Underwood Books (2009).

229   Dick, Tessa, *Philip K. Dick: Remembering Firebright*, Page 182 (2009).

230   Lee, Gwen & Sauter, Doris Elaine, *What if our World Was Their Heaven?: The Final Conversations of Philip K. Dick,* Duckworth (2006).

231   Lee, Gwen & Sauter, Doris Elaine *What if our World Was Their Heaven?: The Final Conversations of Philip K. Dick,* Page 133, Duckworth (2006)

232   Rickman, Gregg, *Philip K. Dick: The Last Testament,* Page 117, Fragments West (1985).

233   Rickman, Gregg, *Philip K. Dick: The Last Testament,* Page 223, Fragments West (1985).

234   Sutin, Lawrence, *Divine Invasions: A Life of Philip K. Dick*, Page 289, Orion Books (2006).

235   *Selected Letters of Philip K. Dick,* 1975-76, Page ix, Underwood-Miller (1992).

236   *Selected Letters of Philip K. Dick,* 1975-76, Page ix, Underwood-Miller (1992).

237   Dick, Tessa, *Philip K. Dick: Remembering Firebright*, Pages 180-181 (2009).

238   Dick, Tessa, *Philip K. Dick: Remembering Firebright*, Pages 183-184 (2009)

239   *Selected Letters of Philip K. Dick,* 1975-76, Page 91, Underwood-Miller (1992).

240   Peake, Anthony, *The Daemon: A Guide To Your Extraordinary Secret Self*, Page 323 (2008).

241   *Selected Letters of Philip K. Dick,* 1975-76, Underwood-Miller (1992).

242 Rickman, Gregg, *Philip K. Dick: The Last Testament,* Page 17, Fragments West (1985).

243 *Selected Letters of Philip K. Dick,* 1974, Page 44, Underwood-Miller (1991).

244 Dick, Tessa, *Philip K. Dick: Remembering Firebright,* Page 46 (2009).

245 Dick, Anne R., *The Search for Philip K. Dick.,* Page 62, The Independent Publishers Group. Kindle Edition.

246 Dick, Tessa, *Philip K. Dick: Remembering Firebright,* Page 109 (2009).

247 *Selected Letters of Philip K. Dick,* 1980-82, Page 226, Underwood-Miller (1991).

248 http://www.claudiax.net/TEMPAUC/pkd-dcLforest.html

249 Carrere, Emmanuel, *I Am Alive And You Are Dead: A Journey Inside The Mind Of Philip K. Dick,* Page 6, Bloomsbury (2006).

250 Dick, Philip K., *The Exegesis of Philip K. Dick* (Loc: 19955-57), Hachette Littlehampton. Kindle Edition.

251 Dick, Philip K., *Eye in the Sky,* Page 70, Vantage eBooks.

252 Purser, Philip, *Even Sheep Can Upset Scientific Detachment,* Pages 27-30, *Daily Telegraph* 506. July 19 1974 – http://www.philipkdick.com/media_london_telegraph.html

253 *Selected Letters of Philip K. Dick,* 1980-1982, Vol. 6, Page 21, Underwood Books (2009).

254 Rickman, Gregg, *Philip K. Dick: The Last Testament,* Page 47, Fragments West (1985).

255 *Selected Letters of Philip K. Dick,* 1974, Page 9, Underwood-Miller (1991).

256 *Selected Letters of Philip K. Dick,* 1974, Page 10, Underwood-Miller (1991).

257 *Selected Letters of Philip K. Dick,* 1974, Page 213, Underwood-Miller (1991).

258 Apel, D. Scott, *Philip K. Dick: The Dream Connection,* Page 88, Permanent Press (1987).

259 Apel, D. Scott, *Philip K. Dick: The Dream Connection,* Page 88, Permanent Press (1987).

260 *Selected Letters of Philip K. Dick,* 1974, Page 254, Underwood-Miller (1991).

261 Sutin, Lawrence (Editor), *The Shifting Realities of Philip K. Dick,* Page 267, Vintage (1995).

262 Sutin, Lawrence (Editor), *The Shifting Realities of Philip K. Dick,* Page 268, Vintage (1995).

263 Sutin, Lawrence (Editor), *The Shifting Realities of Philip K. Dick,* Page 269, Vintage (1995).

264 *Selected Letters of Philip K. Dick,* 1974, Page 157, Underwood-Miller (1991).

265 *Selected Letters of Philip K. Dick,* 1974, Page 157, Underwood-Miller (1991).

266 *Selected Letters of Philip K. Dick,* 1974, Page 156, Underwood-Miller (1991.

267 *Selected Letters of Philip K. Dick,* 1974, Page 101, Underwood-Miller (1991).

268 Dick, Tessa, *Philip K. Dick: Remembering Firebright,* Page 113 (2009).

269 Dick, Tessa, *Philip K. Dick: Remembering Firebright,* Page 113 (2009).

270 Deeley, Michael, *Blade Runners, Deer Hunters & Blowing the Bloody Doors off,* Page 202 Faber & Faber (2008).

271 Deeley, Michael, *Blade Runners, Deer Hunters & Blowing the Bloody Doors off,* Page 224, Faber & Faber (2008).

272 Rickman, Gregg, *Philip K. Dick: In His Own Words,* Page 166, Fragments West (1988)

273 Boonstra, John, *Horselover Fat and The New Messiah,* Page 22, Hartford Advocate, 22 April 1981. Reproduced in PKD Otako #06.

274 Dick, Philip K., *The Exegesis of Philip K. Dick* (Kindle Loc: 3881-3884), Hachette Littlehampton. Kindle Edition.

275 Mavromatis, Andreas, *Hypnagogia,* Thyrsos Press (2010).

276 *Selected Letters of Philip K. Dick,* 1974, Page 144, Underwood-Miller (1991).

277 Apel, D. Scott, *Philip K. Dick: The Dream Connection,* Page 88, Permanent Press (1987)

278 Koestler, Arthur, 'Order From Disorder', *Harper's* magazine, July (1974).

279 *Selected Letters of Philip K. Dick,* 1974, Page 144, Underwood-Miller (1991).

280 *Selected Letters of Philip K. Dick,* 1974, Page 144, Underwood-Miller (1991).

281 *Selected Letters of Philip K. Dick,* 1974, Page 144, Underwood-Miller (1991).

282 Kozyrev, Nikolai, *Possibility of Experimental Study of the Properties of Time* (1967).

283 http://www.rexresearch.com/articles/kozyrev.htm

284 Dick, Philip K., *The Exegesis of Philip K. Dick*, Reference 5:66, Hachette.

285 Dick, Philip K., *The Exegesis of Philip K. Dick*, Reference 5:66, Hachette.

286 Dick, Philip K *The Exegesis of Philip K. Dick*, Reference 48:926, Hachette.

287 Warren, Eugene, *The Search for Absolutes* in Greenberg & Olander, (eds) *Philip K. Dick*, Page 167, Taplinger Publishing Co. (1983).

288 Dick, Philip K., *The Exegesis of Philip K. Dick* (Loc: 20247), Hachette Littlehampton. Kindle Edition.

289 *Selected Letters of Philip K. Dick,* 1975-76, Page 97, Underwood-Miller (1992).

290 Dick, Philip K., *The Exegesis of Philip K. Dick* (Kindle Loc: 3881-3884), Hachette Littlehampton. Kindle Edition.

291 Pais A., *'Subtle is the Lord'*, Page 152, Oxford University Press (1982).

292 Weyl H., *'Space-Time-Matter',* Methuen (1922).

293 Lupoff, Richard A., *A Conversation With Philip K. Dick*, Vol. 1, no. 2, Pages 45-54, August (1987).

294 Rickman, Gregg, *To The High Castle, Philip K. Dick: A Life 1928-1962*, Page 245, Fragments West (1989).

295 *Selected Letters of Philip K. Dick,* 1974, Page 101, Underwood-Miller (1991).

296 Rickman, Gregg, *To The High Castle, Philip K. Dick: A Life 1928-1962*, Page 246, Fragments West (1989).

297 Davies R., *'Doubles, The Enigma of the Second Self'*, Page 121, London – Robert Hale (1998).

298 Rickman, Gregg, *Philip K. Dick: The Last Testament*, Page 39, Fragments West (1985).

299 Rickman, Gregg, *Philip K. Dick: The Last Testament*, Page 39, Fragments West (1985).

300 Dick, Philip K., *The Exegesis of Philip K. Dick* (Kindle Loc: 7002-05), Hachette Littlehampton. Kindle Edition.

301 Cover, Arthur Byron, *Vertex Interviews: Philip K. Dick*, Vertex Vol. 1, no. 6, February (1974).

302 Sutin, Lawrence, *Divine Invasions: A Life of Philip K. Dick*, Page 212, Orion Books (2006).

303 *Selected Letters of Philip K. Dick,* 1980-1982. Vol. 6, Page 262, Underwood Books (2009).

304 Dick, Philip K., *The Divine Invasion*, Page 12, ePub

305 Laszlo, Ervin, *Science and the Akashic Field: An Integral Theory of Everything*, Inner Traditions (2007).

306 *Selected Letters of Philip K. Dick,* 1980-1982. Vol. 6, Page 266, Underwood Books (2009).

307 Sutin, Lawrence, *Divine Invasions: A Life of Philip K. Dick*, Page 201, Orion Books (2006).

308 Sutin, Lawrence, *Divine Invasions: A Life of Philip K. Dick*, Page 201, Orion Books (2006).

309 Dick, Anne R. *The Search for Philip K. Dick,* Page 62, The Independent Publishers Group. Kindle Edition.

310 Dick, Anne R., *The Search for Philip K. Dick,* Page 62, The Independent Publishers Group. Kindle Edition.

311 Dick, Philip K., *The Exegesis of Philip K. Dick* (Kindle Loc: 3890-93), Hachette Littlehampton. Kindle Edition.

312 Rickman, Gregg, *To The High Castle, Philip K. Dick: A Life 1928-1962*, Page 140, Fragments West (1989).

313 Dick, Anne R., *The Search for Philip K. Dick*, Page 250-51, The Independent Publishers Group. Kindle Edition.

314 Rickman, Gregg, *Philip K. Dick: The Last Testament*, Page 23, Fragments West (1985).

315 Boonstra, John, *Horselover Fat and The New Messiah*, Page 22, Hartford Advocate,

22 April 1981. Reproduced in PKD Otako #06.

316 Sperry, R. W., *Lateral specialisation in the surgically separated hemispheres* in Scmitt Fo & Worden F. G., (eds) The Neurosciences 3rd Study Program. MIT Press, Page 11 (1974).

317 '*Mental Phenomena as Causal Determinants in Brain Function*' (in G. Globus 'Consciousness and The Brain', 1976), Page 170.

318 Dick, Philip K., *The Exegesis of Philip K. Dick* (Loc: 1884), Hachette Littlehampton. Kindle Edition.

319 Dick, Philip K., *The Exegesis of Philip K. Dick* (Loc: 1885), Hachette Littlehampton. Kindle Edition.

320 Dick, Philip K., *The Exegesis of Philip K. Dick* (Loc: 1896), Hachette Littlehampton. Kindle Edition.

321 Bergson, Henri, *Mind-Energy*, Lectures and Essays, Page 59, MacMillan (1920).

322 *Selected Letters of Philip K. Dick,* 1974, Page 277, Underwood-Miller (1991).

323 *Selected Letters of Philip K. Dick,* 1977-1979, Underwood Books (1993).

324 Rickman, Gregg, *Philip K. Dick: The Last Testament,* Page 19, Fragments West (1985)

325 Dick, Philip K., *The Exegesis of Philip K. Dick* (Kindle Loc: 5863-66), Hachette Littlehampton. Kindle Edition.

326 Dick, Philip K., *The Exegesis of Philip K. Dick* (Kindle Loc: 17129), Hachette Littlehampton. Kindle Edition.

327 Dick, Philip K., *The Exegesis of Philip K. Dick* (Kindle Loc: 17184-86), Hachette Littlehampton. Kindle Edition.

328 Dick, Philip K., *The Exegesis of Philip K. Dick* (Folder 78. May 1981), Hachette Littlehampton. Kindle Edition.

329 *Selected Letters of Philip K. Dick,* 1980-82, Page 180, Underwood-Miller (1991).

330 Dick, Philip K., *Electric Shepherd*, Norstrilia, Melbourne, Pages 31–2 (1975).

331 Warren, Eugene, *The Search for Absolutes* in Greenberg & Olander, (eds) *Philip K. Dick*, Page 167, Taplinger Publishing Co. (1983).

332 Dick, Philip K., *The Exegesis of Philip K. Dick* (Kindle Loc: 1603-1605), Hachette Littlehampton. Kindle Edition.

333 *Selected Letters of Philip K. Dick,* 1980-82, Page 155, Underwood-Miller (1991).

334 *Selected Letters of Philip K. Dick,* 1980-82, Page156, Underwood-Miller (1991).

335 Luce, Gay Gaer, *Trust Your Body Rhythms*, Pages 52-53, *Psychology Today* April (1975).

336 Dick, Philip K., *The Exegesis of Philip K. Dick* (Loc: 3685-89), Hachette Littlehampton. Kindle Edition.

337 Dick, Philip K., *A Maze of Death*, Page 8, Gollancz (2005).

338 Dick, Tessa, *Philip K. Dick: Remembering Firebright*, Page 74, Create Space (2009).

339 Apel, D. Scott, *Philip K. Dick: The Dream Connection*, Page 96, Permanent Press (1987).

340 Fuller, John G., *The Interrupted Journey: Two Lost Hours Aboard a Flying Saucer*, Souvenir Press (1980).

341 Dick, Tessa, *My Life on the Edge of Reality*, Creative Space (2011).

342 Dick, Philip K., *The Dark-haired Girl*, Page 87, Mark V. Ziesing (1988).

343 Apel, D. Scott, *Philip K. Dick: The Dream Connection*, Page 108, Permanent Press, (1987)

344 Apel, D. Scott, *Philip K. Dick: The Dream Connection*, Page 109, Permanent Press, (1987)

345 Dick, Tessa, *Philip K. Dick: Remembering Firebright*, Page 142 (2009).

346 Keel, John A., *UFOS: Operation Trojan Horse*, Page 267, Abacus (1971)

347 Dick, Philip K., *The Complete Stories of Philip K. Dick Vol 5.*

348 Dick, Philip K., *The Complete Stories of Philip K. Dick Vol 5.*

349 Dick, Philip K., *The Complete Stories of Philip K. Dick Vol 5.*

350 Graham, Kenneth, *The Wind in the Willows*, Chapter 7.

351 DePrez, Daniel, *An Interview With Philip K. Dick, Science Fiction Review*, No 19, Vol. 5, no 3, August (1976).

352 Sutin, Lawrence, *Divine Invasions: A Life of Philip K. Dick*, Page 242, Orion Books (2006).

353 Steiger, Brad, *Philip K. Dick's Phylogenic Memory and the Divine Fire, Alternate Perceptions* magazine, Issue 118, November (2007).

354 Steiger, Brad, *Philip K. Dick's Phylogenic Memory and the Divine Fire, Alternate Perceptions* magazine, Issue 118, November (2007).

355 Sutin, Lawrence, *Divine Invasions: A Life of Philip K. Dick,* Page 210, Orion Books, (2006).

356 Dick, Philip K., *VALIS*, Pages 206-207, Orion Books (2001).

357 *Selected Letters of Philip K. Dick,* 1975-1976, Pages 35-37, Underwood-Miller (1993).

358 Dick, Philip K., *VALIS,* Page 60, Gollancz (2001).

359 Dick, Tessa, *Philip K. Dick: Remembering Firebright*, Page 73/74, Create Space (2009).

360 Dick, Philip K., *The Exegesis of Philip K. Dick* (Kindle Locs:15670-15674), Hachette Littlehampton. Kindle Edition.

361 Rickman, Gregg, *Philip K. Dick: The Last Testament,* Page 69, Fragments West (1985).

362 Dick, Philip K., *The Exegesis of Philip K. Dick* (Loc: 19948-50), Hachette Littlehampton. Kindle Edition

363 Dick, Philip K., *The Exegesis of Philip K. Dick* (Loc: 2720), Hachette Littlehampton. Kindle Edition.

364 Dick, Philip K., *The Exegesis of Philip K. Dick* (Loc: 20247), Hachette Littlehampton. Kindle Edition.

365 *Selected Letters of Philip K. Dick,* 1975-76, Page 92, Underwood-Miller (1992).

366 Ross, Harvey M., *Orthomolecular Psychiatry: Vitamin Pills for Schizophrenics, Psychology Today*, April (1974).

367 Dick, Philip K., *The Exegesis of Philip K. Dick* (Locations 990-991), Hachette Littlehampton. Kindle Edition.

368 Sutin, Lawrence, *Divine Invasions: A Life of Philip K. Dick*, Page 212, Orion Books (2006).

369 Dick, Philip K., *The Exegesis of Philip K. Dick* (Kindle Locs: 546/48), Hachette Littlehampton. Kindle Edition.

370 Peake, Anthony, *The Daemon: A Guide To Your Extraordinary Secret Self*, Arcturus (2008).

371 Dick, Tessa, in 'Good Reads': http://www.goodreads.com/review/show/59389674

372 Dick, Anne R., *The Search for Philip K. Dick.*, Page 135, The Independent Publishers Group. Kindle Edition.

373 Rickman, Gregg, *To The High Castle, Philip K. Dick: A Life 1928-1962*, Page 93, Fragments West (1989).

374 Dick, Philip K *Time Out of Joint* Chapt 3 *Reference needed from book*

375 Rickman, Gregg *To The High Castle Philip K. Dick: A Life 1928-1962*, Page 130 Fragments West, (1989)

376 Sutin, Lawrence, *Divine Invasions: A Life of Philip K. Dick*, Page 63, Orion Books (2006).

377 http://carolinamigrainecenter.com/effect-of-migraine-on-time-perception

378 Sutin, Lawrence, *Divine Invasions: A Life of Philip K. Dick*, Page 49, Orion Books (2006).

379 Hemsley, Rik, *I have Alice in Wonderland Syndrome*, The *Guardian*, 16 February, (2008).

380 Hemsley, Rik, *I have Alice in Wonderland Syndrome*, The *Guardian*, 16 February, (2008).

381 Dick, Anne R., *The Search for Philip K. Dick.*, Pages 236-237, The Independent Publishers Group. Kindle Edition.

382 Yellott, John I. Jr, *Seeing Things Inside Out, Scientific American*, July (1981).

383 *Selected Letters of Philip K. Dick*, 1980-82, Page 192, Underwood-Miller (1991).

384 *Selected Letters of Philip K. Dick*, 1980-82, Page 181, Underwood-Miller (1991).

385 Sacks, Oliver, *Migraine*, Page 63, Picador (1993).

386 http://www.stgemmagalgani.com/2010/07/patron-saint-of-headaches-and-migraines.html

387 Sacks, Oliver, *Migraine*, Page 299, Picador (1993).

388 Hildegard of Bingen, quoted in Sabina Flanagan: *Hildegard of Bingen*, Routledge (1989).

389 Mapson, Robert, *The Speaking Light: Philip K. Dick and the Shamanic Vision* in *SF Commentary*, Aug (2010).

390 Dick, Tessa, *Philip K. Dick: Remembering Firebright*, Page 143 (2009).

391 Mauskop A. & Altura B. M. *Role of magnesium in the pathogenesis and treatment of migraines*, 24-27 Clin Neuros,ci. 5(1) (1998).

392 Moretti G., Manzoni G.C. & Carpeggiani P., Parma *Transitory 150 attacks, migraine and progestogen drugs. Etiopathic correlations*, Pages 2125-9, Minerva Medica, 25 Aug, 71(30) (1980).

393 Solenski, Nina J., *Transient Ischemic Attacks: Part I. Diagnosis and Evaluation*, Page. 1667 Am Fam Physician, 1 Apr 1;69(7). (2004).

394 Dick, Tessa, *Philip K. Dick: Remembering Firebright*, Page 119, Create Space (2009).

395 Prabhakaran SK, Silver A.J., Warrior L, et al. *Misdiagnosis of transient ischemic attacks in the emergency room*, Cerebrovasc Dis, Pages 630-635. No 26. (2008).

396 Samson, Kurt, *Grammy Reporter's Dysphasic Episode Draws Attention to TIA/Migraine Diagnosis Quandary*, Page 20, *Neurology Today*, 17 March (2011).

397 Neppe, V. M., *Anomalistic experience and the cerebral cortex*. In S. Krippner, (Ed.), *Advances in parapsychological research 6*, Pages 168–183 Jefferson, NC: McFarland. (1990).

398 Persinger, M. A., Bureau, Y. R. J., Peredery, O. P., and Richards, P. M., *The Sensed Presence as Right hemisphere Intrusions in the Left Hemisphere Awareness of Self: An Illustrative Case*. Perceptual and Motor Skills, **78**, 999 (1994).

399 Persinger M. A. & Derr J.S., *Geophysical Variables and Behavior: LXII: Temporal Coupling of UFO Reports and Seismic Energy Release within the Rio Grande Rift System: Discriminative Validity of Tectonic Strain Theory*, Perceptual and Motor Skills, 71, 567 (1990).

400 Persinger, M. A. & Makarec K., *Temporal lobe signs and correlative behaviours displayed by normal populations, Journal of General Psychology*, 114, Pages 179-195 (1987).

401 Persinger, M. A., *Vectorial Cerebral Hemisphericity as Differential Sources for the Sensed Presence, Mystical Experiences and Religious Conversion*, Psychological Reports, **76**, 915 (1993).

402 Rickman, Gregg, *To The High Castle, Philip K. Dick: A Life 1928-1962*, Page 56, Fragments West (1989).

403 *Selected Letters of Philip K. Dick*, 1975-76, Page 9, Underwood-Miller (1992).

404 Malzberg, Barr M., Introduction to Greenberg M.H & Olander, J.D Philip K. Dick pp. 11/12 Taplinger Publishing Company, New York (1983).

405 Drevdahl, John E. Cattell & Raymond B., *Personality and Creativity in Artists and Writers,* Pages 107-111, *The Journal of Clinical Psychology*, Vol. XIV, No 2, April (1958).

406 Allport, G.W. & Odbert, H.S. *Trait-names: A psycho-lexical study*, *Psychological Monographs*, 47(211). (1936).

407 Cattell, R. B., *Factor analysis*, Wiley (1952).

408 Karson, Samuel & O'Dell, Jerry, W. *A Guide to the Clinical Use of the 16PF*, Page 47, IPAT (1976).

409 Cattell, Heather Birkett, *The 16PF: Personality in Depth*, Page 223-224, IPAT, (1989).

410 Karson, Samuel & O'Dell, Jerry, W. *A Guide to the Clinical Use of the 16PF*, Page 72/73 IPAT (1976).

411 Cattell, R.B, Eber and H.W & Tatsuoka, M.T. *Handbook for the 16PF*, Page 108, IPAT (1970).

412 Karson, Samuel & O'Dell, Jerry, W. *A Guide to the Clinical Use of the 16PF*, Page 41, IPAT (1976).

413 Cattell, R.B, Eber, H.W & Tatsuoka, M.T., *Handbook for the 16PF*, Page 97, IPAT, (1970).

414 Cattell, Heather Birkett, *The 16PF: Personality in Depth*, Page180, IPAT, (1989).

415 Cattell, Heather Birkett, *The 16PF: Personality in Depth*, Page 193, IPAT (1989).

416 Krug, Samuel L., *Interpreting 16PF Profile Patterns*, IPAT (1981).

417 Dick, Philip K., *Confessions of a Crap Artist*, Page 14.

418 Dick, Philip K., *Confessions of a Crap Artist*, Page 14.

419 Attwood, Tony, *Asperger's Syndrome: A Guide for Parents & Professionals*, Page 124, Jessica Kingsley Publishers (2003).

420 White, B.B. & White, M.S., *Autism from the inside*, Page 244, Medical Hypothesis 24 (1987).

421 Attwood, Tony, *Asperger's Syndrome: A Guide for Parents & Professionals*, Page 148, Jessica Kingsley Publishers (2003).

Index